Holt California
Algebra 1

Review for Mastery Workbook

HOLT, RINEHART AND WINSTON

A Harcourt Education Company

Orlando • Austin • New York • San Diego • London

ISBN 978-0-03-094692-9
ISBN 0-03-094692-1
7 8 9 862 10 09

Contents

Holt Algebra 1

California Standards Prep for ←4.0

Review for Mastery

LESSON 1-1

Variables and Expressions

To translate words into algebraic expressions, find words like these that tell you the operation.

+	−	•	÷
add	subtract	multiply	divide
sum	difference	product	quotient
more	less	times	split
increased	decreased	per	ratio

Kenny owns *v* video games. Stan owns 7 more video games than Kenny. Write an expression for the number of video games Stan owns.

v represents the number of video games Kenny owns.

v + 7   *Think: The word "more" indicates addition.*

Order does not matter for addition. The expression 7 + *v* is also correct.

Jenny is 12 years younger than Candy. Write an expression for Jenny's age if Candy is *c* years old.

c represents Candy's age.

The word "younger" means "less," which indicates subtraction.

c − 12   *Think: Candy is older, so subtract 12 from her age.*

Order does matter for subtraction. The expression 12 − *c* is incorrect.

---

1. Jared can type 35 words per minute. Write an expression for the number of words he can type in *m* minutes.

_____

2. Mr. O'Brien's commute to work is 0.5 hour less than Miss Santos's commute. Write an expression for the length of Mr. O'Brien's commute if Miss Santos's commute is *h* hours.

_____

3. Mrs. Knighten bought a box of *c* crayons and split them evenly between the 25 students in her classroom. Write an expression for the number of crayons each student received.

_____

4. Enrique collected 152 recyclable bottles, and Latasha collected *b* recyclable bottles. Write an expression for the number of bottles they collected altogether.

_____

5. Tammy's current rent is *r* dollars. Next month it will be reduced by $50. Write an expression for next month's rent in dollars.

_____

Holt Algebra 1

California Standards Prep for ←—4.0

Review for Mastery
Variables and Expressions continued

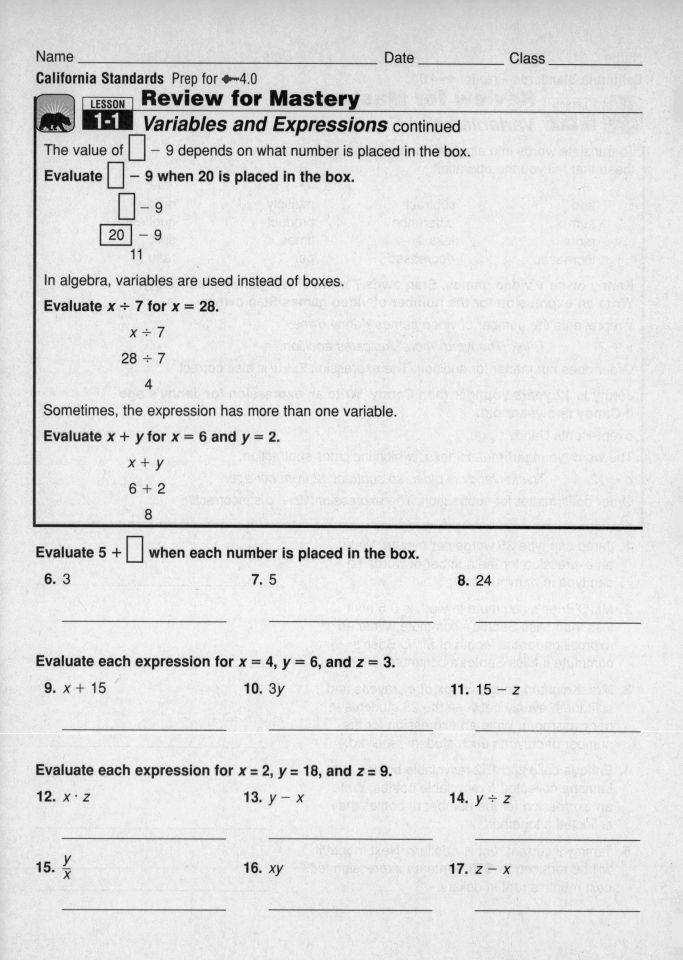

The value of $\boxed{} - 9$ depends on what number is placed in the box.

Evaluate $\boxed{} - 9$ **when 20 is placed in the box.**

$$\boxed{} - 9$$
$$\boxed{20} - 9$$
$$11$$

In algebra, variables are used instead of boxes.

Evaluate $x \div 7$ **for** $x = 28$.

$$x \div 7$$
$$28 \div 7$$
$$4$$

Sometimes, the expression has more than one variable.

Evaluate $x + y$ **for** $x = 6$ **and** $y = 2$.

$$x + y$$
$$6 + 2$$
$$8$$

Evaluate $5 + \boxed{}$ **when each number is placed in the box.**

6. 3   **7.** 5   **8.** 24

_____   _____   _____

Evaluate each expression for $x = 4$, $y = 6$, **and** $z = 3$.

9. $x + 15$ **10.** $3y$ **11.** $15 - z$

_____   _____   _____

Evaluate each expression for $x = 2$, $y = 18$, **and** $z = 9$.

12. $x \cdot z$ **13.** $y - x$ **14.** $y \div z$

_____   _____   _____

15. $\dfrac{y}{x}$ **16.** xy **17.** $z - x$

_____   _____   _____

Holt Algebra 1

California Standards ←2.0

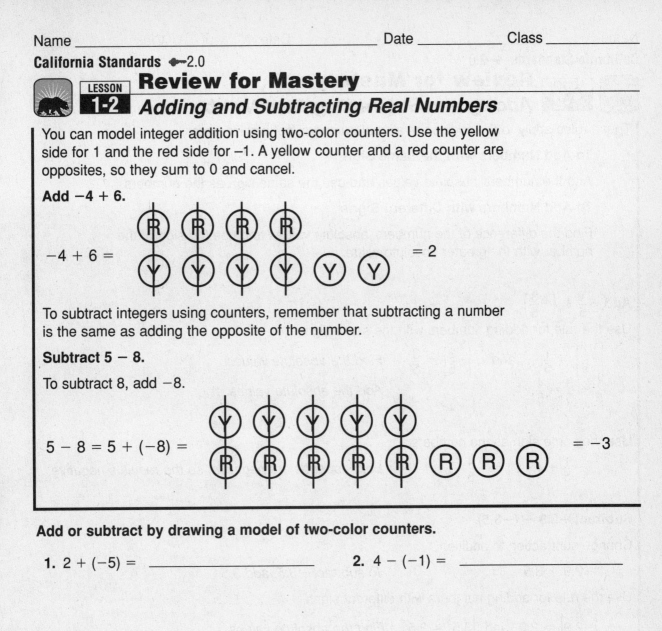

LESSON 1-2

Review for Mastery
Adding and Subtracting Real Numbers

You can model integer addition using two-color counters. Use the yellow side for 1 and the red side for −1. A yellow counter and a red counter are opposites, so they sum to 0 and cancel.

Add −4 + 6.

$$-4 + 6 = \qquad = 2$$

To subtract integers using counters, remember that subtracting a number is the same as adding the opposite of the number.

Subtract 5 − 8.

To subtract 8, add −8.

$$5 - 8 = 5 + (-8) = \qquad = -3$$

Add or subtract by drawing a model of two-color counters.

1. $2 + (-5) =$ _____

2. $4 - (-1) =$ _____

Add or subtract using two color counters.

3. $-3 + 7$

4. $3 + (-4)$

5. $-2 + -6$

_____ _____ _____

6. $8 - 2$

7. $-5 - 3$

8. $7 - (-4)$

_____ _____ _____

9. $-6 - (-4)$

10. $5 + (-5)$

11. $2 - 7$

_____ _____ _____

Holt Algebra 1

California Standards ➛2.0

LESSON 1-2

Review for Mastery

Adding and Subtracting Real Numbers continued

These rules apply to the addition of all real numbers, not just integers:

To Add Numbers with the Same Sign

Add the numbers' absolute values and use the same sign as the numbers.

To Add Numbers with Different Signs

Find the difference of the numbers' absolute values and use the sign of the number with the greater absolute value.

Add $-\dfrac{1}{5} + \left(-\dfrac{3}{5}\right)$.

Use the rule for adding numbers with the same sign.

$\left|-\dfrac{1}{5}\right| = \dfrac{1}{5}$ and $\left|-\dfrac{3}{5}\right| = \dfrac{3}{5}$ *Find the absolute values.*

$\dfrac{1}{5} + \dfrac{3}{5} = \dfrac{4}{5}$ *Add the absolute values.*

Use the same sign as the numbers.

$-\dfrac{1}{5} + \left(-\dfrac{3}{5}\right) = -\dfrac{4}{5}$ *Both addends are negative, so the result is negative.*

Subtract $-2.9 - (-3.5)$.

Change subtraction to addition.

$-2.9 + 3.5$ *To subtract -3.5, add 3.5.*

Use the rule for adding numbers with different signs.

$|-2.9| = 2.9$ and $|3.5| = 3.5$ *Find the absolute values.*

$3.5 - 2.9 = 0.6$ *Find the difference.*

Use the sign of the number with the greater absolute value.

$-2.9 - (-3.5) = 0.6$ *3.5 had the greater absolute value in the addition problem, so the result is positive.*

Add or subtract.

12. $5 + (-9)$

13. $-6.5 + (-3.2)$

14. $-\dfrac{5}{9} + \dfrac{1}{9}$

_____

_____

_____

15. $-12 - (-15)$

16. $-7.8 - 2.5$

17. $\dfrac{3}{8} - \dfrac{5}{8}$

_____

_____

_____

Holt Algebra 1

Name _____ Date _____ Class _____

LESSON 1-3
Review for Mastery
Multiplying and Dividing Real Numbers

To multiply or divide real numbers, first use the rules below to determine the sign of the result. Then operate with the numbers as if they have no signs.

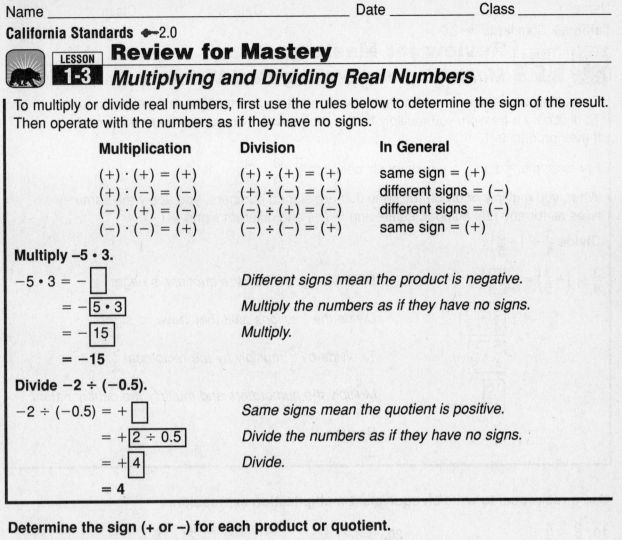

Multiplication	**Division**	**In General**
$(+) \cdot (+) = (+)$	$(+) \div (+) = (+)$	same sign = $(+)$
$(+) \cdot (-) = (-)$	$(+) \div (-) = (-)$	different signs = $(-)$
$(-) \cdot (+) = (-)$	$(-) \div (+) = (-)$	different signs = $(-)$
$(-) \cdot (-) = (+)$	$(-) \div (-) = (+)$	same sign = $(+)$

Multiply $-5 \cdot 3$.

$-5 \cdot 3 = -\boxed{}$ *Different signs mean the product is negative.*

$\qquad = -\boxed{5 \cdot 3}$ *Multiply the numbers as if they have no signs.*

$\qquad = -\boxed{15}$ *Multiply.*

$\qquad = -15$

Divide $-2 \div (-0.5)$.

$-2 \div (-0.5) = +\boxed{}$ *Same signs mean the quotient is positive.*

$\qquad = +\boxed{2 \div 0.5}$ *Divide the numbers as if they have no signs.*

$\qquad = +\boxed{4}$ *Divide.*

$\qquad = 4$

Determine the sign (+ or –) for each product or quotient.

1. $-8 \cdot -4 = $ _____32

2. $156 \div (-8) = $ _____19.5

3. $-15(4) = $ _____60

4. $6.4 \div (-4) = $ _____1.6

5. $-0.5(0.4) = $ _____0.2

6. $29.82 \div 2.1 = $ _____14.2

Multiply or divide.

7. $-3 \cdot 7$

8. $-55 \div -11$

9. $6(-4)$

_____

_____

_____

10. $-100 \div 20$

11. $-6(-8)$

12. $5 \div (-2)$

_____

_____

_____

13. $15.3 \div -3$

14. $-8.2 \cdot -5$

15. $-21 \div 10$

_____

_____

_____

16. $-2.7(4)$

17. $4.5 \div 1.5$

18. $3.4 \cdot (-1.5)$

_____

_____

_____

Holt Algebra 1

California Standards ←2.0

LESSON 1-3 **Review for Mastery**
Multiplying and Dividing Real Numbers continued

To multiply by a fraction, you multiply the numerators and multiply the denominators. To divide by a fraction, you multiply by the **reciprocal**. Two numbers are reciprocals if their product is 1.

For example, $\frac{5}{8}$ and $\frac{8}{5}$ are reciprocals because $\frac{5}{8} \cdot \frac{8}{5} = \frac{40}{40} = 1$.

When you multiply or divide fractions that are signed numbers, you apply the same rules as for any real number: same sign = (+) and different signs = (−).

Divide $\frac{3}{4} \div \left(-\frac{3}{5}\right)$.

$\frac{3}{4} \div \left(-\frac{3}{5}\right) = -\boxed{}$ *Different signs mean the quotient is negative.*

$= -\boxed{\dfrac{3}{4} \div \dfrac{3}{5}}$ *Divide the fractions as if they have no signs.*

$= -\boxed{\dfrac{3}{4} \cdot \dfrac{5}{3}}$ *To divide by $\frac{3}{5}$ multiply by the reciprocal $\frac{5}{3}$.*

$= -\boxed{\dfrac{15}{12}}$ *Multiply the numerators and multiply the denominators.*

$= -\dfrac{5}{4}$ *Reduce.*

Use a reciprocal to write an equivalent multiplication expression.

19. $\frac{2}{5} \div \frac{4}{9} =$ _____

20. $\frac{3}{8} \div \frac{2}{3} =$ _____

21. $18 \div \frac{1}{6} =$ _____

Multiply or divide.

22. $-\frac{3}{8} \cdot \frac{5}{8}$

23. $-\frac{3}{8} \cdot \left(-\frac{2}{3}\right)$

24. $\frac{5}{9} \cdot \left(-\frac{7}{10}\right)$

_____   _____   _____

25. $\frac{3}{8} \div \frac{2}{3}$

26. $\frac{4}{5} \div \left(-\frac{1}{5}\right)$

27. $-7 \div \frac{1}{3}$

_____   _____   _____

28. $-\frac{5}{6} \div \left(-\frac{25}{48}\right)$

29. $\frac{2}{9} \div (-6)$

30. $-\frac{1}{6} \div \left(-2\frac{1}{3}\right)$

_____   _____   _____

Holt Algebra 1

California Standards Prep for ◆━2.0

LESSON 1-4

Review for Mastery
Powers and Exponents

A **power** is an expression that represents repeated multiplication of a factor. The factor is the **base**, and the number of times it is used as a factor is the **exponent**. Pay attention to parentheses, which tell you how much of the expression the exponent influences.

Power	Base	Exponent	Expanded Form
5^4	5	4	$5 \cdot 5 \cdot 5 \cdot 5$
-5^4	5	4	$-(5 \cdot 5 \cdot 5 \cdot 5)$
$(-5)^4$	-5	4	$(-5) \cdot (-5) \cdot (-5) \cdot (-5)$

To evaluate a power, perform the repeated multiplication.

Evaluate $\left(-\dfrac{4}{5}\right)^3$.

There are parentheses, so the exponent influences the negative *and* the fraction.

$$\left(-\frac{4}{5}\right)^3 = \left(-\frac{4}{5}\right)\left(-\frac{4}{5}\right)\left(-\frac{4}{5}\right)$$

$$= \left(+\frac{16}{25}\right)\left(-\frac{4}{5}\right) \qquad \text{\textit{Multiply two of the factors. A negative times a negative is positive.}}$$

$$= -\frac{64}{125} \qquad \text{\textit{Multiply again. A positive times a negative is negative.}}$$

Write the expanded form of each power.

1. 7^6 _____

2. $(-3)^2$ _____

3. $\left(\dfrac{1}{2}\right)^7$ _____

4. -6^5 _____

Evaluate each expression.

5. 3^5

6. -2^4

7. $\left(-\dfrac{2}{9}\right)^2$

_____ _____ _____

8. $(-2)^3$

9. 1^8

10. 0^2

_____ _____ _____

Holt Algebra 1

California Standards Prep for ◆—2.0

LESSON 1-4 Review for Mastery
Powers and Exponents continued

Some numbers can be written as a power of a given base. For example, 8 is a power of 2 because $2^3 = 8$.

If you know that a number is a power of a given base, you can find the exponent by doing repeated multiplication.

Write 81 as a power of −3.

$$-3 = (-3)^1$$
$$(-3)(-3) = 9 = (-3)^2$$
$$(-3)(-3)(-3) = -27 = (-3)^3$$
$$(-3)(-3)(-3)(-3) = 81 = (-3)^4$$
$$81 = (-3)^4$$

Complete each table.

11. powers of 2

Power	Multiplication	Value
2^1	2	
2^2	2 · 2	
2^3		
	2 · 2 · 2 · 2	
		32

12. powers of 3

Power	Multiplication	Value
3^1	3	
		9
	3 · 3 · 3	
3^4		

13. powers of 10

Power	Multiplication	Value
10^1	10	
10^2		
		1000

Write each number as a power of the given base.

14. 16; base 2

_____

15. 27; base 3

_____

16. 1,000,000; base 10

_____

17. 256; base 2

_____

18. −2187; base −3

_____

19. 10,000; base 100

_____

20. 625; base 5

_____

21. 4096; base −4

_____

22. $\frac{1}{8}$; base $\frac{1}{2}$

_____

Holt Algebra 1

California Standards ⬩—2.0

LESSON 1-5

Review for Mastery
Roots and Irrational Numbers

The **square root** of a number is the positive factor that you would square to get that number.

the square root of 9 is 3 because 3 squared is 9

$$\sqrt{9} = 3 \text{ because } 3^2 = 3 \cdot 3 = 9$$

A negative square root is the negative factor that you would square to get the number.

the negative square root of 25 is –5 because –5 squared is 25

$$-\sqrt{25} = -5 \text{ because } (-5)^2 = (-5)(-5) = 25$$

To evaluate a square root, think in reverse. Ask yourself, "What number do I square?"

Find $-\sqrt{36}$.

$(-6)^2 = (-6)(-6) = 36$ *Think: What negative factor do you square to get 36?*

$-\sqrt{36} = -6$

Find $\sqrt{\dfrac{4}{81}}$.

Think about the numerator and denominator separately.

$2^2 = 4$ *Think: What number do I square to get 4?*

$9^2 = 81$ *Think: What number do I square to get 81?*

$\left(\dfrac{2}{9}\right)^2 = \left(\dfrac{2}{9}\right)\left(\dfrac{2}{9}\right) = \dfrac{4}{81}$ *Combine the numerator and denominator to form a positive factor.*

$\sqrt{\dfrac{4}{81}} = \dfrac{2}{9}$

---

1. Complete this table of squares.

1^2	2^2	3^2	4^2			7^2	8^2			11^2	12^2	13^2
				25	36		81	100				

2. Complete this table of square roots.

$\sqrt{1}$	$\sqrt{4}$			$\sqrt{25}$	$\sqrt{36}$	$\sqrt{49}$			$\sqrt{100}$			
		3	4				8	9				13

Find each square root.

3. $\sqrt{121}$ _____

4. $-\sqrt{64}$ _____

5. $\sqrt{256}$ _____

6. $-\sqrt{400}$ _____

7. $\sqrt{\dfrac{1}{169}}$ _____

8. $-\sqrt{\dfrac{25}{144}}$ _____

Holt Algebra 1

California Standards ←2.0

LESSON
1-5

Review for Mastery
Roots and Irrational Numbers continued

This flowchart shows the
subsets of the real numbers
and how they are related.
To identify the classifications of
a real number, start at the
top and work your way down.

```
                    Real Numbers
                   /            \
        Rational Numbers      Irrational Numbers
           /        \
Terminating Decimals   Repeating Decimals
      /         \
Non-Integers      Integers
              /        \
   Negative Integers    Whole Numbers
                       /        \
                    Zero      Natural Numbers
```

Write all of the classifications that apply to the real number –4.

–4 can be shown on a number line. It is real.

–4 can be written as $-\frac{4}{1}$ so it is rational.

Its decimal representation
terminates: $-4 = -4.0$.

–4 is an integer.

–4 is a negative integer. Stop.
There are no more subsets in the
chart below negative integers.

```
                    Real Numbers
                   /            \
        Rational Numbers      Irrational Numbers
           /        \
Terminating Decimals   Repeating Decimals
      /         \
Non-Integers      Integers
              /        \
   Negative Integers    Whole Numbers
                       /        \
                    Zero      Natural Numbers
```

–4: real number, rational number, terminating decimal, integer

Write all classifications that apply to each real number.

9. 24

_____

10. $\frac{1}{3}$

_____

11. $\sqrt{5}$

_____

Holt Algebra 1

California Standards 1.0, 24.3, 25.1

Review for Mastery

LESSON 1-6 *Properties of Real Numbers*

The following properties make it easier to do mental math.

Property	Addition	Multiplication
Commutative Property	$3 + 4 = 4 + 3$	$2 \cdot 5 = 5 \cdot 2$
Associative Property	$(3 + 4) + 5 = 3 + (4 + 5)$	$(2 \cdot 4) \cdot 10 = 2 \cdot (4 \cdot 10)$
Distributive Property	$2(5 + 9) = 2(5) + 2(9)$	

Determine the number that makes the statement true.

$15 + \underline{\hspace{1cm}} = 17 + 15$ illustrates the Commutative Property.

The Commutative Property shows the same numbers rearranged in different ways, so 17 makes the statement true.

$(4 + t) + \underline{\hspace{1cm}} = 4 + (t + 23)$ illustrates the Associative Property.

The Associative Property shows the same numbers grouped in different ways, so 23 makes the statement true.

$3(\underline{\hspace{1cm}} + x) = 3(10) + 3(x)$ illustrates the Distributive Property.

The Distributive Property says that when multiplying a number by a sum, you can multiply by each number in the sum and then add, so 10 makes the statement true.

Determine the number that makes the statement true.

1. $13 + \underline{\hspace{1cm}} = 36 + 13$ illustrates the Commutative Property.

2. $21 + (5 + 7) = (21 + 5) + \underline{\hspace{1cm}}$ illustrates the Associative Property.

3. $12 (\underline{\hspace{1cm}} + 8) = 12(20) + 12(8)$ illustrates the Distributive Property.

4. $(11 + 31) + \underline{\hspace{1cm}} = 11 + (31 + 2)$ illustrates the Associative Property.

5. $22 + 8 = 8 + \underline{\hspace{1cm}}$ illustrates the Commutative Property.

6. $6(30 + 4) = 6(30) + 6(\underline{\hspace{1cm}})$ illustrates the Distributive Property.

Holt Algebra 1

California Standards 1.0, 24.3, 25.1

Review for Mastery
LESSON 1-6
Properties of Real Numbers continued

A set of numbers has **closure** under an operation if the result of the operation on any two numbers in the set is also in the set.

The integers are closed under addition, subtraction, and multiplication.

Operation	Numbers	Algebra
Addition	$5 + 9 = 14$	For integers a and b, $a + b$ is an integer.
Subtraction	$12 - 20 = -8$	For integers a and b, $a - b$ is an integer.
Multiplication	$4 \cdot 3 = 12$	For integers a and b, ab is an integer.

A **counterexample** is an example that proves a statement false.

Find a counterexample to disprove the statement "The natural numbers are closed under subtraction."

Find two natural numbers, a and b, such that their difference is not a natural number.

$a - b = 4 - 9 = -5$

Since -5 is not a natural number, this is a counterexample. The statement is false.

Find a counterexample to show that each statement is false.

7. The whole numbers are closed under division.

_____

8. The set of negative integers is closed under subtraction.

_____

9. The rational numbers are closed under the operation of taking a square root.

_____

12
Holt Algebra 1

California Standards 1.1, 25.1

LESSON
1-7

Review for Mastery
Simplifying Expressions

Expressions can contain more than one operation, and then can also include grouping symbols, like parentheses ( ), brackets [ ], and braces { }. Operations must be performed in a certain order.

I. Perform operations inside grouping symbols, with the innermost group being done first.

II. Evaluate powers (exponents).

III. Perform multiplication and division in order from left to right.

IV. Perform addition and subtraction in order from left to right.

Simplify the expression $6^2 - 3(5 - 1) + 2$.

$6^2 - 3(5 - 1) + 2$

$6^2 - 3 \cdot 4 + 2$ *Evaluate $5 - 1$.*

$36 - 3 \cdot 4 + 2$ *Evaluate 6^2.*

$36 - 12 + 2$ *Evaluate $3 \cdot 4$.*

$24 + 2$ *Add and subtract from left to right.*

26

Simplify each expression.

1. $6 \div 2 \cdot 4 - 3$

2. $18 \div 3^2 - 5 + 2$

3. $3 + 5 \cdot 3 - 8 \div 2$

4. $3 + 3 \div 3 + 3$

5. $7^2 + 4^2 \cdot 3$

6. $6 + 10 \div 2 \cdot 5 - 1$

Simplify each expression.

7. $2^2 + 6(8 - 5) \div 2$

8. $\dfrac{(3 + 2)(4 + 3) + 5^2}{6 - 2^2}$

9. $4(3 - |2 - 6| + 5)$

Holt Algebra 1

Name _____ Date _____ Class _____

California Standards 1.1, 25.1

LESSON 1-7
Review for Mastery
Simplifying Expressions continued

Terms can be combined only if they are **like terms**. Like terms can have different coefficients, but they must have the same variables raised to the same powers.

Like Terms	Not Like Terms
$4x^2$, $7x^2$	$3m$, $5m^3$
$12y$, $18y$	$12y$, $12xy$
$5ab^2$, $-ab^2$	st^4, $3s^4t$

Simplify $24x^3 - 4x^3$.

$24x^3 - 4x^3$

   $20x^3$ *Subtract the coefficients only.*

Simplify $4(x + y) + 5x - 9$.

$4x + 4y + 5x - 9$ *Distribute 4.*

$4x + 5x + 4y - 9$ *Use the Commutative Property.*

$9x + 4y - 9$ *Add the like terms 4x and 5x.*

$9x + 4y - 9$ *No other terms are like terms.*

State whether each pair of terms are like terms.

10. $4xy$ and $3xy$ **11.** $2s^2$ and $5s$ **12.** $-10a$ and $-10b$

_____   _____   _____

If possible, simplify each expression by combining like terms.

13. $7st - 3st$ **14.** $10y^3 + 5y - 4y^3$ **15.** $12x^3 + 6x^4$

_____   _____   _____

Simplify each expression.

16. $3(x + 6) - 2$ **17.** $7y + 2(y - 5) + y$

_____   _____

       Holt Algebra 1

California Standards Prep for ◆─5.0; ◆─2.0

Review for Mastery

LESSON 2-1

Solving One-Step Equations

Any addition equation can be solved by adding the opposite. If the equation involves subtraction, it helps to first rewrite the subtraction as addition.

Solve $x + 4 = 10$.

| Find the opposite of this number. |

Check:

$x + 4 = 10$

$6 + 4 \overset{?}{=} 10$

$10 \overset{?}{=} 10 ✓$

$x + 4 = 10$ The opposite of 4 is -4.

$\underline{-4 \quad -4}$ Add -4 to each side.

$x = \quad 6$

Solve $-5 = x - 8$.

| Find the opposite of this number. |

Check:

$-5 = x - 8$

$-5 \overset{?}{=} 3 - 8$

$-5 \overset{?}{=} -5 ✓$

$-5 = x + -8$ Rewrite subtraction as addition.

                     The opposite of -8 is 8.

$\underline{+8 \qquad +8}$ Add 8 to each side.

$3 = x$

Rewrite each equation with addition. Then state the number that should be added to each side.

1. $x - 7 = 12$ **2.** $x - 8 = -5$ **3.** $-4 = x - 2$

_____ _____ _____

_____ _____ _____

Solve each equation. Check your answers.

4. $x + 4 = 12$ **5.** $21 = x + 2$ **6.** $x + 3 = 8$

_____ _____ _____

7. $x + 10 = -6$ **8.** $-8 = x - 2$ **9.** $x + 5 = -2$

_____ _____ _____

Holt Algebra 1

California Standards Prep for ⬅5.0; ⬅2.0

LESSON 2-1

Review for Mastery
Solving One-Step Equations continued

Solve equations involving multiplication and division by performing the inverse operation.

Solve $\frac{x}{5} = 4$.

$\frac{x}{5} = 4$ *x is <u>divided</u> by 5.*

$5 \cdot \frac{x}{5} = 4 \cdot 5$ *<u>Multiply</u> both sides by 5.*

$\frac{5x}{5} = 20$ *Simplify.*

$x = 20$

Check: $\frac{x}{5} = 4$

$\frac{20}{5} \stackrel{?}{=} 4$

$4 \stackrel{?}{=} 4$ ✓

Solve $-3x = 27$.

$-3x = 27$ *x is <u>multiplied</u> by -3.*

$\frac{-3x}{-3} = \frac{27}{-3}$ *<u>Divide</u> both sides by -3.*

$x = -9$ *Simplify.*

Check: $-3x = 27$

$-3(-9) \stackrel{?}{=} 27$

$27 \stackrel{?}{=} 27$ ✓

Circle the correct word in each sentence. Then solve the equation.

10. $\frac{x}{-2} = 7$

     x is <u>multiplied/divided</u> by -2.

     To solve, <u>multiply/divide</u> both sides by -2.

     x = _____

11. $5m = -40$

     m is <u>multiplied/divided</u> by 5.

     To solve, <u>multiply/divide</u> both sides by 5.

     m = _____

Solve each equation. Check your answers.

12. $-2x = -20$

13. $\frac{w}{5} = -7$

14. $6z = -42$

_____ _____ _____

Holt Algebra 1

California Standards Prep for ◆—5.0

Review for Mastery

LESSON 2-2

Solving Two-Step Equations

When solving two-step equations, first identify the operations and the order in which they are applied to the variable. Then use inverse operations.

	Operations	Solve using Inverse Operations
$4x - 3 = 15$	• x is multiplied by 4. • Then 3 is subtracted.	• Add 3 to both sides. • Then divide both sides by 4.
$\frac{x}{3} + 2 = 9$	• x is divided by 3. • Then 2 is added.	• Add −2 to both sides. • Then multiply both sides by 3.

The order of the inverse operations is the order of operations in reverse.

Solve $5x - 7 = 13$.

		Check:
$5x - 7 = 13$	x is multiplied by 5. Then 7 is subtracted.	$5x - 7 = 13$
$\underline{+7 \quad +7}$	Add 7 to both sides.	$5(4) - 7 \overset{?}{=} 13$
$5x = 20$		$20 - 7 \overset{?}{=} 13$
$\dfrac{5x}{5} = \dfrac{20}{5}$	Divide both sides by 5.	$13 \overset{?}{=} 13$ ✓
$x = 4$		

Solve each equation. Check your answers.

1. $3x - 8 = 4$

2. $\dfrac{b}{2} - 4 = 26$

3. $3y + 4 = 9$

4. $14 = 3x - 1$

Holt Algebra 1

California Standards Prep for ✦─5.0

Review for Mastery

LESSON 2-2

Solving Two-Step Equations   continued

A two-step equation with fractions can be simplified by multiplying each side by the LCD. This will clear the fractions.

Solve $\frac{x}{4} + \frac{2}{3} = 2$.

$$\frac{x}{4} + \frac{2}{3} = 2$$

$$12\left(\frac{x}{4} + \frac{2}{3}\right) = (12)2 \quad \textit{Multiply both sides by the LCD 12.}$$

$$12\left(\frac{x}{4}\right) + 12\left(\frac{2}{3}\right) = 12(2)$$

$$3x + 8 = 24 \quad \textit{x is multiplied by 3. 8 is added.}$$

$$\underline{\quad -8 \quad -8 \quad} \quad \textit{Add} -8 \textit{ to both sides.}$$

$$3x = 16$$

$$\frac{3x}{3} = \frac{16}{3} \quad \textit{Divide both sides by 3.}$$

$$x = \frac{16}{3}$$

Check:

$$\frac{x}{4} + \frac{2}{3} = 2$$

$$\frac{1}{4}x + \frac{2}{3} = 2$$

$$\frac{1}{4}\left(\frac{16}{3}\right) + \frac{2}{3} \stackrel{?}{=} 2$$

$$\frac{16}{12} + \frac{2}{3} \stackrel{?}{=} 2$$

$$\frac{4}{3} + \frac{2}{3} \stackrel{?}{=} 2$$

$$\frac{6}{3} \stackrel{?}{=} 2$$

$$2 \stackrel{?}{=} 2 ✓$$

Solve each equation. Check your answers.

5. $\frac{x}{2} + \frac{3}{8} = 1$

6. $\frac{w}{3} + \frac{2}{5} = \frac{1}{15}$

7. $3 = \frac{a}{5} + \frac{1}{2}$

Holt Algebra 1

California Standards ◄━4.0, ◄━5.0

LESSON 2-3

Review for Mastery
Solving Multi-Step Equations

Solving a multi-step equation is similar to solving a two-step equation. You use inverse operations to write an equivalent equation at each step.

	Operations	Solve Using Inverse Operations
$\dfrac{3x - 1}{2} = 7$	• x is multiplied by 3. • Then 1 is subtracted. • Then the result is divided by 2.	• Multiply both sides by 2. • Add 1 to both sides. • Divide both sides by 3.

Solve $\dfrac{3x - 1}{2} = 7$. **Check your answer.**

Check:

$$2\left(\dfrac{3x - 1}{2}\right) = 2(7) \qquad \textit{Multiply both sides by 2.} \qquad \dfrac{3x - 1}{2} = 7$$

$$3x - 1 = 14 \qquad\qquad\qquad\qquad\qquad\qquad \dfrac{3(5) - 1}{2} \overset{?}{=} 7$$

$$\underline{\quad + 1 = +1\quad} \qquad\qquad \textit{Add 1 to both sides.} \qquad \dfrac{15 - 1}{2} \overset{?}{=} 7$$

$$3x \quad = 15 \qquad\qquad\qquad\qquad\qquad\qquad \dfrac{14}{2} \overset{?}{=} 7$$

$$\dfrac{3x}{3} = \dfrac{15}{3} \qquad\qquad\qquad \textit{Divide both sides by 3.} \qquad 7 \overset{?}{=} 7 \checkmark$$

$$x = 5$$

Solve each equation. Check your answers.

1. $\dfrac{5y + 3}{4} = 7$

2. $\dfrac{3 + 2m}{3} = 9$

3. $\dfrac{6x - 4}{5} = 4$

4. $\dfrac{2r - 3}{5} = 3$

Holt Algebra 1

California Standards ←~4.0, ←~5.0

LESSON 2-3

Review for Mastery

Solving Multi-Step Equations continued

Sometimes you must combine like terms before you can use inverse operations to solve an equation.

	Equivalent Equations	Reasons
$3x + 5 + 4x = 19$ ——→	$3x + 4x + 5 = 19$	Commutative Property of Addition
	$7x + 5 = 19$	Combine like terms.
$15y - 6 - 11y = 2$ ——→	$15y - 11y - 6 = 2$	Commutative Property of Addition
	$4y - 6 = 2$	Combine like terms.

Solve $2x - 7 + 3x = 13$. Check your answer.

$$\begin{aligned} 2x + 3x - 7 &= 13 \\ 5x - 7 &= 13 \\ +7 \quad &+7 \\ \hline 5x &= 20 \\ \frac{5x}{5} &= \frac{20}{5} \\ x &= 4 \end{aligned}$$

Group like terms together.
Combine like terms.
Add 7 to both sides.

Divide both sides by 5.

Check:
$$2x - 7 + 3x = 13$$
$$2(4) - 7 + 3(4) \stackrel{?}{=} 13$$
$$8 - 7 + 12 \stackrel{?}{=} 13$$
$$13 \stackrel{?}{=} 13 \checkmark$$

Solve each equation. Check your answers.

5. $5y + 4 - 2y = 16$

6. $13m - 4 - 10m = 2$

_____

_____

7. $3w - 7 + w = 5$

8. $6 + 7x - 5x = 2$

_____

_____

Holt Algebra 1

Name _____ Date _____ Class _____

California Standards ◆—4.0, ◆—5.0

Review for Mastery

LESSON 2-4

Solving Equations with Variables on Both Sides

Variables must be collected on the same side of the equation before the equation can be solved.

Solve $10x = 2x - 16$.

$$10x = 2x - 16$$

$$\underline{-2x \quad -2x} \qquad \text{Add } -2x \text{ to both sides.}$$

$$8x = -16$$

$$\frac{8x}{8} = \frac{-16}{8} \qquad \text{Divide both sides by 8.}$$

$$x = -2$$

Check:

$$10x = 2x - 16$$

$$10(-2) \overset{?}{=} 2(-2) - 16$$

$$-20 \overset{?}{=} -4 - 16$$

$$-20 \overset{?}{=} -20 \checkmark$$

Solve $3x = 5(x + 2)$.

$$3x = 5x + 10 \qquad \text{Distribute.}$$

$$\underline{-5x \quad -5x} \qquad \text{Add } -5x \text{ to both sides.}$$

$$-2x = 10$$

$$\frac{-2x}{-2} = \frac{10}{-2} \qquad \text{Divide both sides by } -2.$$

$$x = -5$$

Check:

$$3x = 5(x + 2)$$

$$3(-5) \overset{?}{=} 5(-5 + 2)$$

$$-15 \overset{?}{=} 5(-3)$$

$$-15 \overset{?}{=} -15 \checkmark$$

Write the first step you would take to solve each equation.

1. $3x + 2 = 7x$ _____

2. $-4x - 6 = -10x$ _____

3. $15x + 7 = -3x$ _____

Solve each equation. Check your answers.

4. $4x + 2 = 5(x + 10)$ **5.** $-10 + y + 3 = 4y - 13$ **6.** $3(t + 7) + 2 = 6t - 2 + 2t$

Holt Algebra 1

Name _____ Date _____ Class _____

California Standards ←4.0, ←5.0

Review for Mastery

LESSON 2-4

Solving Equations with Variables on Both Sides continued

Some equations have infinitely many solutions. These equations are true for all values of the variable. Some equations have no solutions. There is no value of the variable that will make the equation true.

Solve $-3x + 9 = 4x + 9 - 7x$.

$-3x + 9 = -3x + 9$	Combine like terms.
$\underline{+3x \qquad +3x}$	Add $3x$ to each side.
$9 = 9 ✓$	True statement.

The solution is the set of all real numbers.

Check any value of x:

Try $x = 4$.

$-3x + 9 = 4x + 9 - 7x$

$-3(4) + 9 \overset{?}{=} 4(4) + 9 - 7(4)$

$-12 + 9 \overset{?}{=} 16 + 9 - 28$

$-3 \overset{?}{=} -3 ✓$

Solve $2x + 6 + 3x = 5x - 10$.

$2x + 6 + 3x = 5x - 10$	
$5x + 6 = 5x - 10$	Combine like terms.
$\underline{-5x \qquad -5x}$	Add $-5x$ to each side.
$6 = -10 \; ✗$	False statement.

There is no solution.

Check any value of x:

Try $x = 1$.

$2x + 6 + 3x = 5x - 10$

$2(1) + 6 + 3(1) \overset{?}{=} 5(1) - 10$

$2 + 6 + 3 \overset{?}{=} 5 - 10$

$11 \overset{?}{=} -5 \; ✗$

Solve each equation.

7. $x + 2 = x + 4$

8. $-2x + 8 = 2x + 4$

9. $5 + 3g = 3g + 5$

_____ _____ _____

10. $5x - 1 - 4x = x + 7$

11. $2(f + 3) + 4f = 6 + 6f$

12. $3x + 7 - 2x = 4x + 10$

_____ _____ _____

Holt Algebra 1

California Standards ◆—15.0

LESSON 2-5

Review for Mastery

Solving Proportions

Use cross products to solve proportions.

Solve $\frac{x}{10} = \frac{4}{25}$.

$$\frac{x}{10} \times \frac{4}{25}$$

$25x = 40$ *Multiply x by 25. Write the product on the left.*
                Multiply 10 by 4. Write the product on the right.

$\frac{25x}{25} = \frac{40}{25}$ *Divide both sides by 25.*

$x = 1.6$

Sometimes it is necessary to use the Distributive Property.

Solve $\frac{4}{x + 2} = \frac{2}{5}$.

$$\frac{4}{x + 2} \times \frac{2}{5}$$ *Multiply 4 by 5 and x + 2 by 2.*

$20 = 2(x + 2)$

$20 = 2x + 4$ *Distribute 2.*

$\underline{-4 \qquad\quad -4}$ *Subtract 4 from both sides.*

$\frac{16}{2} = \frac{2x}{2}$ *Divide both sides by 2.*

$8 = x$

Solve each proportion.

1. $\frac{x}{20} = \frac{1}{8}$

2. $\frac{5}{12} = \frac{1.25}{k}$

3. $\frac{3}{4} = \frac{a + 5}{21}$

4. $\frac{3}{y - 3} = \frac{1}{9}$

Holt Algebra 1

California Standards ← 15.0

Review for Mastery

LESSON 2-5

Solving Proportions continued

You can solve percent problems with this proportion: $\dfrac{\text{part}}{\text{whole}} = \dfrac{\text{percent}}{100}$.

Find 30% of 70.

percent   whole

$\dfrac{\text{part}}{\text{whole}} = \dfrac{\text{percent}}{100}$

$\dfrac{x}{70} = \dfrac{30}{100}$ *The part is x.*

$100x = 2100$

$x = 21$

30% of 70 is 21.

What percent of 86 is 64.5?

percent   whole   part

$\dfrac{\text{part}}{\text{whole}} = \dfrac{\text{percent}}{100}$

$\dfrac{64.5}{86} = \dfrac{x}{100}$ *The percent is x.*

$86x = 6450$

$x = 75$

64.5 is 75% of 86.

You can also solve percent problems with this equation:

$$\text{percent} \cdot \text{whole} = \text{part}$$
(as a decimal)

36 is what percent of 50?

Rewrite:	What percent of 50 is 36?	*Use the form "percent of whole is part."*
Translate:	$x \cdot 50 = 36$	*Translate into percent • whole = part.*
Solve:	$x = 0.72$	*Divide both sides by 50.*
	$x = 72\%$	*Write the decimal as a percent.*

36 is 72% of 50.

Complete the labels with the words "part," "whole," and "percent."
Then find each value.

5. Find 16% of 20.

_____

6. What percent of 45 is 6.75?

_____

Rewrite each problem in the form "percent of whole is part."

7. 14 is what percent of 40? _____ of _____ is _____?

8. Find 65% of 80. _____ of _____ is _____?

Holt Algebra 1

California Standards Ext. of ◄─5.0

Review for Mastery

LESSON 2-6

Solving Literal Equations for a Variable

Solving for a variable in a formula can make it easier to use that formula. The process is similar to that of solving multi-step equations. Find the operations being performed on the variable you are solving for, and then use inverse operations.

	Operations	Solve using Inverse Operations
$A = lw$ Solve for w.	• w is multiplied by l.	• Divide both sides by l.
$P = 2l + 2w$ Solve for w.	• w is multiplied by 2. • Then $2l$ is added.	• Add $-2l$ to both sides. • Then divide both sides by 2.

The formula $A = \frac{1}{2}bh$ relates the area A of a triangle to its base b and height h. Solve the formula for b.

> The order of the inverse operations is the order of operations in reverse.

$A = \frac{1}{2}bh$	b is multiplied by $\frac{1}{2}$.
$\left(\frac{2}{1}\right) \cdot A = \left(\frac{2}{1}\right)\frac{1}{2}bh$	Multiply both sides by $\frac{2}{1}$.
$2A = bh$	b is multiplied by h.
$\dfrac{2A}{h} = \dfrac{bh}{h}$	Divide both sides by h.
$\dfrac{2A}{h} = b$	Simplify.

Solve for the indicated variable.

1. $P = 4s$ for s

2. $a + b + c = 180$ for b

3. $P = \frac{KT}{V}$ for K

_____   _____   _____

The formula $V = \frac{1}{3}lwh$ relates the volume of a square pyramid to its base length l, base width w, and height h.

4. Solve the formula for w.   _____

5. A square pyramid has a volume of 560 in^3, a base length of 10 in., and a height of 14 in. What is its base width?   _____

Holt Algebra 1

California Standards Ext. of ◆—5.0

LESSON 2-6 Review for Mastery

Solving Literal Equations for a Variable *continued*

Any equation with two or more variables can be solved for any given variable.

Solve $x = \dfrac{y - z}{10}$ **for y.**

$x = \dfrac{y - z}{10}$ $y - z$ is divided by 10.

$10(x) = 10\left(\dfrac{y - z}{10}\right)$ Multiply both sides by 10.

$10x = y - z$ z is subtracted from y. Add z to both sides.

$\underline{+z \qquad +z}$

$10x + z = y$

Solve $a = b + \dfrac{c}{d}$ **for c.**

$a = b + \dfrac{c}{d}$

$\underline{-b \quad -b}$ Add $-b$ to each side.

$a - b = \dfrac{c}{d}$

$d(a - b) = \left(\dfrac{c}{d}\right)d$ Multiply both sides by d.

$d(a - b) = c$ Simplify.

State the first inverse operation to perform when solving for the indicated variable.

6. $y = x + z$; for z _____

7. $\dfrac{f + g}{2} = h$; for g _____

8. $t = -3r + \dfrac{s}{5}$; for s _____

Solve for the indicated variable.

9. $3ab = c$; for a

10. $y = x + \dfrac{z}{3}$; for z

11. $\dfrac{m + 3}{n} = p$; for m

_____ _____ _____

Holt Algebra 1

California Standards 3.0, ⬅5.0

LESSON 2-7

Review for Mastery
Solving Absolute-Value Equations

There are three steps in solving an absolute-value equation. First use inverse operations to isolate the absolute-value expression. Then rewrite the equation as two cases that do not involve absolute values. Finally, solve these new equations.

Solve $|x - 3| + 4 = 8$.

Step 1: Isolate the absolute-value expression.

$|x - 3| + 4 = 8$

$\underline{\quad\quad -4 \quad -4}$ *Subtract 4 from both sides.*

$|x - 3| = 4$

Step 2: Rewrite the equation as two cases.

$|x - 3| = 4$

Case 1 ⬋   ⬊ **Case 2**

Step 3: $x - 3 = -4$ $x - 3 = 4$

Solve. $\underline{\quad +3 \quad +3}$ $\underline{\quad +3 \quad +3}$ *Add 3 to both sides.*

$x = -1$ $x = 7$

Write the solution set as $\{-1, 7\}$.

Solve each equation.

1. $|x - 2| - 3 = 5$

2. $|x + 7| + 2 = 10$

3. $4|x - 5| = 20$

4. $|2x| + 1 = 7$

Holt Algebra 1

LESSON
2-7

Review for Mastery
Solving Absolute-Value Equations continued

Some absolute-value equations have two solutions. Others have one solution or no solution. To decide how many solutions there are, first isolate the absolute-value expression.

Original Equation	Simplified Equation	Solutions
$\lvert x \rvert + 5 = 7$ ⟶	▶$\begin{aligned}\lvert x \rvert + 5 &= 7 \\ -5 \quad &-5 \\ \hline \lvert x \rvert &= 2\end{aligned}$	$\lvert x \rvert = 2$ has two solutions, $x = -2$ and $x = 2$. The solution set is $\{-2, 2\}$.
$\lvert x - 5 \rvert + 2 = 2$ ⟶	▶$\begin{aligned}\lvert x - 5 \rvert + 2 &= 2 \\ -2 \quad &-2 \\ \hline \lvert x - 5 \rvert &= 0\end{aligned}$	$\lvert x - 5 \rvert = 0$ means $x - 5 = 0$, so there is one solution, $x = 5$. The solution set is $\{5\}$.
$\lvert x + 7 \rvert + 4 = 1$ ⟶	▶$\begin{aligned}\lvert x + 7 \rvert + 4 &= 1 \\ -4 \quad &-4 \\ \hline \lvert x + 7 \rvert &= -3\end{aligned}$	$\lvert x + 7 \rvert = -3$ has no solutions because an absolute-value expression is never negative. The solution set is the empty set, $\varnothing$.

Solve $\lvert 2x + 1 \rvert - 3 = -7$.

$$\lvert 2x + 1 \rvert - 3 = -7$$

$$\underline{+3 \qquad +3} \qquad \textit{Add 3 to both sides.}$$

$$\lvert 2x + 1 \rvert = -4 \qquad \textit{Absolute value cannot be negative.}$$

The solution set is the empty set, $\varnothing$.

Solve each equation.

5. $8 + \lvert x - 2 \rvert = 8$

6. $\lvert x + 1 \rvert + 5 = 2$

_____

7. $4\lvert x - 3 \rvert = -16$

8. $3\lvert x + 10 \rvert = 0$

_____

Holt Algebra 1

Name _____ Date _____ Class _____

California Standards Prep for ✦—5.0

Review for Mastery
LESSON 3-1
Graphing and Writing Inequalities

Describe the solutions of x + 2 < 6.

Choose different values for x. Be sure to choose positive and negative values as well as zero.

	x = 0	x = 2	x = −4	x = 5	x = 4	x = 3	x = 3.5
x + 2 < 6	$0 + 2 \overset{?}{<} 6$ $2 \overset{?}{<} 6$ True	$2 + 2 \overset{?}{<} 6$ $4 \overset{?}{<} 6$ True	$-4 + 2 \overset{?}{<} 6$ $-2 \overset{?}{<} 6$ True	$5 + 2 \overset{?}{<} 6$ $7 \overset{?}{<} 6$ False	$4 + 2 \overset{?}{<} 6$ $6 \overset{?}{<} 6$ False	$3 + 2 \overset{?}{<} 6$ $5 \overset{?}{<} 6$ True	$3.5 + 2 \overset{?}{<} 6$ $5.5 \overset{?}{<} 6$ True

Plot the points on a number line. Use T to label points that make the inequality true.

Use F to label points that make the inequality false.

Look for the point at which the True statements turn to False statements. Numbers less than 4 make the statement true. The solutions are all real numbers less than 4.

Test the inequalities for the values given. Then describe the solutions of the inequality.

1. $5x \le 10$

x = 0	x = 1	x = −3	x = −4	x = 2	x = 3	x = 1.5

2. $m + 1 < -2$

x = 0	x = 3	x = −4	x = −3	x = −2	x = −2.5	x = −5

Describe the solutions of each inequality in words.

3. $\frac{x}{3} > 4$ _____

4. $g - 4 \le -3$ _____

Copyright © by Holt, Rinehart and Winston.
All rights reserved.

29

Holt Algebra 1

California Standards Prep for ➛5.0

Review for Mastery

LESSON
3-1

Graphing and Writing Inequalities continued

Graph $x \le 3$.

Step 1: Draw a circle on the number.

Step 2: Decide whether to fill in the circle.

    If > or <, leave empty.

    If ≥ or ≤, fill in.

Step 3: Draw an arrow.

    If < or ≤, draw arrow to left.

    If > or ≥, draw arrow to the right.

Write the inequality shown by the graph.

Step 1: Write a variable and the number
indicated by the circle.

$x \ ? \ -4$

Step 2: Look at the direction of the arrow.

    If arrow points left, use < or ≤.

    If arrow points right, use > or ≥.

$x >$ or ≥ -4

Step 3: Look at the circle.

    If circle is empty, use > or <.

    If circle is filled in, use ≥ or ≤.

$x > -4$

Graph each inequality.

5. $m \ge 8 - 3$

6. $p < 3.5$

Write the inequality shown by the graph.

7.

_____

8.

_____

Holt Algebra 1

California Standards Prep for ⚜5.0

Review for Mastery

LESSON 3-2

Solving Inequalities by Adding or Subtracting

The method for solving one-step inequalities by adding is just like the method for solving one-step equations by adding.

Solve $x - 2 = 1$ and graph the solution.

$x - 2 = 1$

$\underline{+2 \quad +2}$ Add 2 to each side.

$x = 3$

Solve $x - 2 \geq 1$ and graph the solutions.

$x - 2 \geq 1$

$\underline{+2 \quad +2}$ Add 2 to each side.

$x \geq 3$

Solve $-4 = a - 3$ and graph the solution.

$-4 = a - 3$

$\underline{+3 \qquad +3}$ Add 3 to each side.

$-1 = a$

Solve $-4 > a - 3$ and graph the solutions.

$-4 > a - 3$

$\underline{+3 \qquad +3}$ Add 3 to each side.

$-1 > a$

$a < -1$

Solve each inequality and graph the solutions.

1. $b - 4 < 3$

_____

2. $x - 5 < -2$

_____

3. $-10 > -6 + x$

_____

4. $1 \leq f - 3$

_____

Holt Algebra 1

Name _____ Date _____ Class _____

LESSON 3-2
Review for Mastery
Solving Inequalities by Adding or Subtracting continued

The method for solving one-step inequalities by subtracting is just like the
method for solving one-step equations by subtracting.

Solve $x + 3 = 7$ and graph the solution.

$x + 3 = 7$

$\underline{-3 \quad -3}$ *Subtract 3 from each side.*

$x = 4$

Solve $x + 3 < 7$ and graph the solutions.

$x + 3 < 7$

$\underline{-3 \quad -3}$ *Subtract 3 from each side.*

$x < 4$

Solve $-4 = h + 2$ and graph the solution.

$-4 = h + 2$

$\underline{-2 \qquad -2}$ *Subtract 2 from each side.*

$-6 = h$

Solve $-4 \leq h + 2$ and graph the solutions.

$-4 \leq h + 2$

$\underline{-2 \qquad -2}$ *Subtract 2 from each side.*

$-6 \leq h$

$h \geq -6$

Solve each inequality and graph the solutions.

5. $c + 3 \leq -2$

6. $4 + x < 6$

7. $4 < w + 7$

8. $9 \leq 5 + n$

Holt Algebra 1

California Standards Prep for ←5.0

LESSON
3-3
Review for Mastery
Solving Inequalities by Multiplying or Dividing

The inequality sign must be reversed when multiplying by a negative number.

Multiplying by a positive number:

$2 < 5$ *True*

$3 \cdot 2 \overset{?}{<} 3 \cdot 5$ *Multiply both sides by a positive number.*

$6 \overset{?}{<} 15$ ✓   *Statement is true.*

Multiplying by a negative number:

$2 < 5$ *True*

$(-3) \cdot 2 \overset{?}{<} (-3) \cdot 5$ *Multiply both sides by a negative number.*

$-6 \overset{?}{<} -15$ ✗   *Statement is false.*

$-6 > -15$ ✓   *Reverse inequality sign so statement is true.*

Solve $\frac{x}{3} > -2$ and graph the solution.

$\frac{x}{3} > -2$

$3 \cdot \frac{x}{3} > 3 \cdot (-2)$ *Multiply both sides by 3.*

$x > -6$

Solve $\frac{x}{-4} \geq 1$ and graph the solutions.

$\frac{x}{-4} \geq 1$

$(-4) \cdot \frac{x}{-4} \geq (-4) \cdot 1$ *Multiply both sides by -4.*

$x \leq -4$ *Reverse inequality sign.*

Solve each inequality and graph the solutions.

1. $\frac{x}{3} \geq -2$

2. $-\frac{3}{4}g < -3$

Solve each inequality.

3. $-1 < \frac{v}{-5}$

4. $\frac{5}{6}m > 10$

Holt Algebra 1

LESSON 3-3 Review for Mastery
Solving Inequalities by Multiplying or Dividing continued

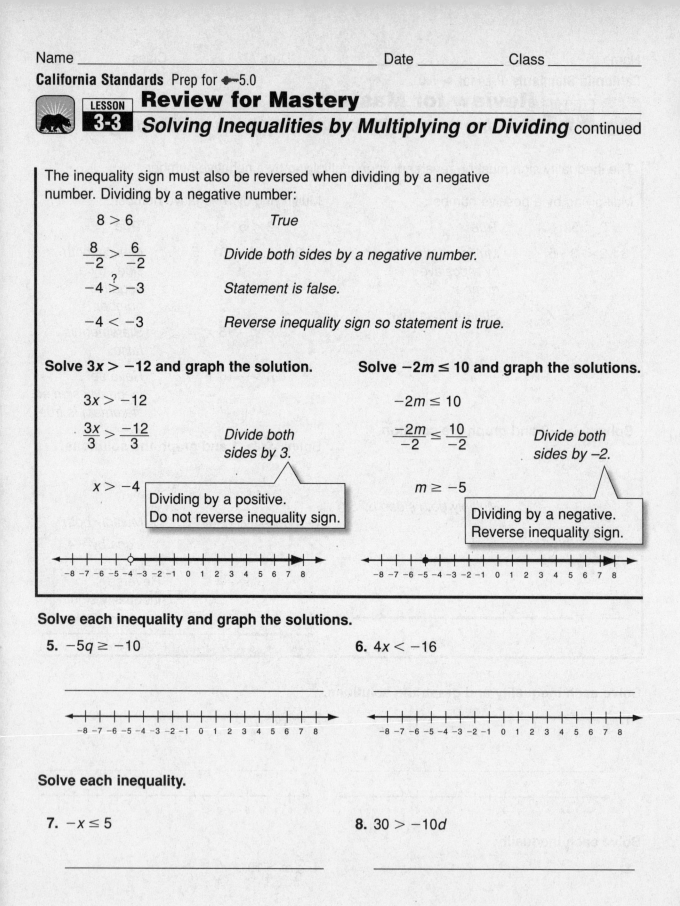

The inequality sign must also be reversed when dividing by a negative number. Dividing by a negative number:

$8 > 6$ *True*

$\dfrac{8}{-2} > \dfrac{6}{-2}$ *Divide both sides by a negative number.*

$-4 \overset{?}{>} -3$ *Statement is false.*

$-4 < -3$ *Reverse inequality sign so statement is true.*

Solve $3x > -12$ and graph the solution.

$3x > -12$

$\dfrac{3x}{3} > \dfrac{-12}{3}$ *Divide both sides by 3.*

$x > -4$

Dividing by a positive.
Do not reverse inequality sign.

Solve $-2m \leq 10$ and graph the solutions.

$-2m \leq 10$

$\dfrac{-2m}{-2} \leq \dfrac{10}{-2}$ *Divide both sides by −2.*

$m \geq -5$

Dividing by a negative.
Reverse inequality sign.

Solve each inequality and graph the solutions.

5. $-5q \geq -10$ 6. $4x < -16$

Solve each inequality.

7. $-x \leq 5$ 8. $30 > -10d$

    34   **Holt Algebra 1**

Name _____ Date _____ Class _____

California Standards ◆—4.0, ◆—5.0

LESSON 3-4

Review for Mastery
Solving Two-Step and Multi-Step Inequalities

When solving inequalities with more than one step, use inverse operations to isolate the variable. The order of the inverse operations is the order of the operations in reverse. You can check your solution by substituting the endpoint and another point in the solution back into the original inequality.

Solve $-5x + 3 < 23$ and graph the solutions.

$-5x + 3 < 23$

$\underline{\quad -3 \quad -3 \quad}$ *Add -3 to each side.*

$-5x < 20$

$\dfrac{-5x}{-5} < \dfrac{20}{-5}$ *Divide both sides by -5.*

$x > -4$ *Reverse the inequality sign.*

Check:

Try -4.   Try 6.

$-5x + 3 < 23$ $-5x + 3 < 23$

$-5(-4) + 3 \overset{?}{<} 23$ $-5(6) + 3 \overset{?}{<} 23$

$20 + 3 \overset{?}{<} 23$ $-30 + 3 \overset{?}{<} 23$

$23 \overset{?}{<} 23$ ✗ $-27 \overset{?}{<} 23$ ✓

The endpoint -4 is not a solution. The open circle on the graph is correct. The value 6 is a solution. The direction of the inequality symbol is correct.

Solve each inequality and graph the solutions.

1. $-3e - 10 \leq -4$

_____

2. $\dfrac{c}{2} + 8 > 11$

_____

3. $15 \leq 3 - 4s$

_____

4. $\dfrac{3}{4}j + 1 > 4$

_____

Holt Algebra 1

Name _____ Date _____ Class _____

California Standards ⬥—4.0, ⬥—5.0

LESSON 3-4
Review for Mastery
Solving Two-Step and Multi-Step Inequalities continued

Solving inequalities may require using the Distributive Property, combining like terms, or clearing fractions. Remember that you can clear fractions by multiplying both sides of the inequality by the least common denominator (LCD).

Solve $\frac{3}{2}x + \frac{1}{6} \geq \frac{5}{3}$.

$$\frac{3}{2}x + \frac{1}{6} \geq \frac{5}{3}$$

$6\left(\frac{3}{2}x + \frac{1}{6}\right) \geq 6\left(\frac{5}{3}\right)$ *Multiply both sides by the LCD 6.*

$6\left(\frac{3}{2}x\right) + 6\left(\frac{1}{6}\right) \geq 6\left(\frac{5}{3}\right)$ *Distribute 6.*

$9x + 1 \geq 10$

$\underline{\quad -1 \quad -1 \quad}$ *Add −1 to both sides.*

$9x \geq 9$

$\frac{9x}{9} \geq \frac{9}{9}$ *Divide both sides by 9.*

$x \geq 1$

Check:

Try 1.	Try 2.
$\frac{3}{2}x + \frac{1}{6} \geq \frac{5}{3}$	$\frac{3}{2}x + \frac{1}{6} \geq \frac{5}{3}$
$\frac{3}{2}(1) + \frac{1}{6} \overset{?}{>} \frac{5}{3}$	$\frac{3}{2}(2) + \frac{1}{6} \overset{?}{\geq} \frac{5}{3}$
$\frac{3}{2} + \frac{1}{6} \overset{?}{\geq} \frac{5}{3}$	$3 + \frac{1}{6} \overset{?}{\geq} \frac{5}{3}$
$\frac{9}{6} + \frac{1}{6} \overset{?}{\geq} \frac{10}{6}$	$3\frac{1}{6} \overset{?}{\geq} 1\frac{2}{3}$ ✓
$\frac{10}{6} \overset{?}{\geq} \frac{10}{6}$ ✓	

The endpoint 1 is a solution. The value 2 is a solution. The direction of the inequality symbol is correct.

Solve each inequality.

5. $-\frac{5}{6}x + 3 < \frac{1}{2}$

6. $2(b - 7) + -4b \geq 30 - 18$

7. $\frac{2}{3}(g + 4) - g > 1$

8. $-\frac{3}{5} + \frac{8}{5}k - (3k - 2) \leq 0$

Holt Algebra 1

Name _____ Date _____ Class _____

LESSON 3-5 **Review for Mastery**
Solving Inequalities with Variables on Both Sides

Variables must be collected on the same side of an inequality before the inequality can be solved. If you collect the variables so that the variable term is positive, you will not have to multiply or divide by a negative number.

Solve $x > 8(x - 7)$.

Collect the variables on the left.

$x > 8(x - 7)$	
$x > 8x - 56$	Distribute.
$\underline{-8x \quad -8x}$	Add $-8x$ to both sides.
$-7x > -56$	
$\dfrac{-7x}{-7} > \dfrac{-56}{-7}$	Divide both sides by -7.
$x < 8$	Reverse the sign.

Notice that if you want to have the variable on the left to make graphing solutions easier, you may still need to switch the inequality sign, even if you did not multiply or divide by a negative number.

Solve $x > 8(x - 7)$.

Collect the variables on the right.

$x > 8(x - 7)$	
$x > 8x - 56$	Distribute.
$\underline{-x \quad -x}$	Add $-x$ to both sides.
$0 > 7x - 56$	
$\underline{+56 \qquad +56}$	
$56 > 7x$	
$\dfrac{56}{7} > \dfrac{7x}{7}$	Divide both sides by 7.
$8 > x$	
$x < 8$	

Write the first step you would take to solve each inequality if you wanted to keep the variable positive.

1. $6y < 10y + 1$ _____

2. $4p - 2 \geq 3p$ _____

3. $5 - 3r \leq 6r$ _____

Solve each inequality.

4. $8c + 4 > 4(c - 3)$ **5.** $5(x - 1) < 3x + 10 - 8x$ **6.** $-8 + 4a - 12 > 2a + 10$

_____ _____ _____ _____

Holt Algebra 1

California Standards ◆–4.0, ◆–5.0

LESSON 3-5

Review for Mastery

Solving Inequalities with Variables on Both Sides continued

An inequality can have infinite solutions.

Solve $-2x - 5 \leq 4x + 8 - 6x$.

$-2x - 5 \leq 4x + 8 - 6x$		
$-2x - 5 \leq -2x + 8$	Combine like terms.
$\underline{+2x \qquad\qquad +2x}$	Add 2x to each side.
$-5 \qquad \leq 8 ✓$	This is a true statement for any number x.

The solution is the set of all real numbers.

Check any value of x:

Try $x = 3$.

$$-2x - 5 \leq 4x + 8 - 6x$$

$$-2(3) - 5 \overset{?}{\leq} 4(3) + 8 - 6(3)$$

$$-6 - 5 \overset{?}{\leq} 12 + 8 - 18$$

$$-11 \overset{?}{\leq} 2 ✓$$

An inequality can also have no solutions.

Solve $3(x - 4) > 7 + 3x$.

$3(x - 4) > 7 + 3x$		
$3x - 12 > 7 + 3x$	Distribute.
$\underline{-3x \qquad\qquad -3x}$	Add −3x to each side.
$-12 > 7 ✗$	No values of x make this inequality true.

There are no solutions. The solution set is ∅.

Check any value of x:

Try $x = 2$.

$$3(x - 4) > 7 + 3x$$

$$3(2 - 4) \overset{?}{>} 7 + 3(2)$$

$$3(-2) \overset{?}{>} 7 + 6$$

$$-6 \overset{?}{>} 13 ✗$$

Solve each inequality.

7. $t + 5 < t + 5$

8. $x + 5 \leq x + 5$

9. $4y + 3(y - 2) < 7y$ 10. $10n - 4 \leq 5(2n + 1)$ 11. $9x + 3 - 5x \geq 2(2x + 5)$

Holt Algebra 1

California Standards ◆—5.0

LESSON 3-6
Review for Mastery
Solving Compound Inequalities

Compound inequalities using AND require you to find solutions so that two inequalities will be satisfied at the same time.

Solve $2 < x + 3 \leq 5$ and graph the solutions.

The two inequalities are: $2 < x + 3$ AND $x + 3 \leq 5$.

Solve $2 < x + 3$.

$$2 < x + 3$$

$$\underline{-3 \qquad -3} \quad \text{Add } -3 \text{ to both sides.}$$

$$-1 < x$$

Solve $x + 3 \leq 5$.

$$x + 3 \leq 5$$

$$\underline{-3 \quad -3} \quad \text{Add } -3 \text{ to both sides.}$$

$$x \leq 2$$

Graph $x > -1$.

Graph $x \leq 2$.

Graph $-1 < x \leq 2$.

Use **overlapping** regions for compound inequalities with **AND**.

Write the two inequalities that must be solved in order to solve each compound inequality.

1. $-3 < x - 4 \leq 10$ _____ AND _____

2. $8 \leq m + 4 \leq 15$ _____ AND _____

3. Graph $-2 \leq w < 6$ by graphing each inequality separately. Then graph the compound inequality.

Solve each compound inequality and graph the solutions.

4. $-5 < k - 1 < 0$

5. $-4 < 2x - 8 \leq 6$

California Standards ◆—5.0

Review for Mastery
Solving Compound Inequalities continued

Compound inequalities using OR require you to find solutions that satisfy either inequality.

Solve $4x > 12$ OR $3x \le -15$ and graph the solutions.

The two inequalities are: $4x > 12$ OR $3x \le -15$.

Solve $4x > 12$.   Solve $3x \le -15$.

$\dfrac{4x}{4} > \dfrac{12}{4}$ *Divide both sides by 4.* $\dfrac{3x}{3} \le \dfrac{-15}{3}$ *Divide both sides by 3.*

$x > 3$. $x \le -5$

Graph $x > 3$.

Graph $x \le -5$.

Graph $x > 3$ OR $x \le -5$.

> Use **both** regions for compound inequalities with **OR**.

Write the compound inequality shown by each graph.

6. _____

7. _____

8. Graph $k \le -1$ OR $k > 4$ by graphing each inequality separately. Then graph the compound inequality.

Solve each compound inequality and graph the solutions.

9. $x + 2 \ge 5$ OR $x + 6 < 2$

10. $6b \ge 42$ OR $3b \le -3$

Holt Algebra 1

California Standards 3.0, ←5.0

LESSON 3-7 **Review for Mastery**

Solving Absolute-Value Inequalities

To solve an absolute-value inequality, first use inverse operations to isolate the absolute-value expression. Then write and solve a compound inequality.

Solve $|x - 2| + 8 < 10$.

Step 1: Isolate the absolute-value expression.

$$|x - 2| + 8 < 10$$

$$\underline{\; -8 \quad -8} \qquad \textit{Subtract 8 from both sides.}$$

$$|x - 2| \qquad < 2$$

Step 2: Solve a compound inequality.

$|x - 2| < 2$ means $x - 2 > -2$ AND $x - 2 < 2$.

$$\underline{\;+2 \quad +2} \qquad \underline{+2 \quad +2} \qquad \textit{Solve each inequality.}$$

$$x \qquad > \quad 0 \;\text{AND}\; x \qquad < 4$$

Graph the solution as shown.

Solve each inequality and graph the solutions.

1. $|x| + 12 < 16$

_____

2. $|x - 1| + 5 \leq 9$

_____

3. $7|x| \leq 21$

_____

4. $|x + 4| - 3 < -2$

_____

Holt Algebra 1

California Standards 3.0, ⬤–5.0

Review for Mastery

LESSON 3-7 *Solving Absolute-Value Inequalities* continued

You can use a similar method to solve absolute-value inequalities that involve a greater-than symbol ($>$). As always, the first step is to isolate the absolute-value expression. Then work with a compound inequality.

Solve $|x - 5| - 4 > -1$.

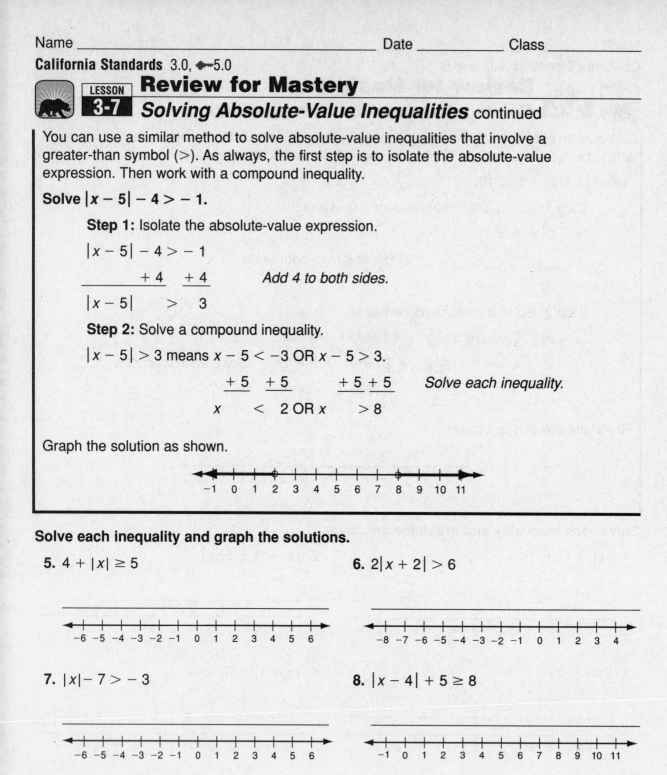

Step 1: Isolate the absolute-value expression.

$$|x - 5| - 4 > -1$$

$$\underline{\ +4 \quad +4}\qquad \textit{Add 4 to both sides.}$$

$$|x - 5| \qquad > \quad 3$$

Step 2: Solve a compound inequality.

$|x - 5| > 3$ means $x - 5 < -3$ OR $x - 5 > 3$.

$$\underline{\quad +5\ +5 \qquad\quad +5 +5}\qquad \textit{Solve each inequality.}$$

$$x \qquad < \quad 2\ \text{OR}\ x \qquad > 8$$

Graph the solution as shown.

Solve each inequality and graph the solutions.

5. $4 + |x| \geq 5$

6. $2|x + 2| > 6$

7. $|x| - 7 > -3$

8. $|x - 4| + 5 \geq 8$

Name _____ Date _____ Class _____

California Standards Rev. of 7AF1.5

Review for Mastery
LESSON 4-1 *Graphing Relationships*

Graphs are a way to turn words into pictures. Be sure to read the graphs from left to right.

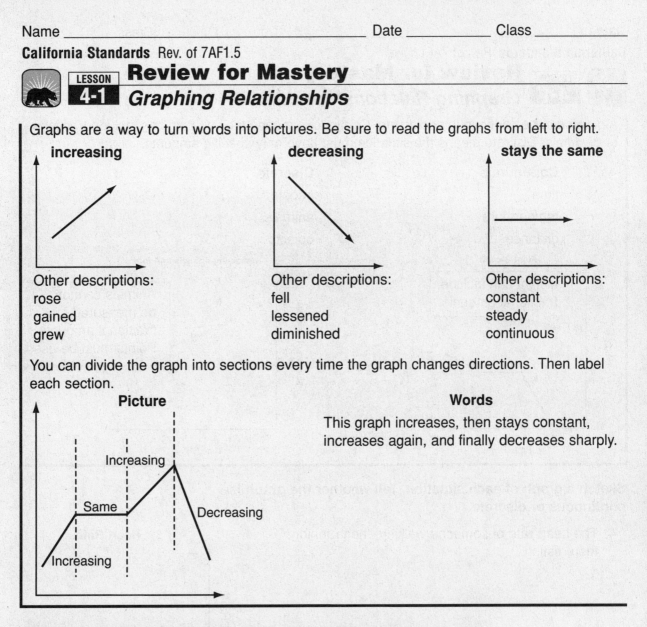

increasing	**decreasing**	**stays the same**
Other descriptions:	Other descriptions:	Other descriptions:
rose	fell	constant
gained	lessened	steady
grew	diminished	continuous

You can divide the graph into sections every time the graph changes directions. Then label each section.

Picture

Increasing
Same
Decreasing
Increasing

Words

This graph increases, then stays constant, increases again, and finally decreases sharply.

**Divide each graph into sections where the graph changes directions.
Then label the sections as *increasing*, *decreasing*, or *same*.**

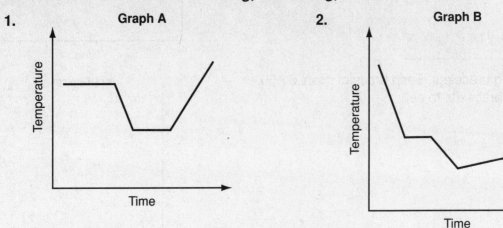

1. Graph A

2. Graph B

3. Which graph above shows that the air temperature
   fell steadily, leveled off, fell again, and then
   increased slightly?

_____

43

Holt Algebra 1

Name _____ Date _____ Class _____

California Standards Rev. of 7AF1.5

LESSON 4-1

Review for Mastery

Graphing Relationships continued

A graph can be continuous or discrete. Continuous means the situation can include fractions or decimals. Discrete means the situation must have only specific amounts.

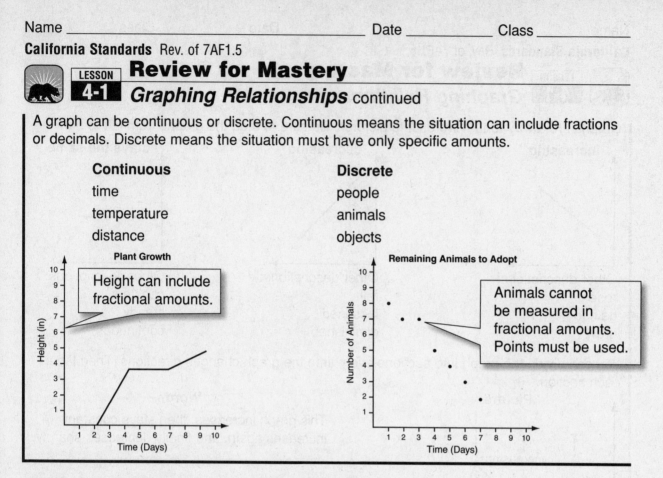

Continuous
- time
- temperature
- distance

Discrete
- people
- animals
- objects

Plant Growth — Height (in) / Time (Days)

Height can include fractional amounts.

Remaining Animals to Adopt — Number of Animals / Time (Days)

Animals cannot be measured in fractional amounts. Points must be used.

Sketch a graph of each situation. Tell whether the graph is continuous or discrete.

4. The heart rate of someone walking, then running, then resting.

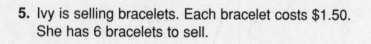

Heart Rate

Heart Rate / Time

_____

5. Ivy is selling bracelets. Each bracelet costs $1.50. She has 6 bracelets to sell.

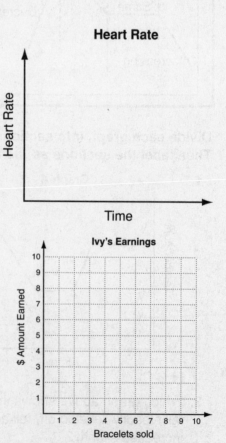

Ivy's Earnings

$ Amount Earned / Bracelets sold

_____

44

Holt Algebra 1

Name _____ Date _____ Class _____

California Standards 16.0, 17.0, 18.0

Review for Mastery
LESSON 4-2 Relations and Functions

A **relation** is a set of ordered pairs. The relation can be in the form of a table, graph, or mapping diagram. The **domain** is all the *x*-values. The **range** is all the *y*-values.

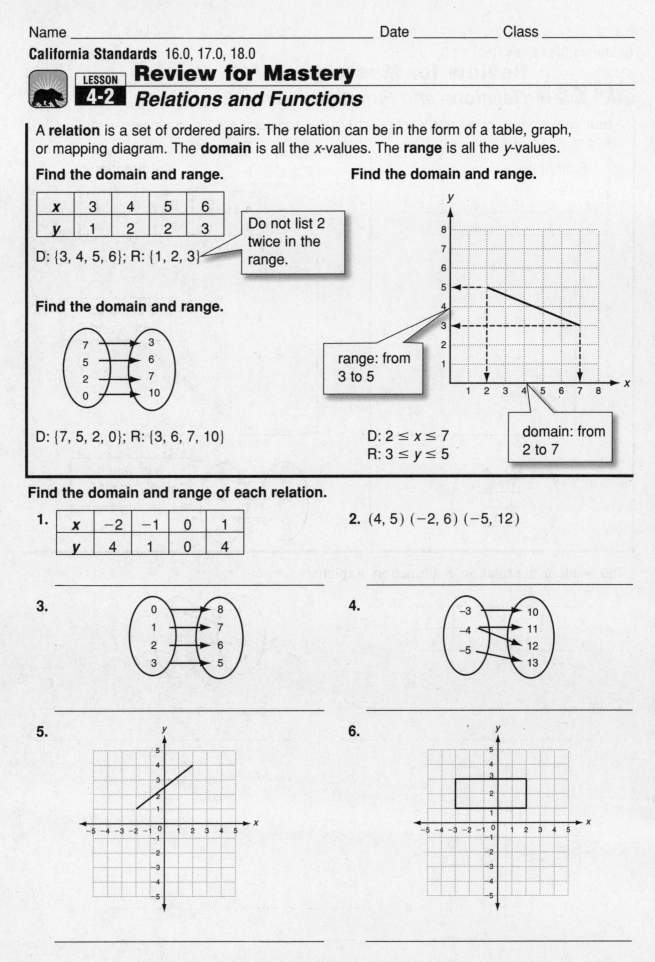

Find the domain and range.

x	3	4	5	6
y	1	2	2	3

D: {3, 4, 5, 6}; R: {1, 2, 3}

Do not list 2 twice in the range.

Find the domain and range.

D: {7, 5, 2, 0}; R: {3, 6, 7, 10}

Find the domain and range.

range: from 3 to 5

domain: from 2 to 7

D: 2 ≤ x ≤ 7
R: 3 ≤ y ≤ 5

Find the domain and range of each relation.

1.

x	−2	−1	0	1
y	4	1	0	4

_____

2. (4, 5) (−2, 6) (−5, 12)

_____

3.

_____

4.

_____

5.

_____

6.

_____

Holt Algebra 1

Name _____ Date _____ Class _____

California Standards 16.0, 17.0, 18.0

LESSON 4-2

Review for Mastery
Relations and Functions continued

A **function** is a type of relation where each *x* value (domain) can be paired with only one *y* value (range).

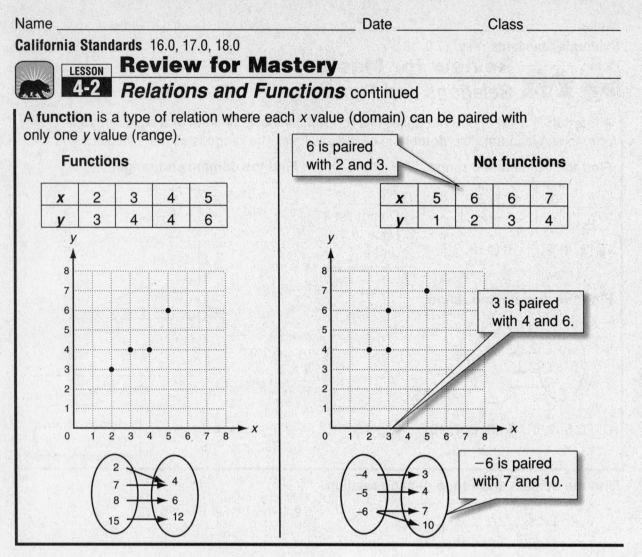

Functions

x	2	3	4	5
y	3	4	4	6

6 is paired with 2 and 3.

Not functions

x	5	6	6	7
y	1	2	3	4

3 is paired with 4 and 6.

−6 is paired with 7 and 10.

Tell whether the relation is a function. Explain.

7.

x	−2	−3	−3	−4
y	1	2	3	4

8.

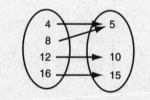

_____   _____

_____   _____

9.

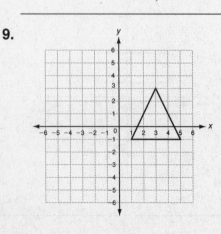

_____

_____

Holt Algebra 1

California Standards 16.0, 17.0, 18.0

Review for Mastery
LESSON 4-3
Writing and Graphing Functions

Functions have dependent and independent variables. The dependent variable will always depend on the independent variable.

Rewrite each situation using the word *depends*. Then identify the dependent and the independent variables.

An employee who works longer hours will receive a larger amount on her paycheck.

Rewrite sentence:

The **amount of a paycheck** *depends* on the **number of hours worked**.

Dependent: amount of paycheck   Independent: number of hours worked

After identifying the independent and dependent variables, you can write a rule in function notation. Remember that $f(x)$ is the **dependent variable** and x is the **independent variable**.

Identify the dependent and independent variables. Write a function rule for each situation.

A zoo charges $6 for parking and $17.50 for each child.

1. *Identify the dependent and independent variables.*

   The **cost of admission** *depends* on **the number of children**.

   Dependent $f(x)$: cost of admission   Independent x: number of children

2. *Write the equation in words.*

   The cost of admission is $17.50 multiplied by the number of children plus $6 for parking.

3. *Write the function using cost of admission = $f(x)$ and number of children = x.*

   $$f(x) = \$17.50x + \$6.00$$

Identify the dependent and the independent variables for each situation below. Write the function. Then evaluate the function for the given input values.

1. A limo service charges $90 for each hour.

   Dependent $f(x)$: _____

   Independent x: _____

   Function: _____

   Evaluate for $x = 2$.

   _____

   Evaluate for $x = 7.5$.

   _____

2. A computer support company charges $295 for the first hour plus $95 for each additional hour.

   Dependent $f(x)$: _____

   Independent x: _____

   Function: _____

   Evaluate for $x = 3.25$.

   _____

   Evaluate for $x = 8$.

   _____

Holt Algebra 1

California Standards 16.0, 17.0, 18.0

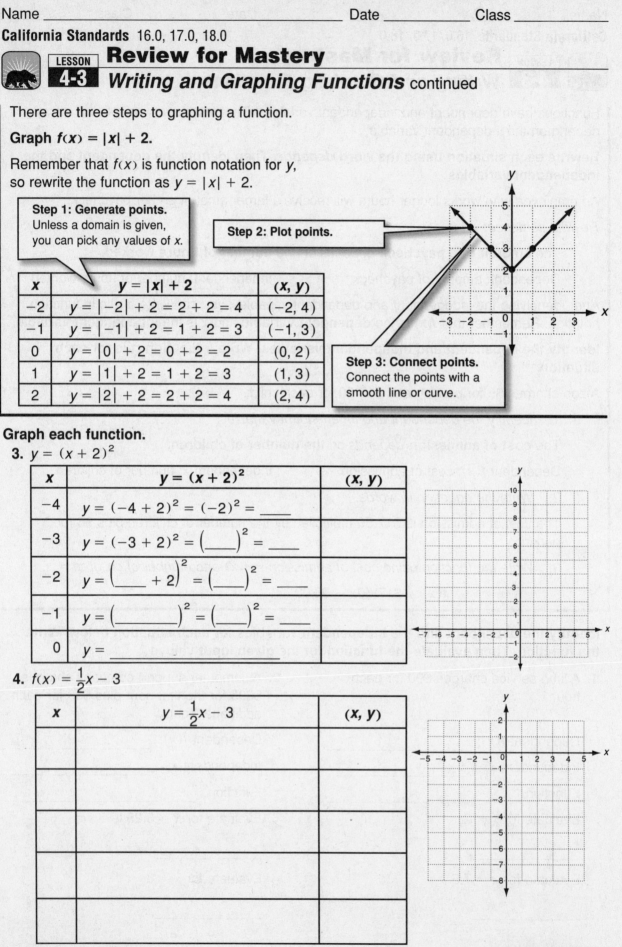

LESSON 4-3

Review for Mastery

Writing and Graphing Functions continued

There are three steps to graphing a function.

Graph $f(x) = |x| + 2$.

Remember that $f(x)$ is function notation for y, so rewrite the function as $y = |x| + 2$.

Step 1: Generate points.
Unless a domain is given, you can pick any values of x.

Step 2: Plot points.

x	$y = |x| + 2$	(x, y)
-2	$y = |-2| + 2 = 2 + 2 = 4$	$(-2, 4)$
-1	$y = |-1| + 2 = 1 + 2 = 3$	$(-1, 3)$
0	$y = |0| + 2 = 0 + 2 = 2$	$(0, 2)$
1	$y = |1| + 2 = 1 + 2 = 3$	$(1, 3)$
2	$y = |2| + 2 = 2 + 2 = 4$	$(2, 4)$

Step 3: Connect points.
Connect the points with a smooth line or curve.

Graph each function.

3. $y = (x + 2)^2$

x	$y = (x + 2)^2$	(x, y)
-4	$y = (-4 + 2)^2 = (-2)^2 = $ ____	
-3	$y = (-3 + 2)^2 = (\underline{})^2 = $ ____	
-2	$y = (\underline{} + 2)^2 = (\underline{})^2 = $ ____	
-1	$y = (\underline{})^2 = (\underline{})^2 = $ ____	
0	$y = $ _____	

4. $f(x) = \frac{1}{2}x - 3$

x	$y = \frac{1}{2}x - 3$	(x, y)

Holt Algebra 1

California Standards Rev. of 7SDAP1.2

LESSON
4-4

Review for Mastery
Scatter Plots and Trend Lines

Correlation is one way to describe the relationship between two sets of data.

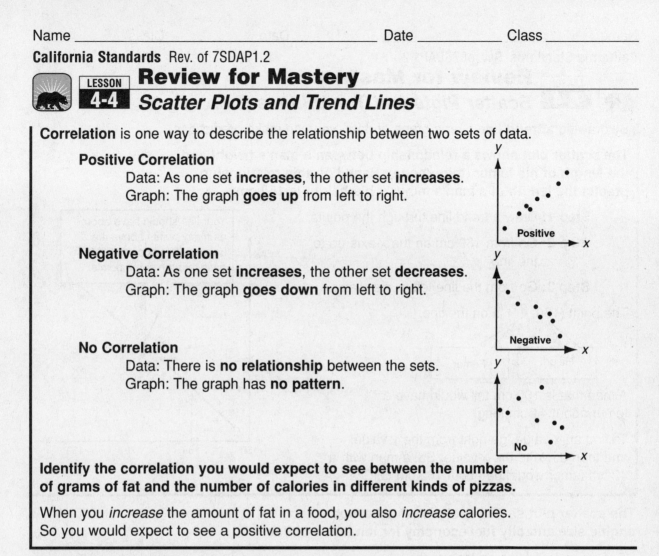

Positive Correlation
    Data: As one set **increases**, the other set **increases**.
    Graph: The graph **goes up** from left to right.

Negative Correlation
    Data: As one set **increases**, the other set **decreases**.
    Graph: The graph **goes down** from left to right.

No Correlation
    Data: There is **no relationship** between the sets.
    Graph: The graph has **no pattern**.

Identify the correlation you would expect to see between the number of grams of fat and the number of calories in different kinds of pizzas.

When you *increase* the amount of fat in a food, you also *increase* calories. So you would expect to see a positive correlation.

Identify the correlation you would expect to see between each pair of data sets. Explain.

1. the number of knots tied in a rope and the length of the rope

_____

2. the height of a woman and her score on an algebra test

_____

Describe the correlation illustrated by each scatter plot.

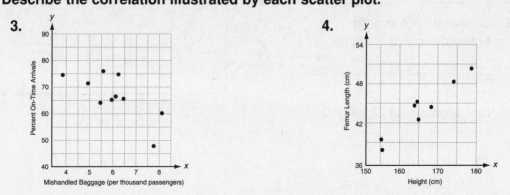

3.

_____

4.

_____

Holt Algebra 1

California Standards Rev. of 7SDAP1.2

LESSON 4-4

Review for Mastery

Scatter Plots and Trend Lines continued

By drawing a **trend line** over a graph of data, you can make predictions.

The scatter plot shows a relationship between a man's height and the length of his femur (thigh bone). Based on this relationship, predict the length of a man's femur if his height is 160 cm.

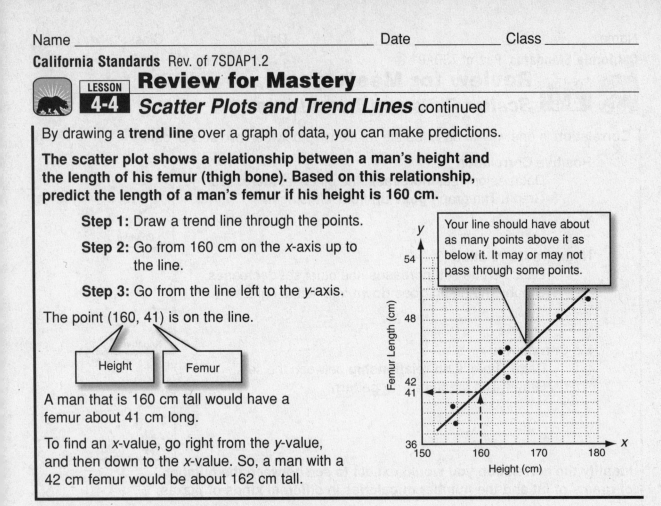

Step 1: Draw a trend line through the points.

Step 2: Go from 160 cm on the *x*-axis up to the line.

Step 3: Go from the line left to the *y*-axis.

The point (160, 41) is on the line.

Height   Femur

A man that is 160 cm tall would have a femur about 41 cm long.

To find an *x*-value, go right from the *y*-value, and then down to the *x*-value. So, a man with a 42 cm femur would be about 162 cm tall.

Your line should have about as many points above it as below it. It may or may not pass through some points.

The scatter plot shows a relationship between engine size and city fuel economy for ten automobiles.

5. Draw a trend line on the graph.

6. Based on the relationship, predict ...

   a. the city fuel economy of an automobile with an engine size of 5 L.

   _____

   b. the city fuel economy of an automobile with an engine size of 2.8 L.

   _____

   c. the engine size of an automobile with a city fuel economy of 11 mi/gal.

   _____

   d. the engine size of an automobile with a city fuel economy of 28 mi/gal.

   _____

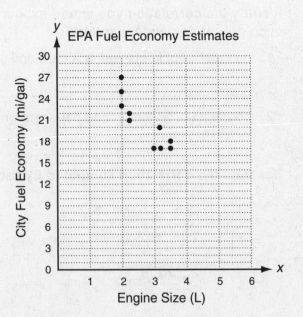

Holt Algebra 1

California Standards Prep for 2A22.0

Review for Mastery

LESSON 4-5

Arithmetic Sequences

An **arithmetic sequence** is a list of numbers (or **terms**) with a **common difference** between each number. After you find the common difference, you can use it to continue the sequence.

Determine whether each sequence is an arithmetic sequence. If so, find the common difference and the next three terms.

1, 2, 4, 8, ...
+1 +2 +4

> Find how much you add or subtract to move from term to term.

The difference between terms is *not* constant.

This sequence is *not* an arithmetic sequence.

0, 6, 12, 18, ...
+6 +6 +6

> Find how much you add or subtract to move from term to term.

The difference between terms is constant.

This sequence is an arithmetic sequence with a common difference of 6.

0, 6, 12, 18, __24__, __30__, __36__
+6 +6 +6

> Use the difference of 6 to find three more terms.

Fill in the blanks with the differences between terms. State whether each sequence is an arithmetic sequence.

1. 14, 12, 10, 8, ...

Is this an arithmetic sequence? _____

____ ____ ____

2. 0.3, 0.6, 1.0, 1.5, ...

Is this an arithmetic sequence? _____

____ ____ ____

Use the common difference to find the next three terms in each arithmetic sequence.

3. 7, 4, 1, −2, ___, ___, ___, ...
   −3 −3 −3 −3 −3 −3

4. −5, 0, 5, 10, ___, ___, ___, ...
   +5 +5 +5

Determine whether each sequence is an arithmetic sequence. If so, find the common difference and the next three terms.

5. −1, 2, −3, 4, ...

_____

6. 1.25, 3.75, 6.25, 8.75, ...

_____

Holt Algebra 1

California Standards Prep for 2A22.0

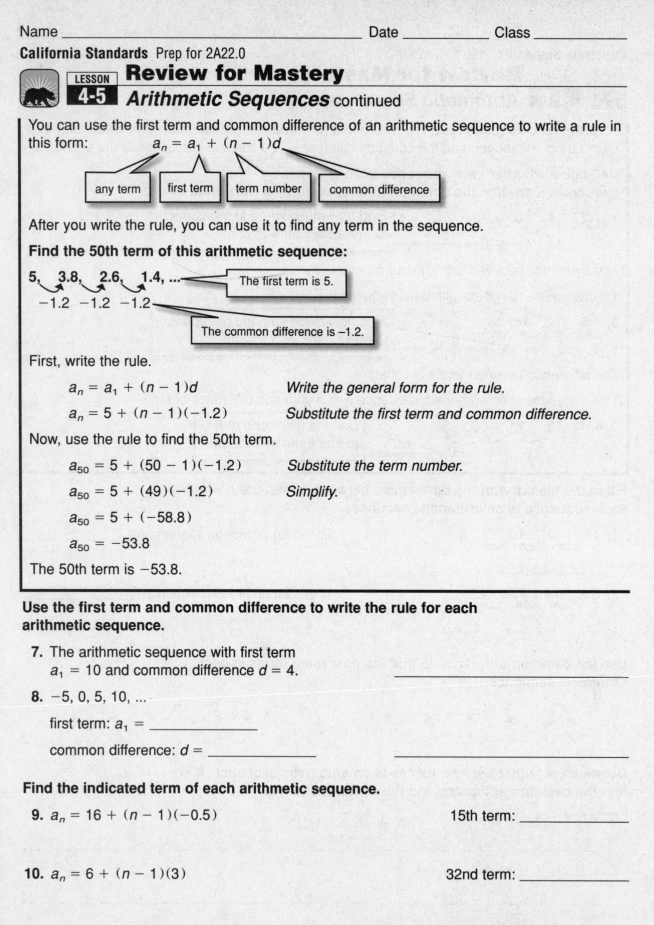

LESSON 4-5

Review for Mastery

Arithmetic Sequences continued

You can use the first term and common difference of an arithmetic sequence to write a rule in this form: $a_n = a_1 + (n - 1)d$

any term | first term | term number | common difference

After you write the rule, you can use it to find any term in the sequence.

Find the 50th term of this arithmetic sequence:

5, 3.8, 2.6, 1.4, ...

The first term is 5.

−1.2 −1.2 −1.2

The common difference is −1.2.

First, write the rule.

$a_n = a_1 + (n - 1)d$	*Write the general form for the rule.*
$a_n = 5 + (n - 1)(-1.2)$	*Substitute the first term and common difference.*

Now, use the rule to find the 50th term.

$a_{50} = 5 + (50 - 1)(-1.2)$	*Substitute the term number.*
$a_{50} = 5 + (49)(-1.2)$	*Simplify.*
$a_{50} = 5 + (-58.8)$	
$a_{50} = -53.8$	

The 50th term is −53.8.

Use the first term and common difference to write the rule for each arithmetic sequence.

7. The arithmetic sequence with first term
$a_1 = 10$ and common difference $d = 4$.

_____

8. −5, 0, 5, 10, ...

first term: $a_1 = $ _____

common difference: $d = $ _____

_____

Find the indicated term of each arithmetic sequence.

9. $a_n = 16 + (n - 1)(-0.5)$

15th term: _____

10. $a_n = 6 + (n - 1)(3)$

32nd term: _____

11. −8, −6, −4, −2, ...

100th term: _____

Holt Algebra 1

California Standards ◆—6.0, ◆—7.0, 17.0, 18.0

LESSON 5-1 Review for Mastery
Linear Equations and Functions

You can determine if a function is linear by its graph, ordered pairs, or equation.

Identify whether the graph represents a linear function.

Step 1: Determine whether the graph is a function.

Every x-value is paired with exactly one y-value; therefore, the graph is a function. Continue to step 2.

Step 2: Determine whether the graph is a straight line.

Conclusion: Because this graph is a function and a straight line, this graph represents a linear function.

Identify whether {(4, 3), (6, 4), (8, 6)} represents a linear function.

Step 1: Write the ordered pairs in a table.

Step 2: Find the amount of change in each variable. Determine if the amounts are constant.

Conclusion: Although the x-values show a constant change, the y-values do not. Therefore, this set of ordered pairs does not represent a linear function.

x	y
4	3
6	4
8	6

+2 / +2 (x) +1 / +2 (y)

Identify whether the function $y = 5x - 2$ is a linear function.

Try to write the equation in standard form ($Ax + By = C$).

$$y = 5x - 2$$
$$\underline{-5x \quad -5x}$$
$$-5x + y = -2$$

In standard form, x and y
• have exponents of 1
• are not multiplied together
• are not in denominators, exponents, or radical signs

Conclusion: Because the function can be written in standard form, ($A = -5$, $B = 1$, $C = -2$), the function is a linear function.

Tell whether each graph, set of ordered pairs, or equation represents a linear function. Write *yes* or *no*.

1.

2.

3.

x	y
−9	5
−5	10
−1	15

_____   _____   _____

4. {(−3, 5), (−2, 8), (−1, 12)}   **5.** $2y = -3x^2$ **6.** $y = 4x - 7$

_____   _____   _____

Holt Algebra 1

LESSON 5-1 **Review for Mastery**

Linear Equations and Functions continued

In real-life problems, the domain and range are sometimes restricted.

Swimming at the park pool costs $2.75 for each person. The total cost is given by $f(x) = 2.75x$ where x is the number of people going swimming. Graph this function and give its domain and range.

Step 1: Graph.

x	$f(x) = 2.75x$
0	$f(0) = 2.75(0) = 0$
1	$f(1) = 2.75(1) = 2.75$
2	$f(2) = 2.75(2) = 5.50$
3	$f(3) = 2.75(3) = 8.25$

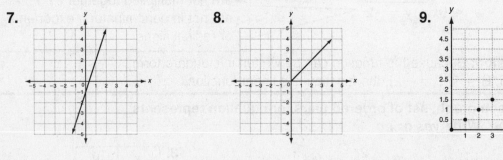

Step 2: Determine the domain and range.

Ask yourself the following questions to help determine the domain.

Can the *x*-value be all fractions or decimals in between the whole numbers?

Can the *x*-value be 0?

Can the *x*-value be negative?

The domain is the number of people. So the domain is restricted to whole numbers.
Because the range is determined by the domain, it is also restricted.
Domain: {0, 1, 2, 3, ...}   Range: {$0, $2.75, $5.50, $8.25, ...}

Give the domain and range for the graphs below.

7.

8.

9.

_____   _____   _____

10. Tyler makes $10 per hour at his job. The function $f(x) = 10x$
    gives the amount of money Tyler makes after *x* hours.
    Graph this function and give its domain and range.

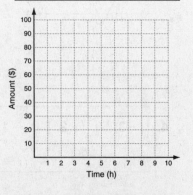

_____

Holt Algebra 1

California Standards ◆—6.0

LESSON 5-2

Review for Mastery
Using Intercepts

The **x-intercept** is the x-coordinate of the point where the graph intersects the x-axis.
The **y-intercept** is the y-coordinate of the point where the graph intersects the y-axis.

At a baseball game, Doug has $12 to spend on popcorn and peanuts.
The peanuts are $4 and the popcorn is $2. The function $4x + 2y = 12$
describes the amount of peanuts x and popcorn y he can buy if he
spends all his money. The function is graphed below. Find the intercepts.
What does each intercept represent?

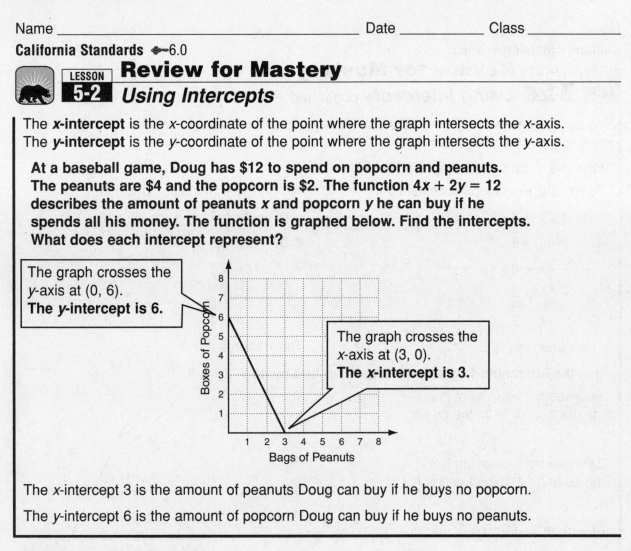

The graph crosses the
y-axis at (0, 6).
The y-intercept is 6.

The graph crosses the
x-axis at (3, 0).
The x-intercept is 3.

The x-intercept 3 is the amount of peanuts Doug can buy if he buys no popcorn.

The y-intercept 6 is the amount of popcorn Doug can buy if he buys no peanuts.

Find the x- and y-intercepts.

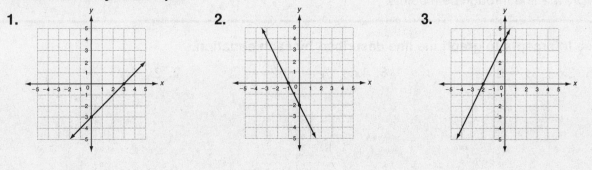

1.

2.

3.

4. The volleyball team is traveling to a game 120 miles away.
Their average speed is 40 mi/h. The graphed line describes
the distance left to travel at any time during the trip. Find the
intercepts. What does each intercept represent?

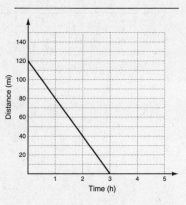

_____

_____

Holt Algebra 1

California Standards ←6.0

LESSON 5-2

Review for Mastery

Using Intercepts continued

You can find the *x*- and *y*-intercepts from an equation. Then you can use the intercepts to graph the equation.

Find the *x*- and *y*-intercepts of $4x + 2y = 8$.

To find the *x*-intercept, substitute 0 for *y*.

$$4x + 2y = 8$$
$$4x + 2(0) = 8$$
$$4x = 8$$
$$\frac{4x}{4} = \frac{8}{4}$$
$$x = 2$$

The *x*-intercept is 2.

To find the *y*-intercept, substitute 0 for *x*.

$$4x + 2y = 8$$
$$4(0) + 2y = 8$$
$$2y = 8$$
$$\frac{2y}{2} = \frac{8}{2}$$
$$y = 4$$

The *y*-intercept is 4.

Use the intercepts to graph the line described by $4x + 2y = 8$.

Because the *x*-intercept is 2,
the point (2, 0) is on the graph.

Because the *y*-intercept is 4,
the point (0, 4) is on the graph.

Plot (2, 0) and (0, 4).

Draw a line through both points.

Use intercepts to graph the line described by each equation.

5. $3x + 9y = 9$

6. $4x + 6y = -12$

7. $2x - y = 4$

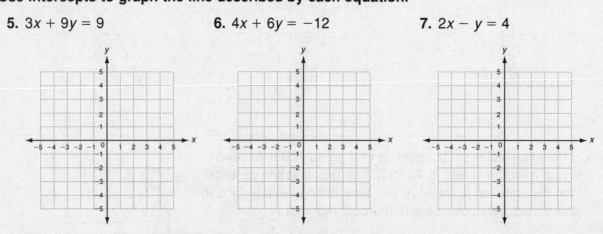

Holt Algebra 1

Name _____ Date _____ Class _____

California Standards Prep for 8.0; ← 6.0

LESSON
5-3

Review for Mastery
Slope

You can find the slope of a line from any two ordered pairs. The ordered pairs can be given to you, or you might need to read them from a table or graph.

Find the slope of the line that contains (–1, 3) and (2, 0).

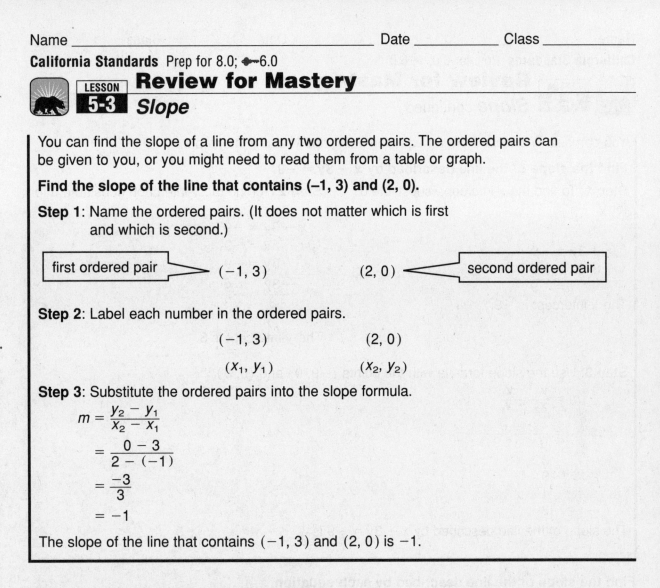

Step 1: Name the ordered pairs. (It does not matter which is first and which is second.)

first ordered pair $(-1, 3)$ $(2, 0)$ second ordered pair

Step 2: Label each number in the ordered pairs.

$$(-1, 3) \qquad (2, 0)$$
$$(x_1, y_1) \qquad (x_2, y_2)$$

Step 3: Substitute the ordered pairs into the slope formula.

$$m = \frac{y_2 - y_1}{x_2 - x_1}$$
$$= \frac{0 - 3}{2 - (-1)}$$
$$= \frac{-3}{3}$$
$$= -1$$

The slope of the line that contains $(-1, 3)$ and $(2, 0)$ is -1.

Find the slope of each linear relationship.

1.

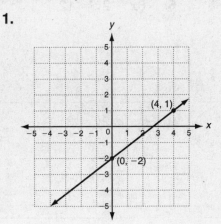

2.

x	y
4	−5
8	−3
12	−1
16	1

3. The line contains $(5, -2)$ and $(7, 6)$.

_____   _____   _____

Holt Algebra 1

California Standards Prep for 8.0; ←—6.0

LESSON 5-3

Review for Mastery

Slope continued

You can also find slope from an equation using the *x*- and *y*-intercepts.

Find the slope of the line described by $x - 3y = -9$.

Step 1: To find the *x*-intercept, substitute 0 for *y*.

$$x - 3y = -9$$
$$x - 3(0) = -9$$
$$x = -9$$

The *x*-intercept is −9.

Step 2: To find the *y*-intercept, substitute 0 for *x*.

$$x - 3y = -9$$
$$(0) - 3y = -9$$
$$-3y = -9$$
$$\frac{-3y}{-3} = \frac{-9}{-3}$$
$$y = 3$$

The *y*-intercept is 3.

Step 3: Use the slope formula with the points $(-9, 0)$ and $(0, 3)$.

$$m = \frac{y_2 - y_1}{x_2 - x_1}$$
$$= \frac{3 - 0}{0 - (-9)}$$
$$= \frac{3}{9}$$
$$= \frac{1}{3}$$

The slope of the line described by $x - 3y = -9$ is $\frac{1}{3}$.

Find the slope of the line described by each equation.

4. $-2x - 5y = 10$

5. $4x + 2y = 8$

6. $-6x + 2y = 12$

_____

7. $8y - 4x = 32$

8. $6y + 8x = 24$

9. $-\frac{1}{2}x + 2y = 3$

_____

Holt Algebra 1

California Standards ←—6.0

LESSON
5-4
Review for Mastery
Direct Variation

A direct variation is a special type of linear relationship. It can be written in the form $y = kx$ where k is a nonzero constant called the constant of variation.

You can identify direct variations from equations or from ordered pairs.

Tell whether $2x + 4y = 0$ is a direct variation. If so, identify the constant of variation.

First, put the equation in the form $y = kx$.

$2x + 4y = 0$

$\underline{-2x \qquad -2x}$ *Add $-2x$ to each side.*

$4y = -2x$

$\dfrac{4y}{4} = -\dfrac{2x}{4}$ *Divide both sides by 4.*

$y = -\dfrac{1}{2}x$

Because the equation can be written in the form $y = kx$, it is a direct variation.

The constant of variation is $-\dfrac{1}{2}$.

Tell whether the relationship is a direct variation. If so, identify the constant of variation.

x	2	4	6
y	1	2	3

If we solve $y = kx$ for k, we get:

$y = kx \longrightarrow \dfrac{y}{x} = \dfrac{kx}{x} \longrightarrow \dfrac{y}{x} = k$

Find k for each ordered pair. This means find $\dfrac{y}{x}$ for each ordered pair. If they are the same, the relationship is a direct variation.

$\dfrac{1}{2} \qquad \dfrac{2}{4} = \dfrac{1}{2} \qquad \dfrac{3}{6} = \dfrac{1}{2}$

This is a direct variation.

Tell whether each equation or relationship is a direct variation. If so, identify the constant of variation.

1. $x + y = 7$ **2.** $4x - 3y = 0$ **3.** $-8y = 24x$

4.

x	−4	2	10
y	2	−1	−5

5.

x	5	12	8
y	17.5	42	28

6.

x	6	8	10
y	8	10	12

Holt Algebra 1

California Standards ←—6.0

LESSON 5-4
Review for Mastery
Direct Variation continued

If you know one ordered pair that satisfies a direct variation, you can find and graph other ordered pairs that will also satisfy the direct variation.

The value of *y* varies directly with *x*, and *y* = 8 when *x* = 24. Find *y* when *x* = 27.

We have to find how the *y* varies with the change in *x*. Then we can find the value of *y* when *x* = 27.

$y = kx$	Use the equation for direct variation.
$8 = k(24)$	Substitute 8 for *y* and 24 for *x*
$\dfrac{8}{24} = \dfrac{k(24)}{24}$	Solve for *k*.
$\dfrac{1}{3} = k$	Simplify.
$y = \dfrac{1}{3}x$	Write the direct variation equation.
$y = \dfrac{1}{3}(27)$	Substitute 27 for *x*.
$y = 9$	

A garden snail can travel about 2.6 feet per minute. Write a direct variation equation for the distance *y* a snail will travel in *x* minutes. Then graph.

Step 1: Write an equation.

distance = 2.6 feet × minutes

$$y = 2.6x$$

Step 2: Generate ordered pairs.

x	*y* = 2.6*x*	(*x, y*)
0	$y = 2.6(0)$	(0, 0)
1	$y = 2.6(1)$	(1, 2.6)
2	$y = 2.6(2)$	(2, 5.2)

Step 3: Graph.

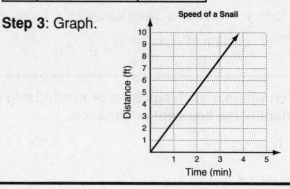

7. The value of *y* varies directly with *x*, and *y* = 8 when *x* = 2. Find y when *x* = 10.

_____

8. The value of *y* varies directly with *x*, and *y* = 5 when *x* = −20. Find *y* when *x* = 35.

_____

9. The cost of electricity to run a personal computer is about $2.13 per day. Write a direct variation equation for the electrical cost *y* of running a computer each day *x*. Then graph.

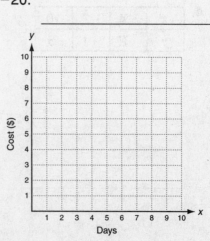

_____

Holt Algebra 1

California Standards ◆—6.0

Review for Mastery
Slope-Intercept Form

An equation is in **slope-intercept form** if it is written as:

$$y = mx + b.$$

> m is the slope.
> b is the y-intercept.

A line has a slope of –4 and a y-intercept of 3. Write the equation in slope-intercept form.

$y = mx + b$	*Substitute the given values for m and b.*
$y = -4x + 3$	

A line has a slope of 2. The ordered pair (3, 1) is on the line. Write the equation in slope-intercept form.

Step 1: Find the y-intercept.

$y = mx + b$	
$y = 2x + b$	*Substitute the given value for m.*
$1 = 2(3) + b$	*Substitute the given values for x and y.*
$1 = 6 + b$	*Solve for b.*
$\underline{-6 \quad -6}$	
$-5 = b$	

Step 2: Write the equation.

$y = mx + b$	
$y = 2x - 5$	*Substitute the given value for m and the value you found for b.*

Write the equation that describes each line in slope-intercept form.

1. slope $= \dfrac{1}{4}$, y-intercept $= 3$ _____

2. slope $= -5$, y-intercept $= 0$ _____

3. slope $= 7$, y-intercept $= -2$ _____

4. slope is 3, (4, 6) is on the line. _____

5. slope is $\dfrac{1}{2}$, (−2, 8) is on the line. _____

6. slope is −1, (5, −2) is on the line. _____

Holt Algebra 1

California Standards ←6.0

LESSON 5-5 Review for Mastery

Slope-Intercept Form continued

You can use the slope and *y*-intercept to graph a line.

Write 2*x* + 6*y* = 12 in slope-intercept form. Then graph the line.

Step 1: Solve for *y*.

$2x + 6y = 12$ *Subtract 2x from both sides.*

$\underline{-2x \qquad -2x}$

$6y = -2x + 12$

$\dfrac{6y}{6} = \dfrac{-2x + 12}{6}$ *Divide both sides by 6.*

$y = -\dfrac{1}{3}x + 2$ *Simplify.*

Step 2: Find the slope and *y*-intercept.

slope: $m = -\dfrac{1}{3} = \dfrac{-1}{3}$

y-intercept: $b = 2$

Step 3: Graph the line.

• Plot (0, 2).

• Then count 1 **down** (because the rise is **negative**) and 3 **right** (because the run is **positive**) and plot another point.

• Draw a line connecting the points.

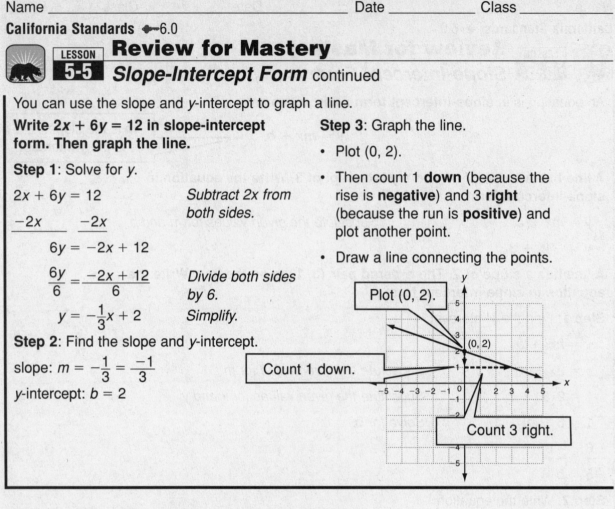

Plot (0, 2).

Count 1 down.

Count 3 right.

Write the following equations in slope-intercept form.

7. $5x + y = 30$

8. $x - y = 7$

9. $-4x + 3y = 12$

_____   _____   _____

10. Write $2x - y = 3$ in slope-intercept form. Then graph the line.

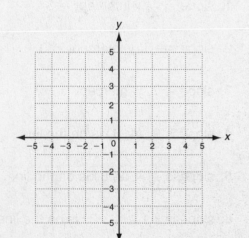

_____

Holt Algebra 1

LESSON 5-6

Review for Mastery
Point-Slope Form

You can graph a line if you know the slope and any point on the line.

Graph the line with slope 2 that contains the point (3, 1).

Step 1: Plot (3, 1).

Step 2: The slope is 2 or $\frac{2}{1}$. Count 2 **up** and **1 right** and plot another point.

Step 3: Draw a line connecting the points.

Write an equation in point-slope form for the line with slope $-\frac{1}{3}$ that contains the point (5, 2).

The **point-slope form** of a linear equation is

$$y - y_1 = m(x - x_1).$$

> m is the given slope.
> (x_1, y_1) is the given point.

$$y - y_1 = m(x - x_1).$$

$$y - 2 = -\frac{1}{3}(x - 5)$$ *Substitute $-\frac{1}{3}$ for m, 5 for x_1 and 2 for y_1.*

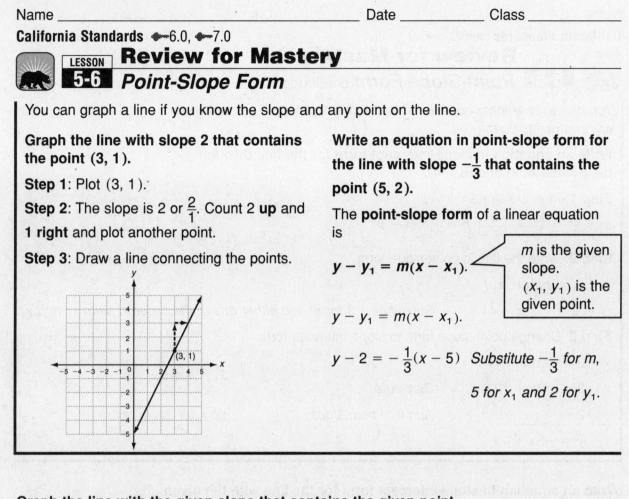

Graph the line with the given slope that contains the given point.

1. slope = $\frac{2}{3}$; (−3, −3)

2. slope = $\frac{-1}{2}$; (−2, 4)

3. slope = 3; (−2, −2)

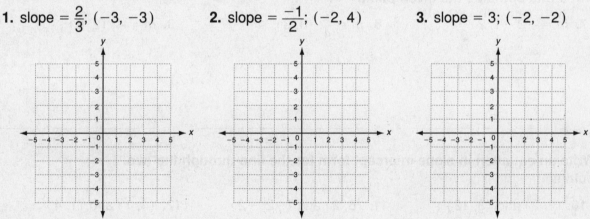

Write an equation in point-slope form for the line with the given slope that contains the given point.

4. slope = $-\frac{2}{5}$; (5, 1)

5. slope = 5; (−2, 6)

6. slope = $\frac{1}{6}$; (−4, 0)

Holt Algebra 1

California Standards ●—6.0, ●—7.0

LESSON 5-6 Review for Mastery
Point-Slope Form continued

You can write a linear equation in slope-intercept form if you are given any two points on the line.

Write an equation in slope-intercept form for the line through the points (4, 2) and (6, −4).

Step 1: Find the slope.

$$m = \frac{y_2 - y_1}{x_2 - x_1} = \frac{-4 - 2}{6 - 4} = \frac{-6}{2} = -3$$

Step 2: Write the line in point-slope form.

$y - y_1 = m(x - x_1)$

$y - 2 = -3(x - 4)$ *Substitute −3 for m and either one of the ordered pairs x_1 and y_1.*

Step 3: Change point-slope form to slope-intercept form.

$y - 2 = -3(x - 4)$

$y - 2 = -3x + 12$ *Distribute.*

$\underline{ +2 +2}$ *Add 2 to both sides.*

$y = -3x + 14$

Write an equation in slope-intercept form for the line with the given slope that contains the given point.

7. $m = -3$; (1, 2)   **8.** $m = \frac{1}{4}$; (8, 3)   **9.** $m = 4$; (2, 8)

_____   _____   _____

Write an equation in slope-intercept form for the line through the two points.

10. (1, 2) and (3, 12)   **11.** (6, 2) and (−2, −2)   **12.** (4, 1) and (1, 4)

_____   _____   _____

Holt Algebra 1

California Standards 8.0, 25.1

Review for Mastery

LESSON 5-7

Slopes of Parallel and Perpendicular Lines

Two lines are **parallel** if they lie in the same plane and have no points in common. The lines will never intersect.

Identify which lines are parallel.

$y = -2x + 4$; $y = 3x + 4$; $y = -2x - 1$

If lines have the same slope, but different y-intercepts, they are parallel lines.

$y = -2x + 4$; $y = 3x + 4$; $y = -2x - 1$

$m = -2$, $m = 3$ $m = -2$

$b = 4$ $b = 4$ $b = -1$

$y = -2x + 4$ and $y = -2x - 1$ are parallel.

Two lines are **perpendicular** if they intersect to form right angles.

Identify which lines are perpendicular.

If the product of the slopes of two lines is -1, the two lines are perpendicular.

$y = -3x + 1$; $y = 3x + 2$; $y = -\frac{1}{3}x + 3$

$m = -3$ $m = 3$ $m = -\frac{1}{3}$

Because $3\left(-\frac{1}{3}\right) = -1$, $y = 3x + 2$ and

$y = -\frac{1}{3}x + 3$ are perpendicular.

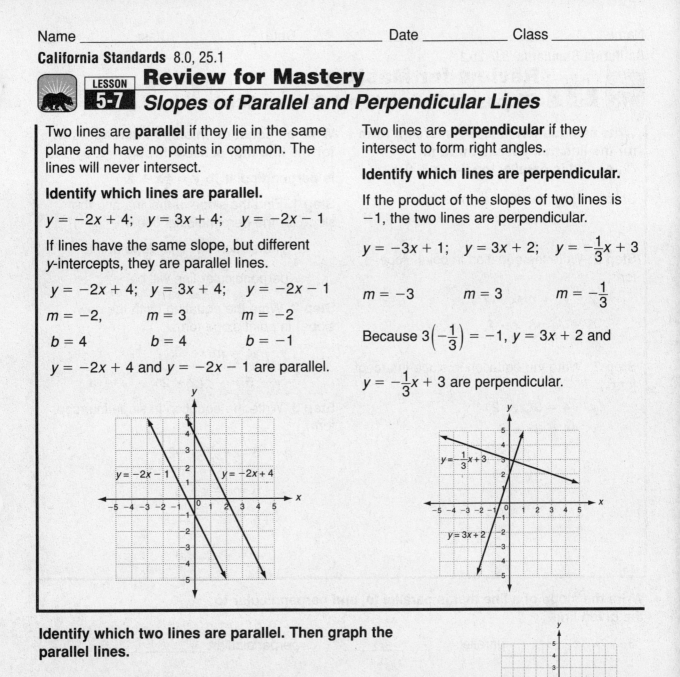

Identify which two lines are parallel. Then graph the parallel lines.

1. $y = 4x + 2$; $y = 2x + 1$; $y = 2x - 3$

_____

Identify which two lines are perpendicular. Then graph the perpendicular lines.

2. $y = -\frac{2}{3}x + 2$; $y = \frac{3}{2}x + 1$; $y = \frac{2}{3}x - 3$

_____

Holt Algebra 1

California Standards 8.0, 25.1

LESSON 5-7

Review for Mastery

Slopes of Parallel and Perpendicular Lines continued

Write an equation in slope-intercept form for the line that passes through (2, 4) and is parallel to $y = 3x + 2$.

Step 1: Find the slope of the line.
The slope is 3.

Step 2: Write the equation in point-slope form.

$$y - y_1 = m(x - x_1)$$
$$y - 4 = 3(x - 2)$$

Step 3: Write the equation in slope-intercept form.

$$y - 4 = 3(x - 2)$$
$$y - 4 = 3x - 6$$
$$\underline{+4 \qquad\quad +4}$$
$$y = 3x - 2$$

Write an equation in slope-intercept form for the line that passes through (2, 5) and is perpendicular to $y = \frac{2}{3}x + 2$.

Step 1: Find the slope of the line and the slope for the perpendicular line.

The slope is $\frac{2}{3}$. The slope of the perpendicular line will be $-\frac{3}{2}$.

Step 2: Write the equation (with the new slope) in point-slope form.

$$y - y_1 = m(x - x_1)$$
$$y - 5 = -\frac{3}{2}(x - 2)$$

Step 3: Write the equation in slope-intercept form.

$$y - 5 = -\frac{3}{2}(x - 2)$$
$$y - 5 = -\frac{3}{2}x + 3$$
$$\underline{+5 \qquad\quad +5}$$
$$y = -\frac{3}{2}x + 8$$

Write the slope of a line that is parallel to, and perpendicular to, the given line.

3. $y = 6x - 3$ parallel: _____   perpendicular: _____

4. $y = \frac{4}{3}x - 1$ parallel: _____   perpendicular: _____

5. Write an equation in slope-intercept form for the line that passes through (6, 5) and is parallel to $y = -x + 4$.

_____

6. Write an equation in slope-intercept form for the line that passes through (8, −1) and is perpendicular to $y = -4x - 7$.

_____

Holt Algebra 1

California Standards ●─6.0, ●─9.0

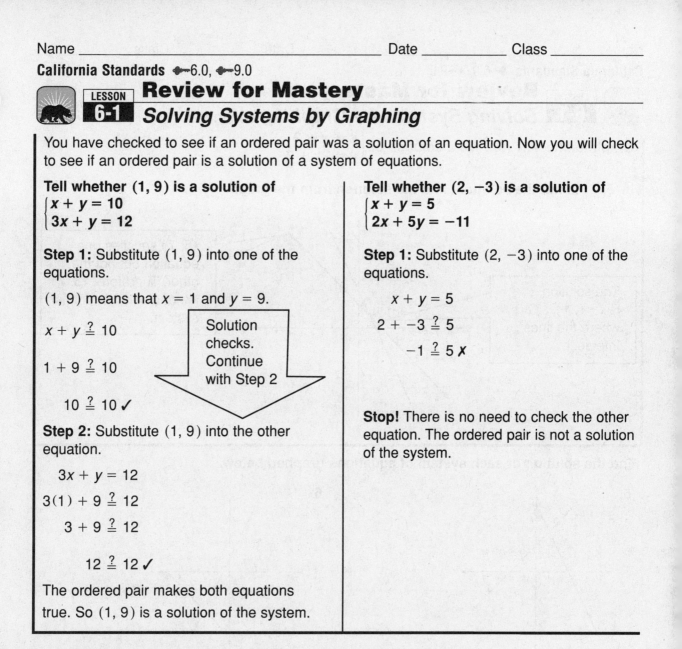

LESSON 6-1
Review for Mastery
Solving Systems by Graphing

You have checked to see if an ordered pair was a solution of an equation. Now you will check to see if an ordered pair is a solution of a system of equations.

Tell whether (1, 9) is a solution of
$$\begin{cases} x + y = 10 \\ 3x + y = 12 \end{cases}$$

Step 1: Substitute (1, 9) into one of the equations.

(1, 9) means that $x = 1$ and $y = 9$.

$x + y \overset{?}{=} 10$

$1 + 9 \overset{?}{=} 10$

$10 \overset{?}{=} 10$ ✓

Solution checks. Continue with Step 2

Step 2: Substitute (1, 9) into the other equation.

$3x + y = 12$

$3(1) + 9 \overset{?}{=} 12$

$3 + 9 \overset{?}{=} 12$

$12 \overset{?}{=} 12$ ✓

The ordered pair makes both equations true. So (1, 9) is a solution of the system.

Tell whether (2, −3) is a solution of
$$\begin{cases} x + y = 5 \\ 2x + 5y = -11 \end{cases}$$

Step 1: Substitute (2, −3) into one of the equations.

$x + y = 5$

$2 + -3 \overset{?}{=} 5$

$-1 \overset{?}{=} 5$ ✗

Stop! There is no need to check the other equation. The ordered pair is not a solution of the system.

Tell whether the ordered pair is a solution of the given system.

1. $(0, -4);\begin{cases} x + 2y = -8 \\ x = 4 + y \end{cases}$

2. $(2, 5);\begin{cases} x + y = 7 \\ 3x + y = 10 \end{cases}$

_____

3. $(-3, 1);\begin{cases} 2x + y = 5 \\ x + 3y = -6 \end{cases}$

4. $(-3, 9);\begin{cases} y = x + 12 \\ y = -3x \end{cases}$

_____

Holt Algebra 1

California Standards ●—6.0, ●—9.0

LESSON
6-1
Review for Mastery
Solving Systems by Graphing continued

Graph to check if $(5, 7)$ is a solution of $\begin{cases} y = x + 2 \\ y = 2x + 3 \end{cases}$.

If $(5, 7)$ is not the solution, find the solution from the graph.

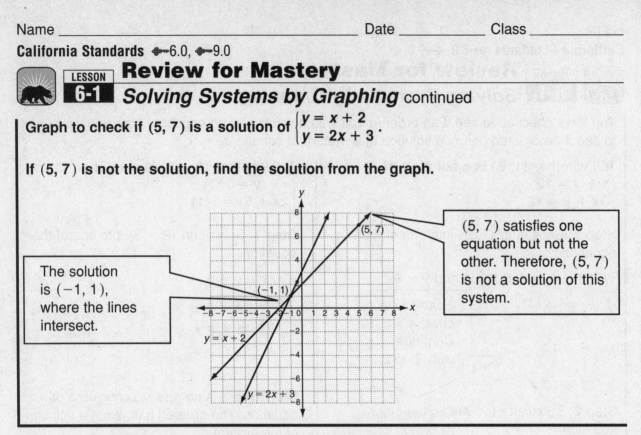

The solution is $(-1, 1)$, where the lines intersect.

$(5, 7)$ satisfies one equation but not the other. Therefore, $(5, 7)$ is not a solution of this system.

Find the solution of each system of equations graphed below.

5.

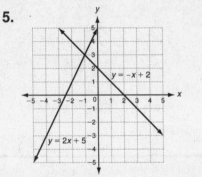

$y = -x + 2$

$y = 2x + 5$

6.

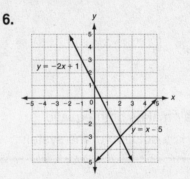

$y = -2x + 1$

$y = x - 5$

Solve each system by graphing.

7. $\begin{cases} y = -3 \\ y = x + 2 \end{cases}$

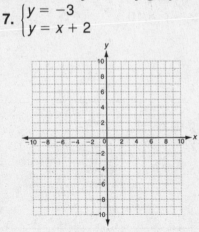

8. $\begin{cases} y = x - 6 \\ y = -x \end{cases}$

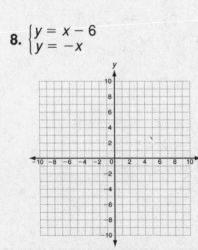

Holt Algebra 1

California Standards ⬅—9.0

Review for Mastery

LESSON 6-2

Solving Systems by Substitution

You can use substitution to solve a system of equations if one of the equations is already solved for a variable.

Solve $\begin{cases} y = x + 2 \\ 3x + y = 10 \end{cases}$

Step 1: Choose the equation to use as the substitute.

Use the first equation $y = x + 2$ because it is already solved for a variable.

Step 2: Solve by substitution.

$$\boxed{x + 2}$$

$$3x + \overset{\downarrow}{y} = 10$$

$3x + (x + 2) = 10$ *Substitute x + 2 for y.*

$4x + 2 = 10$ *Combine like terms.*

$$\underline{\quad -2 \quad -2}$$

$$4x = 8$$

$$\frac{4x}{4} = \frac{8}{4}$$

$$x = 2$$

Step 3: Now substitute $x = 2$ back into one of the original equations to find the value of y.

$$y = x + 2$$

$$y = 2 + 2$$

$$y = 4$$

The solution is $(2, 4)$.

Check:

Substitute $(2, 4)$ into both equations.

$y = x + 2$	$3x + y = 10$
$4 \overset{?}{=} 2 + 2$	$3(2) + 4 \overset{?}{=} 10$
$4 \overset{?}{=} 4$ ✓	$6 + 4 \overset{?}{=} 10$
	$10 \overset{?}{=} 10$ ✓

Solve each system by substitution. Check your answer.

1. $\begin{cases} x = y - 1 \\ x + 2y = 8 \end{cases}$

2. $\begin{cases} y = x + 2 \\ y = 2x - 5 \end{cases}$

3. $\begin{cases} y = x + 5 \\ 3x + y = -11 \end{cases}$

4. $\begin{cases} x = y + 10 \\ x = 2y + 3 \end{cases}$

Holt Algebra 1

California Standards ←—9.0

LESSON 6-2 Review for Mastery
Solving Systems by Substitution continued

You may need to solve one of the equations for a variable before solving with substitution.

Solve $\begin{cases} y - x = 4 \\ 2x + 3y = 27. \end{cases}$

Step 1: Solve the first equation for y.

$y - x = 4$

$\underline{\quad +x \quad +x}$

$\qquad y = x + 4$

Step 2: Solve by substitution.

$\boxed{x + 4}$

$2x + 3y = 27$

$2x + 3(x + 4) = 27$ *Substitute $x + 4$ for y.*

$2x + 3x + 12 = 27$ *Distribute.*

$5x + 12 = 27$ *Combine like terms.*

$\underline{\qquad -12 \quad -12}$

$\qquad 5x = 15$

$\qquad \dfrac{5x}{5} = \dfrac{15}{5}$

$\qquad x = 3$

Step 3: Now substitute $x = 3$ back into one of the original equations to find the value of y.

$y - x = 4$

$y - 3 = 4$

$\underline{\quad +3 \quad +3}$

$\qquad y = 7$

The solution is $(3, 7)$.

Check:

Substitute $(3, 7)$ into both equations.

$y - x = 4 \qquad\qquad 2x + 3y = 27$

$7 - 3 \overset{?}{=} 4 \qquad\qquad 2(3) + 3(7) \overset{?}{=} 27$

$4 \overset{?}{=} 4 \checkmark \qquad\qquad 6 + 21 \overset{?}{=} 27$

$\qquad\qquad\qquad\qquad 27 \overset{?}{=} 27 \checkmark$

Solve each system by substitution. Check your answer.

5. $\begin{cases} x - y = -3 \\ 2x + y = 12 \end{cases}$

6. $\begin{cases} y - x = 8 \\ 5x + 2y = 9 \end{cases}$

Holt Algebra 1

California Standards ◆–9.0

LESSON 6-3

Review for Mastery

Solving Systems by Elimination

Elimination can be used to solve a system of equations by adding terms vertically. This will cause one of the variables to be eliminated. It may be necessary to multiply one or both equations by some number to use this method.

I. Elimination may require no change to either equation.

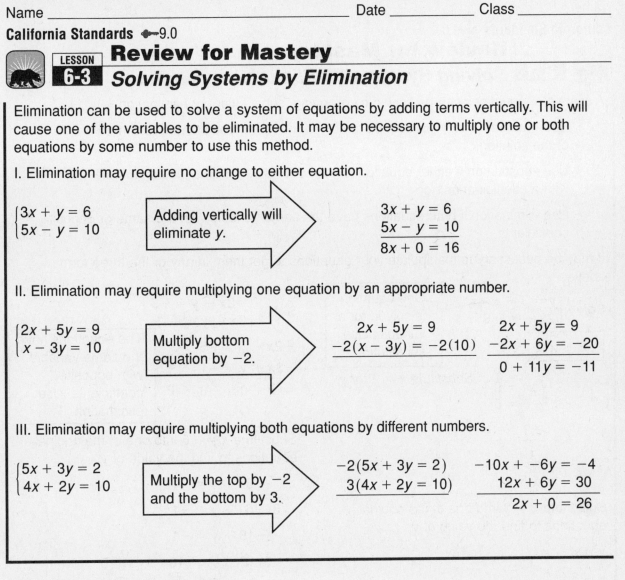

$\begin{cases} 3x + y = 6 \\ 5x - y = 10 \end{cases}$

Adding vertically will eliminate y.

$\begin{array}{r} 3x + y = 6 \\ 5x - y = 10 \\ \hline 8x + 0 = 16 \end{array}$

II. Elimination may require multiplying one equation by an appropriate number.

$\begin{cases} 2x + 5y = 9 \\ x - 3y = 10 \end{cases}$

Multiply bottom equation by -2.

$\begin{array}{r} 2x + 5y = 9 \\ -2(x - 3y) = -2(10) \\ \hline \end{array}$

$\begin{array}{r} 2x + 5y = 9 \\ -2x + 6y = -20 \\ \hline 0 + 11y = -11 \end{array}$

III. Elimination may require multiplying both equations by different numbers.

$\begin{cases} 5x + 3y = 2 \\ 4x + 2y = 10 \end{cases}$

Multiply the top by -2 and the bottom by 3.

$\begin{array}{r} -2(5x + 3y = 2) \\ 3(4x + 2y = 10) \\ \hline \end{array}$

$\begin{array}{r} -10x + -6y = -4 \\ 12x + 6y = 30 \\ \hline 2x + 0 = 26 \end{array}$

Solve each system by elimination.

1. $\begin{cases} 2x - y = 20 \\ 3x + 2y = -19 \end{cases}$

2. $\begin{cases} 3x + 2y = 10 \\ 3x - 2y = 14 \end{cases}$

_____

3. $\begin{cases} x + y = 12 \\ 2x + y = 6 \end{cases}$

4. $\begin{cases} 3x - y = 2 \\ -8x + 2y = 4 \end{cases}$

_____

Holt Algebra 1

California Standards ✦9.0

Review for Mastery

LESSON 6-3

Solving Systems by Elimination continued

A system of equations can be solved by graphing, substitution, or elimination.

- Use graphing if both equations are solved for y, or if you want an estimate of the solution.

- Use substitution if either equation is solved for a variable, or has a variable with a coefficient of 1 or −1.

- Use elimination if both equations have the same variable with the same or opposite coefficients.

It may be necessary to manipulate your equations to get them in any of the three forms above.

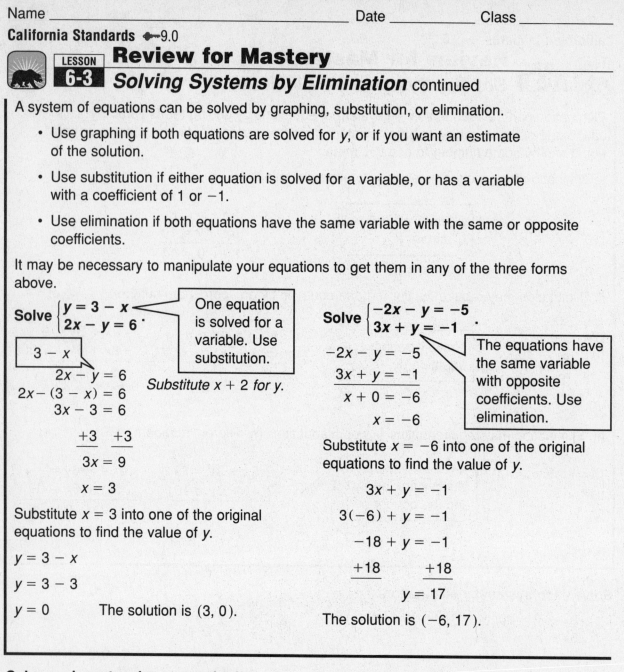

Solve $\begin{cases} y = 3 - x \\ 2x - y = 6 \end{cases}$

One equation is solved for a variable. Use substitution.

$3 - x$

$2x - y = 6$

$2x - (3 - x) = 6$

$3x - 3 = 6$

$\underline{+3 \quad +3}$

$3x = 9$

$x = 3$

Substitute $x + 2$ for y.

Substitute $x = 3$ into one of the original equations to find the value of y.

$y = 3 - x$

$y = 3 - 3$

$y = 0$ The solution is (3, 0).

Solve $\begin{cases} -2x - y = -5 \\ 3x + y = -1 \end{cases}$

$-2x - y = -5$

$3x + y = -1$

$\overline{x + 0 = -6}$

$x = -6$

The equations have the same variable with opposite coefficients. Use elimination.

Substitute $x = -6$ into one of the original equations to find the value of y.

$3x + y = -1$

$3(-6) + y = -1$

$-18 + y = -1$

$\underline{+18 \qquad +18}$

$y = 17$

The solution is (−6, 17).

Solve each system by any method.

5. $\begin{cases} y = x + 3 \\ -2x + y = -4 \end{cases}$

6. $\begin{cases} 4x + y = 10 \\ -2x - y = 4 \end{cases}$

7. $\begin{cases} 2x + y = 8 \\ 3x + 5y = 5 \end{cases}$

_____   _____   _____

Holt Algebra 1

California Standards 8.0, ⚷9.0

LESSON 6-4 Review for Mastery
Solving Special Systems

When solving equations in one variable, it is possible to have one solution, no solutions, or infinitely many solutions. The same results can occur when graphing systems of equations.

Solve $\begin{cases} 4x + 2y = 2 \\ 2x + y = 4 \end{cases}$.

Multiplying the second equation by -2 will eliminate the x-terms.

$$4x + 2y = 2 \qquad\qquad 4x + 2y = 2$$
$$-2(2x + y = 4) \longrightarrow \underline{-4x - 2y = -8}$$
$$0 + 0 = -6$$
$$0 = -6 \, ✗$$

The equation is a contradiction. **There is no solution.**

Solve $\begin{cases} y = 4 - 3x \\ 3x + y = 4 \end{cases}$.

Because the first equation is solved for a variable, use substitution.

$$3x + y = 4$$
$$3x + (4 - 3x) = 4 \quad \textit{Substitute } 4 - 3x \textit{ for } y$$
$$0 + 4 = 4$$
$$4 = 4 \, ✓$$

The equation is true for all values of x and y. **There are infinitely many solutions.**

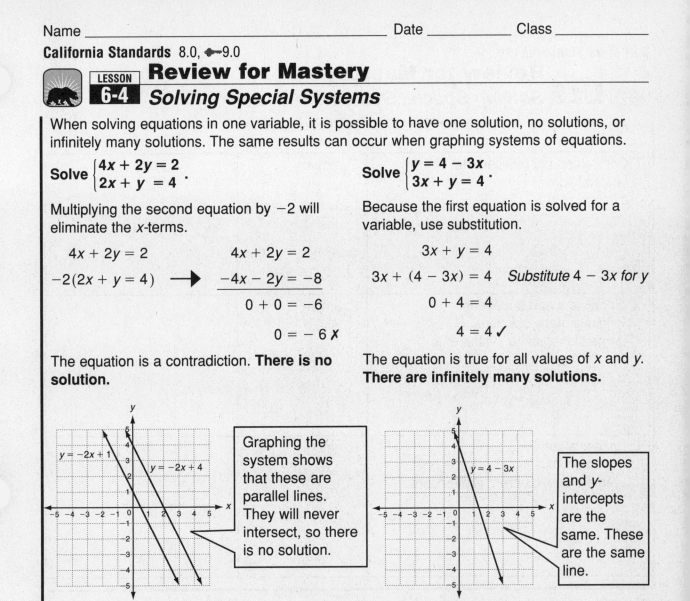

Graphing the system shows that these are parallel lines. They will never intersect, so there is no solution.

The slopes and y-intercepts are the same. These are the same line.

Solve each system of linear equations algebraically.

1. $\begin{cases} y = 3x \\ 2y = 6x \end{cases}$

2. $\begin{cases} y = 2x + 5 \\ y - 2x = 1 \end{cases}$

3. $\begin{cases} 3x - 2y = 9 \\ -6x + 4y = 1 \end{cases}$

_____ _____ _____

Holt Algebra 1

California Standards 8.0, ⬥–9.0

LESSON 6-4

Review for Mastery

Solving Special Systems continued

A system of linear equations can be classified in three ways.

I. Consistent and independent
  one solution
  different slopes
	Example:
	$\begin{cases} y = x + 3 \\ y = -x + 6 \end{cases}$	

II. Consistent and dependent
  infinitely many solutions
  same slope, same y-intercepts
	Example
	$\begin{cases} y = 3x + 4 \\ y - 3x = 4 \end{cases}$	

III. Inconsistent
  no solutions
  same slope, different y-intercepts
	Example
	$\begin{cases} y = 2x + 5 \\ y = 2x + 2 \end{cases}$	

Classify each system below by comparing the slopes and y-intercepts. Then give the number of solutions.

4. $\begin{cases} y = -3x - 2 \\ y = -3x - 4 \end{cases}$

5. $\begin{cases} y = 2x + 5 \\ y = 5 + 2x \end{cases}$

6. $\begin{cases} y = -4x + 3 \\ y = 2x + 7 \end{cases}$

_____ _____ _____

_____ _____ _____

Classify each system and give the number of solutions. If there is one solution, provide it.

7. $\begin{cases} y = 2x + 8 \\ y - 4x = 8 \end{cases}$

8. $\begin{cases} y + 3x - 2 = 0 \\ 9x + 3y = 6 \end{cases}$

_____ _____

_____ _____

Holt Algebra 1

California Standards ◆—9.0, ◆—15.0

LESSON 6-5

Review for Mastery
Applying Systems

When you solve a mixture problem, you can use a table to help you set up the system of equations. Each row of the table gives you one of the equations in the system.

A chemist mixes a 12% alcohol solution with a 20% alcohol solution to make 300 milliliters of an 18% alcohol solution. How many milliliters of each solution does the chemist use?

Let a be the number of milliliters of the 12% solution. Let b be the number of milliliters of the 20% solution.

	12% Solution	+	20% Solution	=	18% Solution
Amount of Solution (mL)	a	+	b	=	300
Amount of Alcohol (mL)	$0.12a$	+	$0.2b$	=	$(0.18)300$

Write a system of equations by reading each row of the table: $\begin{cases} a + b = 300 \\ 0.12a + 0.2b = 54 \end{cases}$

Now use elimination or substitution to solve the system.

The solution is $(75, 225)$. The chemist uses 75 milliliters of the 12% solution and 225 milliliters of the 20% solution.

Write a system of equations for each mixture problem. Then solve the problem.

1. Jenny mixes a 30% saline solution with a 50% saline solution to make 800 milliliters of a 45% saline solution. How many milliliters of each solution does she use?

_____

2. A pharmacist wants to mix a medicine that is 10% aspirin with a medicine that is 25% aspirin to make 10 grams of a medicine that is 16% aspirin. How many grams of each medicine should the pharmacist mix together?

_____

3. Peanuts cost $1.60 per pound and raisins cost $2.40 per pound. Brad wants to make 8 pounds of a peanut-raisin mixture that costs $2.20 per pound. How many pounds of peanuts and raisins should he use?

_____

Holt Algebra 1

California Standards ✦9.0, ✦15.0

LESSON 6-5
Review for Mastery
Applying Systems continued

A table is also helpful in setting up a system of equations when you solve a money problem. Each row of the table gives you one of the equations in the system.

A cashier is counting money at the end of the day. She has a stack that contains $5 bills and $10 bills. The stack contains a total of 45 bills and the value of the bills is $290. How many $5 bills and $10 bills are in the stack?

Let f be the number of $5 bills and let t be the number of $10 bills.

	$5 Bills	+	$10 Bills	=	Total
Number of Bills	f	+	t	=	45
Value of Bills ($)	$5f$	+	$10t$	=	290

Write a system of equations by reading each row of the table: $\begin{cases} f + t = 45 \\ 5f + 10t = 290 \end{cases}$

Now use elimination or substitution to solve the system.

The solution is $(32, 13)$. There are 32 $5 bills and 13 $10 bills.

Write a system of equations for each money problem. Then solve the problem.

4. Miguel has some quarters and dimes. There are 38 coins altogether and the total value of the coins is $6.80. How many quarters and how many dimes does he have?

_____

5. The drawer of a cash register contains 55 bills. All of the bills are either $10 bills or $20 bills. The total value of the bills is $810. How many $10 bills and how many $20 bills are in the drawer?

_____

6. Kenisha is selling tickets to a school play. Adult tickets cost $12 and student tickets cost $6. Kenisha sells a total of 48 tickets and collects a total of $336. How many of each type of ticket does she sell?

_____

Holt Algebra 1

California Standards ◆━6.0

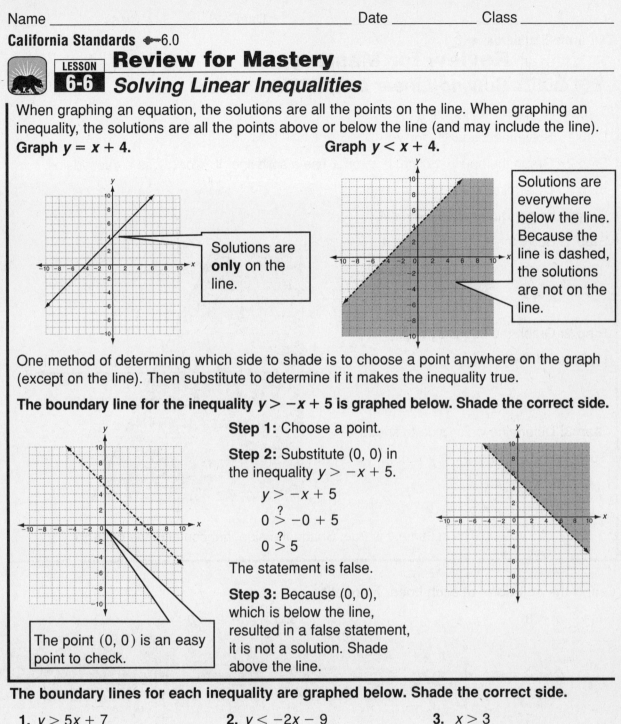

LESSON 6-6

Review for Mastery
Solving Linear Inequalities

When graphing an equation, the solutions are all the points on the line. When graphing an inequality, the solutions are all the points above or below the line (and may include the line).

Graph $y = x + 4$.

Solutions are **only** on the line.

Graph $y < x + 4$.

Solutions are everywhere below the line. Because the line is dashed, the solutions are not on the line.

One method of determining which side to shade is to choose a point anywhere on the graph (except on the line). Then substitute to determine if it makes the inequality true.

The boundary line for the inequality $y > -x + 5$ is graphed below. Shade the correct side.

Step 1: Choose a point.

Step 2: Substitute $(0, 0)$ in the inequality $y > -x + 5$.

$$y > -x + 5$$
$$0 \overset{?}{>} -0 + 5$$
$$0 \overset{?}{>} 5$$

The statement is false.

Step 3: Because $(0, 0)$, which is below the line, resulted in a false statement, it is not a solution. Shade above the line.

The point $(0, 0)$ is an easy point to check.

The boundary lines for each inequality are graphed below. Shade the correct side.

1. $y > 5x + 7$

2. $y < -2x - 9$

3. $x > 3$

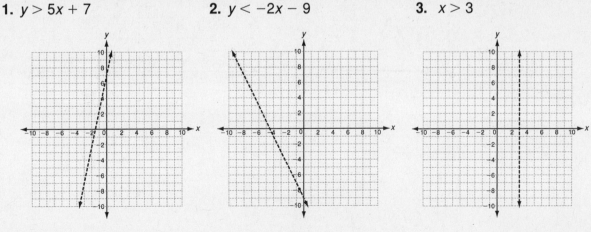

Holt Algebra 1

California Standards ◆―6.0

LESSON 6-6

Review for Mastery
Solving Linear Inequalities continued

To graph a linear inequality:

Step 1: Solve the inequality for *y*.

Step 2: Graph the boundary line. If ≤, or ≥ use a solid line. If < or > use a dashed line.

Step 3: Determine which side to shade.

Graph the solutions of 2*x* + *y* ≤ 4.

Step 1: Solve for *y*.

$$2x + y \le 4$$
$$\underline{-2x \quad \quad -2x}$$
$$y \le -2x + 4$$

Step 2: Graph the boundary line.

Use a solid line for ≤.

Step 3: Determine which side to shade.

Substitute (0, 0) into 2*x* + *y* ≤ 4.

$$2x + y \le 4$$
$$2(0) + 0 \overset{?}{\le} 4$$
$$0 \overset{?}{\le} 4.$$ The statement is true. Shade the side that contains the point (0, 0).

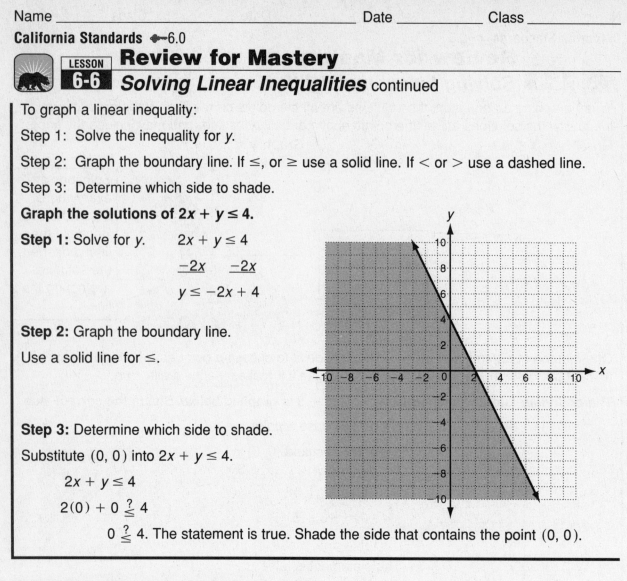

Graph the solutions of each linear inequality.

4. *y* − *x* < 3

5. *x* + *y* + 2 ≥ 0

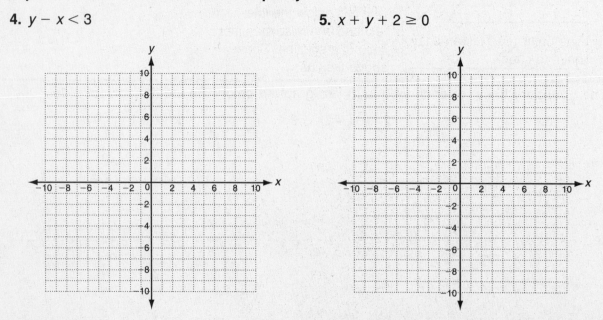

Holt Algebra 1

Name _____ Date _____ Class _____

California Standards ◆—6.0, ◆—9.0

LESSON 6-7
Review for Mastery
Solving Systems of Linear Inequalities

You can graph a system of linear inequalities by combining the graphs of the inequalities.

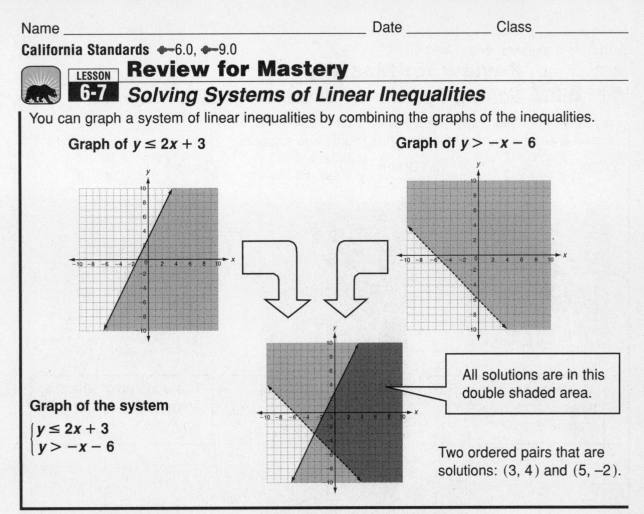

Graph of $y \leq 2x + 3$

Graph of $y > -x - 6$

Graph of the system

$$\begin{cases} y \leq 2x + 3 \\ y > -x - 6 \end{cases}$$

All solutions are in this double shaded area.

Two ordered pairs that are solutions: $(3, 4)$ and $(5, -2)$.

For each system below, give two ordered pairs that are solutions and two that are not solutions.

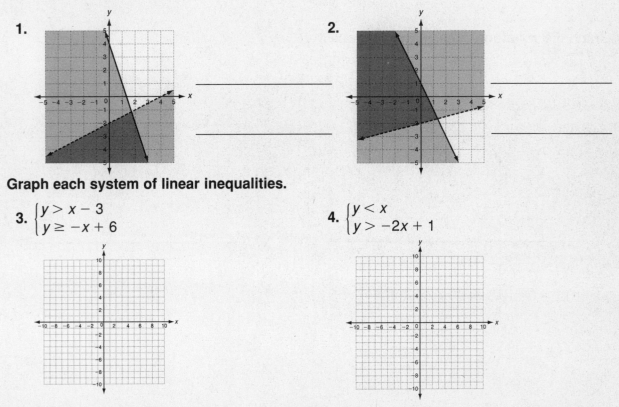

1.

_____

_____

2.

_____

_____

Graph each system of linear inequalities.

3. $\begin{cases} y > x - 3 \\ y \geq -x + 6 \end{cases}$

4. $\begin{cases} y < x \\ y > -2x + 1 \end{cases}$

Holt Algebra 1

Name _____ Date _____ Class _____

California Standards ◆–6.0, ◆–9.0

LESSON 6-7 Review for Mastery
Solving Systems of Linear Inequalities continued

A system of equations with parallel lines has no solutions.
Parallel lines in a system of inequalities might have solutions.

Graph $\begin{cases} y < x + 4 \\ y > x - 2 \end{cases}$.

Graph $\begin{cases} y \geq 2x + 4 \\ y > 2x - 1 \end{cases}$.

Graph $\begin{cases} y > -3x + 5 \\ y < -3x - 3 \end{cases}$.

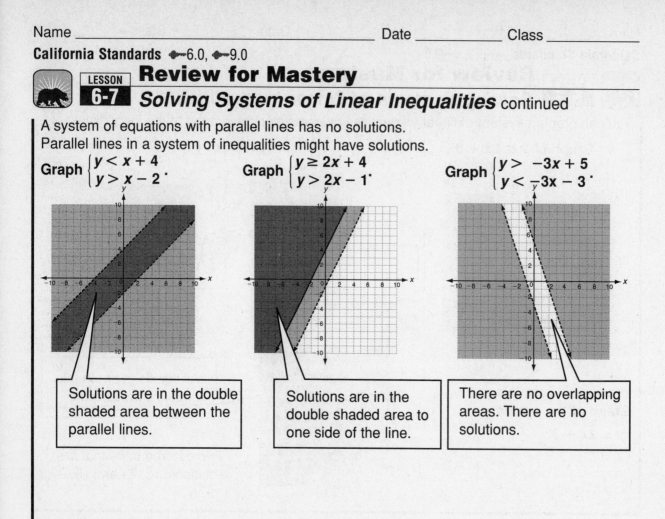

Solutions are in the double shaded area between the parallel lines.

Solutions are in the double shaded area to one side of the line.

There are no overlapping areas. There are no solutions.

Graph the solutions of each linear inequality.

5. $\begin{cases} y \leq x - 3 \\ y > x + 3 \end{cases}$

6. $\begin{cases} y > 2x - 2 \\ y \leq 2x + 3 \end{cases}$

7. $\begin{cases} y > -x - 1 \\ y > -x - 5 \end{cases}$

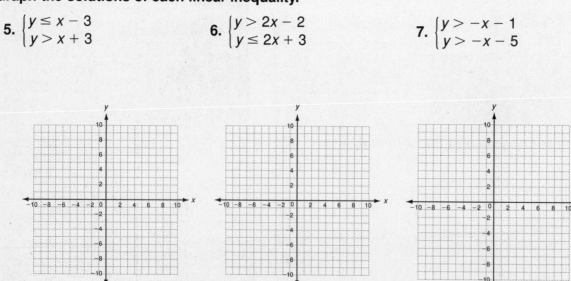

Holt Algebra 1

California Standards ←—2.0

LESSON 7-1

Review for Mastery
Integer Exponents

Remember that 2^3 means $2 \times 2 \times 2 = 8$. The base is 2, the exponent is positive 3. Exponents can also be 0 or negative.

	Zero Exponents	Negative Exponents	Negative Exponents in the Denominator
Definition	For any nonzero number x, $x^0 = 1$.	For any nonzero number x and any integer n, $x^{-n} = \dfrac{1}{x^n}$.	For any nonzero number x and any integer n, $\dfrac{1}{x^{-n}} = x^n$.
Examples	$6^0 = 1 \qquad \left(\dfrac{1}{2}\right)^0 = 1$	$5^{-3} = \dfrac{1}{5^3} \qquad 2^{-4} = \dfrac{1}{2^4}$	$\dfrac{1}{8^{-2}} = 8^2 \qquad \dfrac{1}{2^{-4}} = 2^4$
	0^0 and 0^{-n} are undefined.		

Simplify 4^{-2}.

4^{-2}

$\dfrac{1}{4^2}$ *Write without negative exponents.*

$\dfrac{1}{4 \cdot 4}$ *Write in expanded form.*

$\dfrac{1}{16}$ *Simplify.*

Simplify $x^2 y^{-3} z^0$.

$x^2 y^{-3} z^0$

$\dfrac{x^2 z^0}{y^3}$ *Write without negative exponents.*

$\dfrac{x^2(1)}{y^3}$ $z^0 = 1$.

$\dfrac{x^2}{y^3}$ *Simplify.*

Fill in the blanks to simplify each expression.

1. 2^{-5}

$2^{-5} = \dfrac{1}{2^{\square}}$

$\dfrac{1}{2^5} = \dfrac{1}{\boxed{}}$

$= \underline{}$

2. 10^{-3}

$10^{-3} = \dfrac{1}{10^{\square}}$

$\dfrac{1}{10^3} = \dfrac{1}{\boxed{}}$

$= \underline{}$

3. $\dfrac{1}{5^{-4}}$

$\dfrac{1}{5^{-4}} = 5^{\square}$

$5^{\square} = \boxed{}$

$= \underline{}$

Simplify.

4. $5y^{-4}$ _____

5. $\dfrac{8}{a^{-3}}$ _____

6. $9x^3 y^{-2}$ _____

7. $\dfrac{x^3}{x^{-1}y}$ _____

8. $\dfrac{b^2}{a^{-1}b^3}$ _____

9. $5x^{-4}y^2$ _____

Holt Algebra 1

California Standards ← 2.0

LESSON 7-1

Review for Mastery

Integer Exponents continued

Evaluate $a^{-3}b^4$ for $a = 5$ and $b = 2$.

$a^{-3}b^4$

$(5^{-3})(2^4)$ *Substitute.*

$\dfrac{2^4}{5^3}$ *Write without negative exponents.*

$\dfrac{16}{125}$ *Simplify.*

When evaluating, it is important to determine whether the negative is raised to the power.

Evaluate $-x^{-2}$ for $x = 10$.

The negative is not raised to the power.

$-x^{-2}$

-10^{-2} *Substitute.*

$-\dfrac{1}{10^2}$ *Write without negative exponents.*

$-\dfrac{1}{10 \cdot 10}$ *Write in expanded form.*

$-\dfrac{1}{100}$ *Simplify.*

Evaluate $(-x)^{-2}$ for $x = 10$.

The negative is raised to the power.

$(-x)^{-2}$

$(-10)^{-2}$ *Substitute.*

$\dfrac{1}{(-10)^2}$ *Write without negative exponents.*

$\dfrac{1}{(-10) \cdot (-10)}$ *Write in expanded form.*

$\dfrac{1}{100}$ *Simplify.*

Evaluate each expression for the given values of the variables.

10. $x^2 y^0$ for $x = -2$ and $y = 5$

11. $a^3 b^3$ for $a = 4$ and $b = 2$

_____   _____

12. $\dfrac{z^3}{y^{-2}}$ for $z = 2$ and $y = 5$

13. $-a^3 b^{-4}$ for $a = 2$ and $b = -1$

_____   _____

14. $\dfrac{n^{-2}}{m^{-4}}$ for $m = 6$ and $n = 2$

15. $(-u)^2 v^{-6}$ for $u = 2$ and $v = 2$

_____   _____

Holt Algebra 1

California Standards ⬅2.0

Review for Mastery

LESSON 7-2

Powers of 10 and Scientific Notation

Powers of 10 are used to write large numbers in a simple way.

The exponent will tell you how many places to move the decimal when finding the value of a power of 10.

Find the value of 10^5.

Step 1: Start with the number 1.

1.0

Step 2: The exponent is **positive** 5. Move the decimal 5 spaces to the **right**.

1.00000 = 100,000

Write 100,000,000 as a power of 10.

100000000.

The decimal point is 8 places to the right of the 1. The exponent is 8.

$$100,000,000 = 10^8$$

Numbers greater than 1 will have a positive exponent.

Find the value of 10^{-4}.

Step 1: Start with the number 1.

1.0

Step 2: The exponent is **negative** 4. Move the decimal 4 spaces to the **left**.

0001 = 0.0001

Write 0.00001 as a power of 10.

0.00001

The decimal point is 5 places to the left of the one. The exponent is −5.

$$0.00001 = 10^{-5}$$

Numbers less than 1 will have a negative exponent.

First determine whether the decimal point will move to the right or to the left. Then find the value of each power of 10.

1. 10^6

2. 10^{-2}

3. 10^4

_____

_____

_____

_____

_____

_____

First determine whether the exponent will be positive or negative when each number is written as a power of 10. Then write each number as a power of 10.

4. 1000

5. 0.0001

6. 10,000,000

_____

_____

_____

_____

_____

_____

Holt Algebra 1

California Standards ↤2.0

Review for Mastery
LESSON 7-2 Powers of 10 and Scientific Notation continued

Scientific notation is used for writing very large or very small numbers.

| The first factor must be between 1 and 10. | → 3.2×10^5 ← | The second factor must be a power of 10. |

Write 7,230,000,000 in scientific notation.

Step 1: Write the first factor.   7.23

Step 2: Count the number of places you need to move the decimal point to make the given value.

7.2 3 0 0 0 0 0 0 0

Step 3: Because you moved to the right, the exponent will be positive.

7.23×10^9

Write 0.00062 in scientific notation.

Step 1: Write the first factor.   6.2

Step 2: Count the number of places you need to move the decimal point to make the given value.

0 . 0 0 0 6 2

Step 3: Because you moved to the left, the exponent will be negative.

6.2×10^{-4}

Write 8.24×10^{-6} in standard notation.

Step 1: Write the first factor.   8.24

Step 2: Because the exponent is −6, move the decimal point 6 places to the left.

0 0 0 0 0 8 . 2 4

Step 3: Write the number.   0.00000824

First determine whether the exponent will be positive or negative when each number is written in scientific notation. Then write the number in scientific notation.

7. 61,200,000   **8.** 0.00045   **9.** 4,670,000

_____   _____   _____

_____   _____   _____

Write each number in standard notation.

10. 7.451×10^3 **11.** 4.231×10^{-5} **12.** 2.93×10^8

_____   _____   _____

Holt Algebra 1

California Standards ⬤━2.0

Review for Mastery

LESSON 7-3

Multiplication Properties of Exponents

You can multiply a power by a power by expanding each factor.

Simplify $(4^3)(4^5)$.

$$(4^3)(4^5)$$

$(4 \cdot 4 \cdot 4)(4 \cdot 4 \cdot 4 \cdot 4 \cdot 4)$ *Expand each factor.*

$\qquad\qquad 4^8$ *Count the number of factors.*
The number of factors is the exponent.

Or you can use the **Product of Powers Property**:

$$a^m \cdot a^n = a^{m+n} \quad (a \neq 0, \ m \text{ and } n \text{ are integers.})$$

Simplify $(4^3)(4^5)$.   **Simplify $a^4 \cdot b^5 \cdot a^{-2}$.**

$\qquad (4^3)(4^5)$ $a^{4+(-2)} \cdot b^5$

$\qquad 4^{3+5}$ $a^2 \cdot b^5$

$\qquad 4^8$ $a^2 b^5$

You can use the **Power of a Power Property** to find a power raised to another power.

$$(a^m)^n = a^{mn} \quad (a \neq 0, \ m \text{ and } n \text{ are integers.})$$

Simplify $(2^3)^2$.   **Simplify $(x^5)^4 \cdot y$.**

$\qquad (2^3)^2$ $x^{5 \cdot 4} \cdot y$

$\qquad 2^{3 \cdot 2}$ $x^{20} y$

$\qquad 2^6$

Simplify.

1. $2^3 \cdot 2^4$ **2.** $8^{-2} \cdot 5^3 \cdot 8^6$ **3.** $2^4 \cdot 3^5 \cdot 2^8 \cdot 3^{-2}$

_____   _____   _____

4. $m^8 \cdot n^4 \cdot m^7$ **5.** $(6^4)^2$ **6.** $(4^{-3})^2$

_____   _____   _____

7. $(5^{-3})^3 \cdot 4^0$ **8.** $(x^2)^{-4} \cdot y^{-3}$ **9.** $(u^5)^{-2} \cdot (v^3)^4$

_____   _____   _____

Holt Algebra 1

California Standards ←―2.0

LESSON
7-3

Review for Mastery

Multiplication Properties of Exponents continued

In the **Power of a Product Property,** each factor is raised to that power.

$$(ab)^n = a^n b^n \quad (a \neq 0, b \neq 0, n \text{ is any integer.})$$

Simplify $(x^3 y^{-5})^2$.

$(x^3 y^{-5})^2$

$x^{3 \cdot 2} \cdot y^{-5 \cdot 2}$ *Use the Power of a Product Property.*

$x^6 y^{-10}$ *Simplify.*

$\dfrac{x^6}{y^{10}}$ *Write with positive exponents.*

Exponential expressions are simplified if:

- there are no negative exponents.

- the same base does not appear more than once in a product or a quotient.

- no powers, products or quotients are raised to powers.

- all fractions have been simplified.

Simplified				Not Simplified			
$\dfrac{x}{y}$	$a^2 b^3$	$\dfrac{m^3}{n^3}$	$\dfrac{2g}{3h^4}$	x^{-2}	$(y^2)^4$	$(st)^4$	$\dfrac{2d^4}{6}$

Tell if each expression is simplified. If not, simplify.

10. $\dfrac{-3a^2}{8b}$ **11.** $(2h^3)^2$ **12.** $m^3 \cdot m^0$

_____   _____   _____

_____   _____   _____

Simplify.

13. $(-4x^5)^2$ **14.** $(s^4 t^3)^3$ **15.** $(-2x^{-4}y)^5$

_____   _____   _____

Holt Algebra 1

California Standards ✦2.0

Review for Mastery

LESSON 7-4

Division Properties of Exponents

The **Quotient of Powers Property** can be used to divide terms with exponents.

$$\frac{a^m}{a^n} = a^{m-n} \text{ (} a \neq 0, \text{ } m \text{ and } n \text{ are integers.)}$$

Simplify $\frac{7^5}{7^2}$.

$$\frac{7^5}{7^2} = 7^{5-2}$$

$$= 7^3$$

Simplify $\frac{x^7 y}{x^3}$.

$$\frac{x^7 y}{x^3} = x^{7-3} \cdot y$$

$$= x^4 y$$

The **Positive Power of a Quotient Property** can be used to raise quotients to positive powers.

$$\left(\frac{a}{b}\right)^n = \frac{a^n}{b^n} \text{ (} a \neq 0, \text{ } b \neq 0, \text{ } n \text{ is a positive integer.)}$$

Simplify $\left(\frac{2}{5}\right)^4$.

$$\left(\frac{2}{5}\right)^4 = \frac{2^4}{5^4}$$ *Use the Positive Power of a Quotient Property.*

$$= \frac{16}{625}$$ *Simplify.*

Simplify $\left(\frac{2x^5}{y^4}\right)^3$.

$$\left(\frac{2x^5}{y^4}\right)^3 = \frac{(2x^5)^3}{(y^4)^3}$$ *Use the Positive Power of a Quotient Property.*

$$= \frac{2^3(x^5)^3}{(y^4)^3}$$ *Use the Power of a Product Property.*

$$= \frac{8x^{15}}{y^{12}}$$ *Simplify.*

Simplify.

1. $\frac{5^6}{5^4}$

2. $\frac{x^6 y^5}{y^3}$

3. $\frac{a^2 b^4}{(ab)^3}$

4. $\left(\frac{2}{5}\right)^3$

5. $\left(\frac{x^3}{y^2}\right)^6$

6. $\left(\frac{3m^3}{n^2}\right)^2$

7. $\left(\frac{a}{b^2}\right)^3$

8. $\left(\frac{x^3}{xy}\right)^2$

9. $\left(\frac{30}{20}\right)^2$

Holt Algebra 1

California Standards ⬟2.0

LESSON 7-4

Review for Mastery

Division Properties of Exponents continued

You can divide quotients raised to a negative power by using the
Negative Power of a Quotient Property.

$$\left(\frac{a}{b}\right)^{-n} = \left(\frac{b}{a}\right)^{n} = \frac{b^n}{a^n} \quad (a \neq 0,\ b \neq 0,\ n \text{ is a positive integer})$$

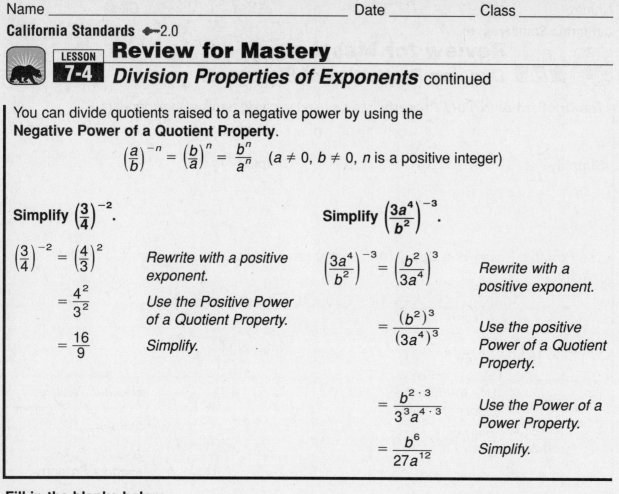

Simplify $\left(\frac{3}{4}\right)^{-2}$.

$\left(\frac{3}{4}\right)^{-2} = \left(\frac{4}{3}\right)^{2}$ *Rewrite with a positive exponent.*

$= \frac{4^2}{3^2}$ *Use the Positive Power of a Quotient Property.*

$= \frac{16}{9}$ *Simplify.*

Simplify $\left(\frac{3a^4}{b^2}\right)^{-3}$.

$\left(\frac{3a^4}{b^2}\right)^{-3} = \left(\frac{b^2}{3a^4}\right)^{3}$ *Rewrite with a positive exponent.*

$= \frac{(b^2)^3}{(3a^4)^3}$ *Use the positive Power of a Quotient Property.*

$= \frac{b^{2 \cdot 3}}{3^3 a^{4 \cdot 3}}$ *Use the Power of a Power Property.*

$= \frac{b^6}{27a^{12}}$ *Simplify.*

Fill in the blanks below.

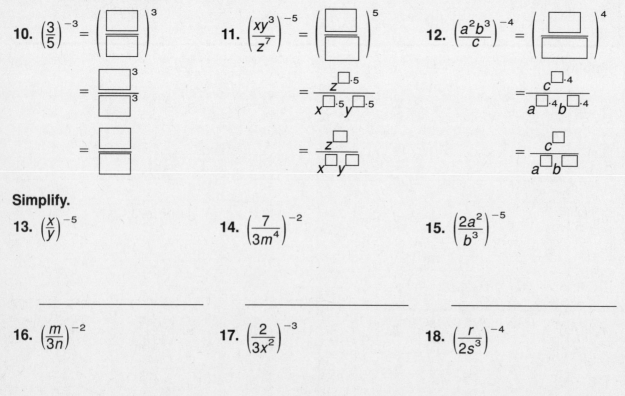

10. $\left(\frac{3}{5}\right)^{-3} = \left(\dfrac{\square}{\square}\right)^{3}$

$= \dfrac{\square^3}{\square^3}$

$= \dfrac{\square}{\square}$

11. $\left(\frac{xy^3}{z^7}\right)^{-5} = \left(\dfrac{\square}{\square}\right)^{5}$

$= \dfrac{z^{\square \cdot 5}}{x^{\square \cdot 5} y^{\square \cdot 5}}$

$= \dfrac{z^{\square}}{x^{\square} y^{\square}}$

12. $\left(\frac{a^2 b^3}{c}\right)^{-4} = \left(\dfrac{\square}{\square}\right)^{4}$

$= \dfrac{c^{\square \cdot 4}}{a^{\square \cdot 4} b^{\square \cdot 4}}$

$= \dfrac{c^{\square}}{a^{\square} b^{\square}}$

Simplify.

13. $\left(\frac{x}{y}\right)^{-5}$

14. $\left(\frac{7}{3m^4}\right)^{-2}$

15. $\left(\frac{2a^2}{b^3}\right)^{-5}$

_____

_____

_____

16. $\left(\frac{m}{3n}\right)^{-2}$

17. $\left(\frac{2}{3x^2}\right)^{-3}$

18. $\left(\frac{r}{2s^3}\right)^{-4}$

_____

_____

_____

Holt Algebra 1

California Standards ⊸2.0

Review for Mastery
LESSON 7-5 Fractional Exponents

To simplify a number raised to the power of $\frac{1}{n}$, write the nth root of the number.

Simplify $216^{\frac{1}{3}}$.

$$216^{\frac{1}{3}} = \sqrt[3]{216} = 6$$

Think: What number, when taken as a factor 3 times, is equal to 216?

$6^3 = 6 \times 6 \times 6 = 216$, so $\sqrt[3]{216} = 6$.

When an expression contains two or more expressions with fractional exponents, evaluate the expressions with the exponents first, then add or subtract.

Simplify $81^{\frac{1}{2}} + 32^{\frac{1}{5}}$.

$$81^{\frac{1}{2}} + 32^{\frac{1}{5}} = \sqrt{81} + \sqrt[5]{32}$$
$$= 9 + 2$$
$$= 11$$

Simplify each expression.

1. $64^{\frac{1}{2}}$

2. $1000^{\frac{1}{3}}$

3. $1^{\frac{1}{5}}$

_____   _____   _____

4. $256^{\frac{1}{4}}$

5. $32^{\frac{1}{5}}$

6. $49^{\frac{1}{2}}$

_____   _____   _____

7. $8^{\frac{1}{3}} + 16^{\frac{1}{2}}$

8. $121^{\frac{1}{2}} + 27^{\frac{1}{3}}$

9. $32^{\frac{1}{5}} + 1^{\frac{1}{2}}$

_____   _____   _____

10. $81^{\frac{1}{4}} - 16^{\frac{1}{4}}$

11. $144^{\frac{1}{2}} - 125^{\frac{1}{3}}$

12. $625^{\frac{1}{4}} - 0^{\frac{1}{2}}$

_____   _____   _____

Holt Algebra 1

California Standards ◆–2.0

![bear logo] **LESSON 7-5** # Review for Mastery
Fractional Exponents continued

A fractional exponent may have a numerator other than 1. To simplify a number raised to the power of $\frac{m}{n}$, write the nth root of the number raised to the mth power.

Simplify $125^{\frac{4}{3}}$.

$$125^{\frac{4}{3}} = \left(\sqrt[3]{125}\right)^4 = (5)^4 = 625$$

To find $\sqrt[3]{125}$, think: what number, when taken as a factor 3 times, equals 125?
$5^3 = 5 \times 5 \times 5 = 125$, so $\sqrt[3]{125} = 5$.

Simplify $64^{\frac{5}{6}}$.

$$64^{\frac{5}{6}} = \left(\sqrt[6]{64}\right)^5 = (2)^5 = 32$$

To find $\sqrt[6]{64}$, think: what number, when taken as a factor 6 times, equals 64?
$2^6 = 2 \times 2 \times 2 \times 2 \times 2 \times 2 = 64$, so $\sqrt[6]{64} = 2$.

Simplify each expression.

13. $4^{\frac{3}{2}}$

14. $16^{\frac{3}{4}}$

15. $32^{\frac{2}{5}}$

_____   _____   _____

16. $1^{\frac{3}{5}}$

17. $27^{\frac{4}{3}}$

18. $100^{\frac{3}{2}}$

_____   _____   _____

19. $8^{\frac{2}{3}}$

20. $81^{\frac{5}{4}}$

21. $128^{\frac{3}{7}}$

_____   _____   _____

22. $16^{\frac{5}{4}}$

23. $49^{\frac{3}{2}}$

24. $8^{\frac{8}{3}}$

_____   _____   _____

Holt Algebra 1

California Standards Prep for ◆—10.0

LESSON 7-6 **Review for Mastery**
Polynomials

A **monomial** is a number, a variable, or a product of numbers and variables with whole-number exponents. A **polynomial** is a monomial or a sum or difference of monomials.

The degree of the monomial is the sum of the exponents in the monomial.

Find the degree of $8x^2y^3$.	**Find the degree of $-4a^6b$.**
$8x^2y^3$ The exponents are 2 and 3.	$-4a^6b$ The exponents are 6 and 1.
The degree of the monomial is $2 + 3 = 5$.	The degree of the monomial is $6 + 1 = 7$.

The **standard form of a polynomial** is written with the terms in order from the greatest degree to the least degree. The coefficient of the first term is the **leading coefficient**.

Write $5x + 6x^3 + 4 + 2x^4$ in standard form.

$\underbrace{5x}_{1} + \underbrace{6x^3}_{3} + \underbrace{4}_{0} - \underbrace{2x^4}_{4}$ *Find the degree of each term.*

$2x^4 + 6x^3 + 5x + 4$ *Write the terms in order of degree.*

The leading coefficient is 2.

Find the degree of each monomial.

1. $7m^3n^5$

2. $6xyz$

3. $4x^2y^2$

_____   _____   _____

Write each polynomial in standard form. Then give the leading coefficient.

4. $x^3 - 5x^4 - 6x^5$

5. $2x + 5x^2 - x^3$

6. $8x + 7x^2 - 1$

_____   _____   _____

_____   _____   _____

7. $-2x^2 + 3x^4 + 7x$

8. $-8 + 3x^3 + 6x^5$

9. $4x^2 - 6x - 5x^5$

_____   _____   _____

_____   _____   _____

Holt Algebra 1

California Standards Prep for ◆—10.0

Polynomials have special names based on their degree and the number of terms they have.

The degree of the polynomial is the degree of the term with the greatest degree.

Degree	0	1	2	3	4	5	6 or more
Name	Constant	Linear	Quadratic	Cubic	Quartic	Quintic	6th degree ...

Terms	1	2	3	4 or more
Name	Monomial	Binomial	Trinomial	Polynomial

Classify $7x^4 + 5x + 3$ according to its degree and number of terms.

$7x^4 + 5x + 3$ is a quartic trinomial. ⟶ Degree: 4 / Terms: 3

A **root** of a polynomial is a value of the variable for which the polynomial is equal to 0.

Tell whether 4 is a root of $-16t^2 + 65t - 4$.

$$-16t^2 + 65t - 4$$

$$-16(4)^2 + 65(4) - 4$$ ⟵ Substitute 4 for t.

$$-16(16) + 65(4) - 4$$

$$-256 + 260 - 4$$ ⟵ Follow the order of operations to simplify.

$$0$$

4 is a root of $-16t^2 + 65t - 4$.

Classify each polynomial according to its degree and number of terms.

10. $7x^2 - 5x$

11. $b^3 + 2b^2 - 4b + 1$

_____   _____

Tell whether each number is a root of $3x^3 - 10x - 4$.

12. 5

13. −1

14. 2

_____   _____   _____

Holt Algebra 1

California Standards ⬤━10.0

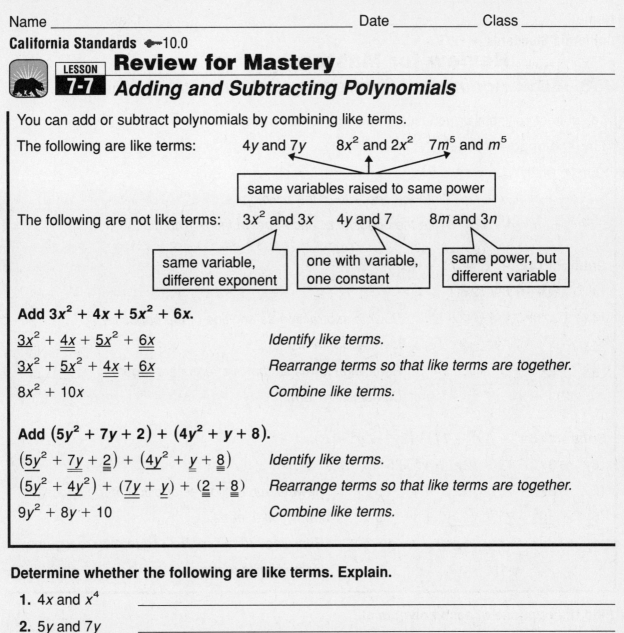

LESSON 7-7

Review for Mastery
Adding and Subtracting Polynomials

You can add or subtract polynomials by combining like terms.

The following are like terms: $4y$ and $7y$ $8x^2$ and $2x^2$ $7m^5$ and m^5

same variables raised to same power

The following are not like terms: $3x^2$ and $3x$ $4y$ and 7 $8m$ and $3n$

same variable, different exponent

one with variable, one constant

same power, but different variable

Add $3x^2 + 4x + 5x^2 + 6x$.

$\underline{3x^2} + \underline{4x} + \underline{5x^2} + \underline{6x}$	*Identify like terms.*
$\underline{3x^2} + \underline{5x^2} + \underline{4x} + \underline{6x}$	*Rearrange terms so that like terms are together.*
$8x^2 + 10x$	*Combine like terms.*

Add $(5y^2 + 7y + 2) + (4y^2 + y + 8)$.

$(\underline{5y^2} + \underline{7y} + \underline{2}) + (\underline{4y^2} + \underline{y} + \underline{8})$	*Identify like terms.*
$(\underline{5y^2} + \underline{4y^2}) + (\underline{7y} + \underline{y}) + (\underline{2} + \underline{8})$	*Rearrange terms so that like terms are together.*
$9y^2 + 8y + 10$	*Combine like terms.*

Determine whether the following are like terms. Explain.

1. $4x$ and x^4 _____

2. $5y$ and $7y$ _____

3. $2z^3$ and $4x^3$ _____

Add.

4. $2y^2 + 3y + 7y + y^2$ **5.** $8m^4 + 3m - 4m^4$ **6.** $12x^5 + 10x^4 + 8x^4$

_____   _____   _____

7. $(6x^2 + 3x) + (2x^2 + 6x)$ _____

8. $(m^2 - 10m + 5) + (8m + 2)$ _____

9. $(6x^3 + 5x) + (4x^3 + x^2 - 2x + 9)$ _____

10. $(2y^5 - 6y^3 + 1) + (y^5 + 8y^4 - 2y^3 - 1)$ _____

Holt Algebra 1

California Standards ⬥━10.0

LESSON 7-7

Review for Mastery

Adding and Subtracting Polynomials continued

To subtract polynomials you must remember to add the opposite.

Find the opposite of $(5m^3 - m + 4)$.

$(5m^3 - m + 4)$	
$-(5m^3 - m + 4)$	Write the opposite of the polynomial.
$-5m^3 + m - 4$	Write the opposite of each term in the polynomial.

Subtract $(4x^3 + x^2 + 7) - (2x^3)$.

$(4x^3 + x^2 + 7) - (2x^3)$	
$(4x^3 + x^2 + 7) + (-2x^3)$	Rewrite subtraction as addition of the opposite.
$(\underline{4x^3} + x^2 + 7) + (\underline{-2x^3})$	Identify like terms.
$(\underline{4x^3} - \underline{2x^3}) + x^2 + 7$	Rearrange terms so that like terms are together.
$2x^3 + x^2 + 7$	Combine like terms.

Subtract $(6y^4 + 3y^2 - 7) - (2y^4 - y^2 + 5)$.

$(6y^4 + 3y^2 - 7) - (2y^4 - y^2 + 5)$	
$(6y^4 + 3y^2 - 7) + (-2y^4 + y^2 - 5)$	Rewrite subtraction as addition of the opposite.
$(\underline{6y^4} + \underline{\underline{3y^2}} - \underline{\underline{\underline{7}}}) + (\underline{-2y^4} + \underline{\underline{y^2}} - \underline{\underline{\underline{5}}})$	Identify like terms.
$(\underline{6y^4} - \underline{2y^4}) + (\underline{\underline{3y^2}} + \underline{\underline{y^2}}) + (-\underline{\underline{\underline{7}}} - \underline{\underline{\underline{5}}})$	Rearrange terms so that like terms are together.
$4y^4 + 4y^2 - 12$	Combine like terms.

Find the opposite of each polynomial.

11. $x^2 + 7x$ **12.** $-3x^3 + 4x - 8$ **13.** $-5x^4 + x^3 - 7x^2 - 3$

_____   _____   _____

Subtract.

14. $(9x^3 - 5x) - (3x)$ _____

15. $(6t^4 + 3) - (-2t^4 + 2)$ _____

16. $(2x^3 + 4x - 2) - (4x^3 - 6)$ _____

17. $(t^3 - 2t) - (t^2 + 2t + 6)$ _____

18. $(4c^5 + 8c^2 - 2c - 2) - (c^3 - 2c + 5)$ _____

Holt Algebra 1

California Standards ●—10.0

LESSON 7-8

Review for Mastery
Multiplying Polynomials

To multiply monomials, multiply the constants, then multiply variables with the same base.

Multiply $(3a^2b)(4ab^3)$.

$(3a^2b)(4ab^3)$

$(3 \cdot 4)(a^2 \cdot a)(b \cdot b^3)$ *Rearrange so that the constants and the variables with the same bases are together.*

$12a^3b^4$ *Multiply.*

To multiply a polynomial by a monomial, distribute the monomial to each term in the polynomial.

Multiply $2x(x^2 + 3x + 7)$.

$2x(x^2 + 3x + 7)$

$(2x)x^2 + (2x)3x + (2x)7$ *Distribute.*

$2x^3 + 6x^2 + 14x$ *Multiply.*

Multiply.

1. $(-5x^2y^3)(2xy)$ 2. $(2xyz)(-4x^2yz)$ 3. $(3x)(x^2y^3)$

_____   _____   _____

Fill in the blanks below. Then finish multiplying.

4. $4(x - 5)$ 5. $3x(x + 8)$ 6. $2x(x^2 - 6x + 3)$

$(\Box)x - (\Box)5$ $(\Box)x + (\Box)8$ $(\Box)x^2 - (\Box)6x + (\Box)3$

_____   _____   _____

Multiply.

7. $5(x + 9)$ 8. $-4x(x^2 + 8)$ 9. $3x^2(2x^2 + 5x + 4)$

_____   _____   _____

10. $-3(5 - x^2 + 2)$ 11. $(5a^3b)(2ab)$ 12. $5y(-y^2 + 7y - 2)$

_____   _____   _____

Holt Algebra 1

California Standards ⬅—10.0

LESSON 7-8 Review for Mastery
Multiplying Polynomials continued

Use the Distributive Property to multiply binomials and polynomials.

Multiply $(x + 3)(x - 7)$.

$(x + 3)(x - 7)$

$x(x - 7) + 3(x - 7)$　　　　　*Distribute each term of the first binomial.*

$(x)x - (x)7 + (3)x - (3)7$

$x^2 - \underline{7x} + \underline{3x} - 21$　　　　*Multiply.*

$x^2 - 4x - 21$　　　　　　　*Combine like terms.*

Multiply $(x + 5)(x^2 + 3x + 4)$.

$(x + 5)(x^2 + 3x + 4)$

$x(x^2 + 3x + 4) + 5(x^2 + 3x + 4)$　　　*Distribute each term of the first binomial.*

$(x)x^2 + (x)3x + (x)4 + (5)x^2 + (5)3x + (5)4$　*Distribute again.*

$x^3 + \underline{3x^2} + \underline{4x} + \underline{5x^2} + \underline{15x} + 20$　　　*Multiply.*

$x^3 + 8x^2 + 19x + 20$　　　　　　　*Combine like terms.*

Fill in the blanks below. Then finish multiplying.

13. $(x + 4)(x - 5)$

$\boxed{}(x - 5) + \boxed{}(x - 5)$

_____

14. $(x - 2)(x + 8)$

$\boxed{}(x + 8) - \boxed{}(x + 8)$

_____

15. $(x - 3)(x - 6)$

$\boxed{}(x - 6) - \boxed{}(x - 6)$

_____

Multiply.

16. $(x - 2)(x - 3)$

17. $(x - 7)(x + 7)$

18. $(x + 2)(x + 1)$

_____

_____

_____

Fill in the blanks below. Then finish multiplying.

19. $(x + 3)(2x^2 + 4x + 8)$

$\boxed{}(2x^2 + 4x + 8) + \boxed{}(2x^2 + 4x + 8)$

_____

20. $(x + 2)(6x^2 + 4x + 5)$

$\boxed{}(6x^2 + 4x + 5) + \boxed{}(6x^2 + 4x + 5)$

_____

Holt Algebra 1

Name _____ Date _____ Class _____

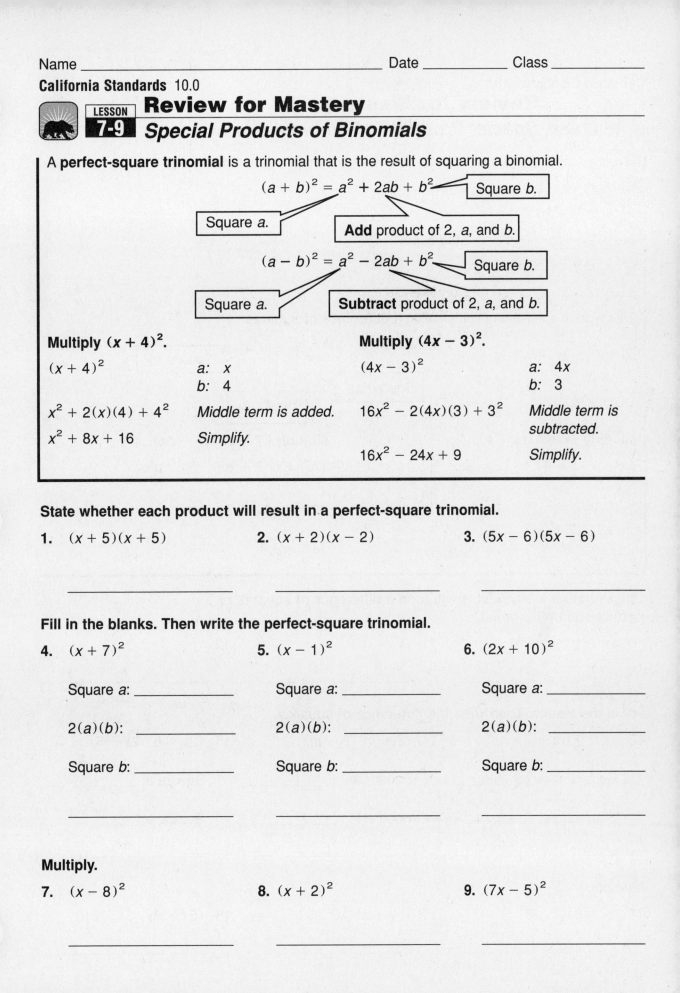

LESSON 7-9
Review for Mastery
Special Products of Binomials

A **perfect-square trinomial** is a trinomial that is the result of squaring a binomial.

$(a + b)^2 = a^2 + 2ab + b^2$ ← Square b.

Square a.

Add product of 2, a, and b.

$(a - b)^2 = a^2 - 2ab + b^2$ ← Square b.

Square a.

Subtract product of 2, a, and b.

Multiply $(x + 4)^2$.

$(x + 4)^2$ a: x
            b: 4

$x^2 + 2(x)(4) + 4^2$ *Middle term is added.*

$x^2 + 8x + 16$ *Simplify.*

Multiply $(4x - 3)^2$.

$(4x - 3)^2$ a: 4x
            b: 3

$16x^2 - 2(4x)(3) + 3^2$ *Middle term is subtracted.*

$16x^2 - 24x + 9$ *Simplify.*

State whether each product will result in a perfect-square trinomial.

1. $(x + 5)(x + 5)$

2. $(x + 2)(x - 2)$

3. $(5x - 6)(5x - 6)$

_____

_____

_____

Fill in the blanks. Then write the perfect-square trinomial.

4. $(x + 7)^2$

   Square a: _____

   $2(a)(b)$: _____

   Square b: _____

5. $(x - 1)^2$

   Square a: _____

   $2(a)(b)$: _____

   Square b: _____

6. $(2x + 10)^2$

   Square a: _____

   $2(a)(b)$: _____

   Square b: _____

_____

_____

_____

Multiply.

7. $(x - 8)^2$

8. $(x + 2)^2$

9. $(7x - 5)^2$

_____

_____

_____

Holt Algebra 1

California Standards 10.0

When you multiply certain types of binomials, the middle term will be zero.

Multiply $(a + b)(a - b)$.

$(a + b)(a - b)$

$a(a - b) + b(a - b)$ *Distribute.*

$a^2 - ab + ab - b^2$

$a^2 - b^2$ *Combine like terms.*

This type of special product is called a **difference of squares**.

$$(a + b)(a - b) = a^2 - b^2$$

Square b.

Square a.

Subtract.

Multiply $(x + 4)(x - 4)$.

$(x + 4)(x - 4)$ $a: x$
                      $b: 4$

$(x)^2 - (4)^2$

$x^2 - 16$ *Simplify.*

Multiply $(7 + 8x)(7 - 8x)$.

$(7 + 8x)(7 - 8x)$ $a: 7$
                        $b: 8x$

$(7)^2 - (8x)^2$

$49 - 64x^2$ *Simplify.*

State whether the products will form a difference of squares or a perfect-square trinomial.

10. $(x + 10)(x - 10)$ **11.** $(y + 6)(y + 6)$ **12.** $(z - 3)(z - 3)$

_____   _____   _____

Fill in the blanks. Then write the difference of squares.

13. $(a + 7)(a - 7)$ **14.** $(2 + m)(2 - m)$ **15.** $(2x + 5)(2x - 5)$

Square *a*: _____   Square *a*: _____   Square *a*: _____

Square *b*: _____   Square *b*: _____   Square *b*: _____

_____   _____   _____

Multiply.

16. $(x + 8)(x - 8)$ **17.** $(10 + x)(10 - x)$ **18.** $(5x + 2y)(5x - 2y)$

_____   _____   _____

Holt Algebra 1

California Standards Prep for 11.0

LESSON 8-1

Review for Mastery
Factors and Greatest Common Factors

A prime number has exactly two factors, itself and 1. The number 1 is not a prime number. To write the **prime factorization** of a number, factor the number into its prime factors only.

Find the prime factorization of 30.

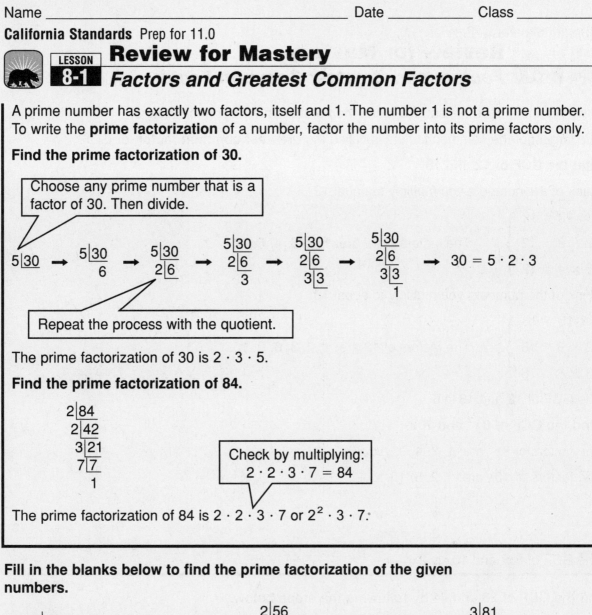

Choose any prime number that is a factor of 30. Then divide.

$$5\overline{)30} \rightarrow \frac{5\overline{)30}}{6} \rightarrow \frac{5\overline{)30}}{2\overline{)6}} \rightarrow \frac{\begin{array}{c}5\overline{)30}\\2\overline{)6}\end{array}}{3} \rightarrow \frac{\begin{array}{c}5\overline{)30}\\2\overline{)6}\end{array}}{3\overline{)3}} \rightarrow \frac{\begin{array}{c}5\overline{)30}\\2\overline{)6}\\3\overline{)3}\end{array}}{1} \rightarrow 30 = 5 \cdot 2 \cdot 3$$

Repeat the process with the quotient.

The prime factorization of 30 is $2 \cdot 3 \cdot 5$.

Find the prime factorization of 84.

$$\begin{array}{c}2\overline{)84}\\2\overline{)42}\\3\overline{)21}\\7\overline{)7}\\1\end{array}$$

Check by multiplying:
$2 \cdot 2 \cdot 3 \cdot 7 = 84$

The prime factorization of 84 is $2 \cdot 2 \cdot 3 \cdot 7$ or $2^2 \cdot 3 \cdot 7$.

Fill in the blanks below to find the prime factorization of the given numbers.

1.

2.

3.

_____   _____   _____

Write the prime factorization of each number.

4. 99   **5.** 75   **6.** 84

_____   _____   _____

Holt Algebra 1

California Standards Prep for 11.0

LESSON 8-1

Review for Mastery

Factors and Greatest Common Factors continued

If two numbers have the same factors, the numbers have common factors.

The largest of the common factors is called the **greatest common factor**, or GCF.

Find the GCF of 12 and 18.

Think of the numbers you multiply to equal 12.

$\left.\begin{array}{l} 1 \times 12 = 12 \\ 2 \times 6 = 12 \\ 3 \times 4 = 12 \end{array}\right\}$ The factors of 12 are: **1**, **2**, **3**, 4, **6**, 12

Think of the numbers you multiply to equal 18.

$\left.\begin{array}{l} 1 \times 18 = 18 \\ 2 \times 9 = 18 \\ 3 \times 6 = 18 \end{array}\right\}$ The factors of 18 are: **1**, **2**, **3**, **6**, 9, 18.

The GCF of 12 and 18 is 6.

Find the GCF of $8x^2$ and $10x$.

The factors of $8x^2$ are: **1**, **2**, 4, 8, *x*, x

The factors of $10x$ are: **1**, **2**, 5, 10, *x*

↓   ↓

2   *x*

The GCF of $8x^2$ and $10x$ is $2x$.

Find the GCF of 28 and 44 by following the steps below.

7. Find the factors of 28.   _____

8. Find the factors of 44.   _____

9. Find the GCF of 28 and 44.   _____

Find the GCF of each pair of numbers.

10. 15 and 20   **11.** 16 and 28   **12.** 24 and 60

_____   _____   _____

Find the GCF of each pair of monomials.

13. $4a$ and $10a$ **14.** $15x^3$ and $21x^2$ **15.** $5y^2$ and $8y$

_____   _____   _____

Holt Algebra 1

California Standards 11.0

LESSON 8-2

Review for Mastery
Factoring by GCF

The Distributive Property states: $a(b + c) = ab + ac$

Factoring by GCF reverses the Distributive Property:

$$ab + ac = a(b + c)$$

Factor $12x^3 + 21x^2 + 15x$. Check your answer.

Step 1: Find the GCF of all the terms in the polynomial.

The factors of $12x^3$ are: 1, 2, **3**, 4, 6, 12, **x**, x, x

The factors of $21x^2$ are: 1, **3**, 7, 21, **x**, x   } The GCF is **3x**.

The factors of $15x$ are: 1, **3**, 5, 15, **x**

Step 2: Write terms as products using the GCF.

$12x^3 + \ 21x^2 + \ \ \ 15x$

$(3x)4x^2 + (3x)7x + (3x)5$

Step 3: Use the Distributive Property to factor out the GCF.

$3x(4x^2 + 7x + 5)$

Check:

$3x(4x^2 + 7x + 5) = 12x^3 + 21x^2 + 15x$ ✓

Factor $5(x - 3) + 4x(x - 3)$.

Step 1: Find the GCF of all the terms in the polynomial.

The factors of $5(x - 3)$ are: 5, $(x - 3)$ }

The factors of $4x(x - 3)$ are: 4, x, $(x - 3)$ } The GCF is $(x - 3)$.

The terms are already written as products with the GCF.

Step 2: Use the Distributive Property to factor out the GCF.

$(x - 3)(5 + 4x)$

Factor each polynomial.

1. $20x^2 - 15x$

2. $44a^2 + 11a$

3. $24y - 36x$

Factor each expression.

4. $5x(x + 7) + 2(x + 7)$

5. $3a(a + 4) - 2(a + 4)$

6. $4y(4y + 1) + (4y + 1)$

Holt Algebra 1

California Standards 11.0

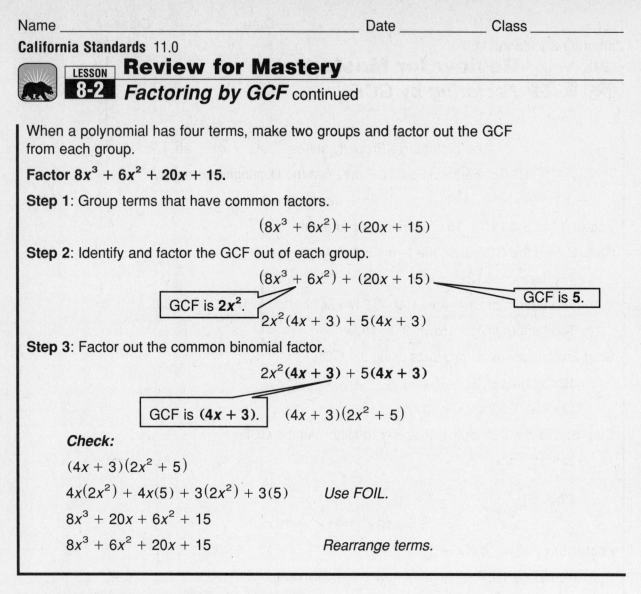

LESSON 8-2 ## Review for Mastery

Factoring by GCF continued

When a polynomial has four terms, make two groups and factor out the GCF from each group.

Factor $8x^3 + 6x^2 + 20x + 15$.

Step 1: Group terms that have common factors.

$$(8x^3 + 6x^2) + (20x + 15)$$

Step 2: Identify and factor the GCF out of each group.

$$(8x^3 + 6x^2) + (20x + 15)$$

GCF is **$2x^2$**.   GCF is **5**.

$$2x^2(4x + 3) + 5(4x + 3)$$

Step 3: Factor out the common binomial factor.

$$2x^2(4x + 3) + 5(4x + 3)$$

GCF is **$(4x + 3)$**. $(4x + 3)(2x^2 + 5)$

Check:

$(4x + 3)(2x^2 + 5)$

$4x(2x^2) + 4x(5) + 3(2x^2) + 3(5)$ *Use FOIL.*

$8x^3 + 20x + 6x^2 + 15$

$8x^3 + 6x^2 + 20x + 15$ *Rearrange terms.*

Factor each polynomial filling in the blanks.

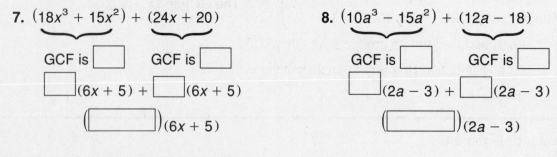

7. $(18x^3 + 15x^2) + (24x + 20)$

GCF is ☐   GCF is ☐

☐$(6x + 5) + $☐$(6x + 5)$

$($☐$)(6x + 5)$

8. $(10a^3 - 15a^2) + (12a - 18)$

GCF is ☐   GCF is ☐

☐$(2a - 3) + $☐$(2a - 3)$

$($☐$)(2a - 3)$

Factor each polynomial by grouping.

9. $21x^3 + 12x^2 + 14x + 8$

10. $40x^3 - 50x^2 + 12x - 15$

Holt Algebra 1

California Standards 11.0

LESSON 8-3

Review for Mastery
Factoring $x^2 + bx + c$

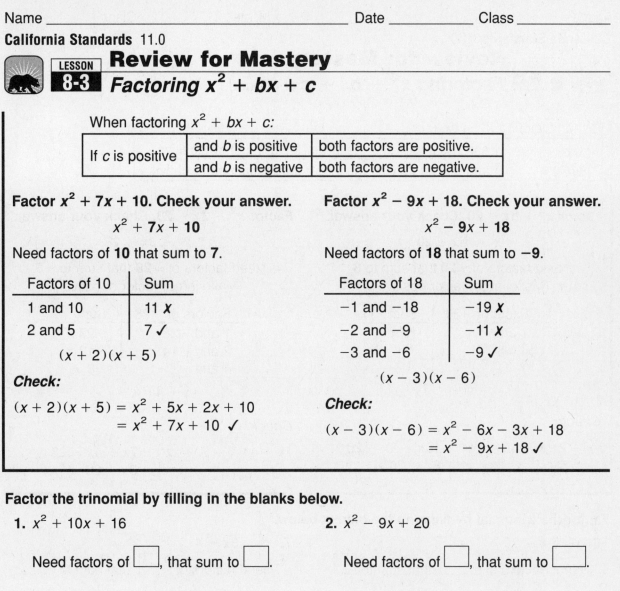

When factoring $x^2 + bx + c$:

If c is positive	and b is positive	both factors are positive.
	and b is negative	both factors are negative.

Factor $x^2 + 7x + 10$. Check your answer.

$$x^2 + 7x + 10$$

Need factors of **10** that sum to **7**.

Factors of 10	Sum
1 and 10	11 ✗
2 and 5	7 ✓

$$(x + 2)(x + 5)$$

Check:

$$(x + 2)(x + 5) = x^2 + 5x + 2x + 10$$
$$= x^2 + 7x + 10 ✓$$

Factor $x^2 - 9x + 18$. Check your answer.

$$x^2 - 9x + 18$$

Need factors of **18** that sum to **−9**.

Factors of 18	Sum
−1 and −18	−19 ✗
−2 and −9	−11 ✗
−3 and −6	−9 ✓

$$(x - 3)(x - 6)$$

Check:

$$(x - 3)(x - 6) = x^2 - 6x - 3x + 18$$
$$= x^2 - 9x + 18 ✓$$

Factor the trinomial by filling in the blanks below.

1. $x^2 + 10x + 16$

Need factors of ☐, that sum to ☐.

2. $x^2 - 9x + 20$

Need factors of ☐, that sum to ☐.

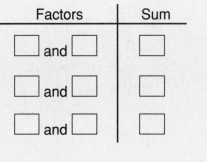

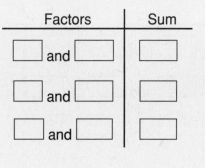

Factor each trinomial.

3. $x^2 + 13x + 12$ **4.** $x^2 + 15x + 50$ **5.** $x^2 - 13x + 36$

Holt Algebra 1

California Standards 11.0

LESSON 8-3 Review for Mastery
Factoring $x^2 + bx + c$ continued

When factoring $x^2 + bx + c$:

If c is negative	and b is positive	the larger factor must be positive.
	and b is negative	the larger factor must be negative.

Factor $x^2 + 8x - 20$. Check your answer.

$$x^2 + 8x - 20$$

Need factors of **−20** that sum to **8**.
(Make larger factor positive.)

Factors of −20	Sum
−1 and 20	19 ✗
−2 and 10	8 ✓
−4 and 5	1 ✗

$$(x - 2)(x + 10)$$

Check:

$$(x - 2)(x + 10) = x^2 + 10x - 2x - 20$$
$$= x^2 + 8x - 20 \checkmark$$

Factor $x^2 - 3x - 28$. Check your answer.

$$x^2 - 3x - 28$$

Need factors of **−28** that sum to **−3**.
(Make larger factor negative.)

Factors of −28	Sum
1 and −28	−27 ✗
2 and −14	−12 ✗
4 and −7	−3 ✓

$$(x + 4)(x - 7)$$

Check:

$$(x + 4)(x - 7) = x^2 - 7x + 4x - 28$$
$$= x^2 - 3x - 28 \checkmark$$

Factor the trinomial by filling in the blanks below.

6. $x^2 + x - 20$

Need factors of ⬜, that sum to ⬜.

Factors		Sum
⬜ and ⬜		⬜
⬜ and ⬜		⬜
⬜ and ⬜		⬜

7. $x^2 - 3x - 4$

Need factors of ⬜, that sum to ⬜.

Factors		Sum
⬜ and ⬜		⬜
⬜ and ⬜		⬜

Factor each trinomial.

8. $x^2 + 3x - 18$

9. $x^2 - 5x - 14$

10. $x^2 + 4x - 45$

Holt Algebra 1

California Standards 11.0

Review for Mastery
Factoring $ax^2 + bx + c$

When factoring $ax^2 + bx + c$, first find factors of a and c. Then check the products of the inner and outer terms to see if the sum is b.

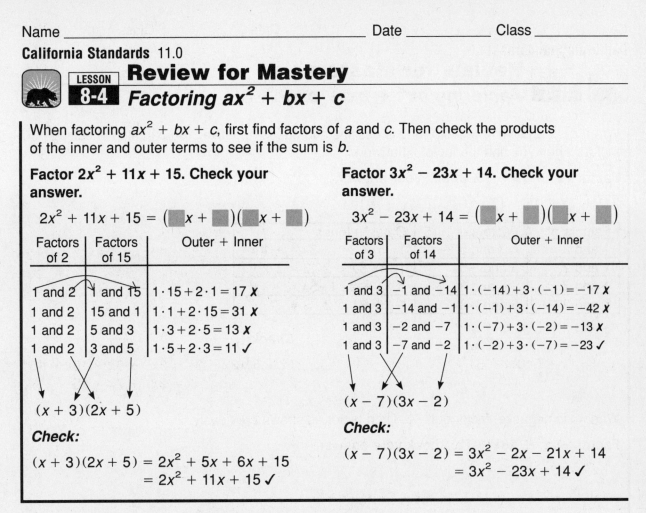

Factor $2x^2 + 11x + 15$. Check your answer.

$2x^2 + 11x + 15 = (\blacksquare x + \blacksquare)(\blacksquare x + \blacksquare)$

Factors of 2	Factors of 15	Outer + Inner
1 and 2	1 and 15	$1 \cdot 15 + 2 \cdot 1 = 17$ ✗
1 and 2	15 and 1	$1 \cdot 1 + 2 \cdot 15 = 31$ ✗
1 and 2	5 and 3	$1 \cdot 3 + 2 \cdot 5 = 13$ ✗
1 and 2	3 and 5	$1 \cdot 5 + 2 \cdot 3 = 11$ ✓

$(x + 3)(2x + 5)$

Check:

$(x + 3)(2x + 5) = 2x^2 + 5x + 6x + 15$
$= 2x^2 + 11x + 15$ ✓

Factor $3x^2 - 23x + 14$. Check your answer.

$3x^2 - 23x + 14 = (\blacksquare x + \blacksquare)(\blacksquare x + \blacksquare)$

Factors of 3	Factors of 14	Outer + Inner
1 and 3	−1 and −14	$1 \cdot (-14) + 3 \cdot (-1) = -17$ ✗
1 and 3	−14 and −1	$1 \cdot (-1) + 3 \cdot (-14) = -42$ ✗
1 and 3	−2 and −7	$1 \cdot (-7) + 3 \cdot (-2) = -13$ ✗
1 and 3	−7 and −2	$1 \cdot (-2) + 3 \cdot (-7) = -23$ ✓

$(x - 7)(3x - 2)$

Check:

$(x - 7)(3x - 2) = 3x^2 - 2x - 21x + 14$
$= 3x^2 - 23x + 14$ ✓

---

1. Factor $5x^2 + 12x + 4$ by filling in the blanks below.

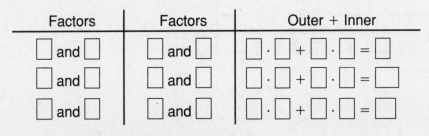

Factors	Factors	Outer + Inner
☐ and ☐	☐ and ☐	☐ · ☐ + ☐ · ☐ = ☐
☐ and ☐	☐ and ☐	☐ · ☐ + ☐ · ☐ = ☐
☐ and ☐	☐ and ☐	☐ · ☐ + ☐ · ☐ = ☐

_____

Factor each trinomial.

2. $3x^2 + 7x + 4$

3. $2x^2 - 13x + 21$

4. $4x^2 + 8x + 3$

Holt Algebra 1

California Standards 11.0

Review for Mastery

LESSON 8-4

Factoring $ax^2 + bx + c$ continued

When c is negative, one factor of c is positive and one is negative. You can stop checking factors when you find the factors that work.

Factor $2x^2 + 7x - 15$. Check your answer.

$2x^2 + 7x - 15 = (\blacksquare x + \blacksquare)(\blacksquare x + \blacksquare)$

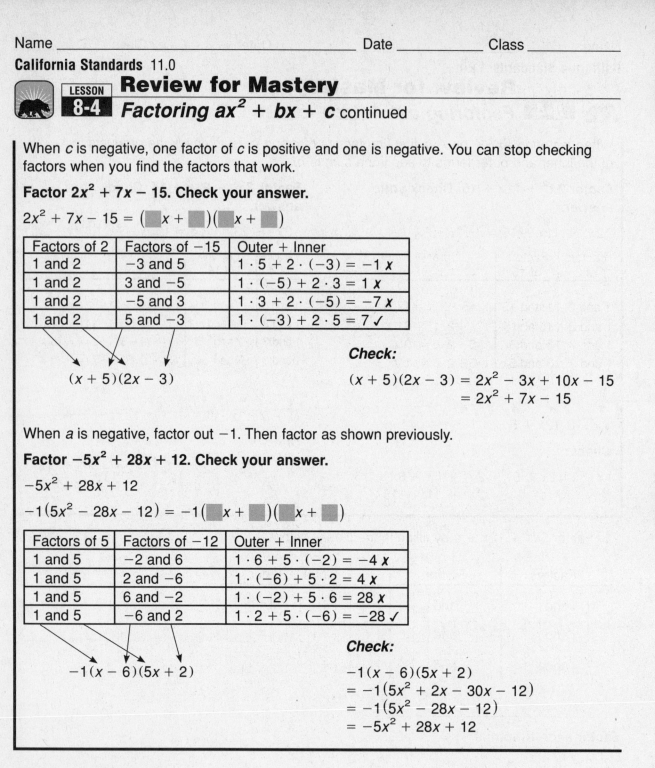

Factors of 2	Factors of -15	Outer + Inner
1 and 2	-3 and 5	$1 \cdot 5 + 2 \cdot (-3) = -1\ x$
1 and 2	3 and -5	$1 \cdot (-5) + 2 \cdot 3 = 1\ x$
1 and 2	-5 and 3	$1 \cdot 3 + 2 \cdot (-5) = -7\ x$
1 and 2	5 and -3	$1 \cdot (-3) + 2 \cdot 5 = 7\ ✓$

$(x + 5)(2x - 3)$

Check:

$(x + 5)(2x - 3) = 2x^2 - 3x + 10x - 15$
$= 2x^2 + 7x - 15$

When a is negative, factor out -1. Then factor as shown previously.

Factor $-5x^2 + 28x + 12$. Check your answer.

$-5x^2 + 28x + 12$

$-1(5x^2 - 28x - 12) = -1(\blacksquare x + \blacksquare)(\blacksquare x + \blacksquare)$

Factors of 5	Factors of -12	Outer + Inner
1 and 5	-2 and 6	$1 \cdot 6 + 5 \cdot (-2) = -4\ x$
1 and 5	2 and -6	$1 \cdot (-6) + 5 \cdot 2 = 4\ x$
1 and 5	6 and -2	$1 \cdot (-2) + 5 \cdot 6 = 28\ x$
1 and 5	-6 and 2	$1 \cdot 2 + 5 \cdot (-6) = -28\ ✓$

$-1(x - 6)(5x + 2)$

Check:

$-1(x - 6)(5x + 2)$
$= -1(5x^2 + 2x - 30x - 12)$
$= -1(5x^2 - 28x - 12)$
$= -5x^2 + 28x + 12$

Factor each trinomial.

5. $3x^2 - 7x - 20$

6. $5x^2 + 34x - 7$

7. $-2x^2 + 3x + 5$

_____ _____ _____

Holt Algebra 1

California Standards 11.0

Review for Mastery
LESSON 8-5

Factoring Special Products

If a polynomial is a perfect square trinomial, the polynomial can be factored using a pattern.

$$a^2 + 2ab + b^2 = (a + b)^2$$

$$a^2 - 2ab + b^2 = (a - b)^2$$

Determine whether $4x^2 + 20x + 25$ is a perfect square trinomial. If so, factor it. If not, explain why.

Step 1: Find a, b, then $2ab$.

$a = \sqrt{4x^2} = 2x$	*The first term is a perfect square.*
$b = \sqrt{25} = 5$	*The last term is a perfect square.*
$2ab = 2(2x)(5) = 20x$	*Middle term $(20x) = 2ab$.*

Therefore, $4x^2 + 20x + 25$ is a perfect square trinomial.

Step 2: Substitute expressions for a and b into $(a + b)^2$.

$$(2x + 5)^2$$

Determine whether $9x^2 + 25x + 36$ is a perfect square trinomial. If so, factor it. If not, explain why.

Step 1: Find a, b, then $2ab$.

$a = \sqrt{9x^2} = 3x$	*The first term is a perfect square.*
$b = \sqrt{36} = 6$	*The last term is a perfect square.*
$2ab = 2(3x)(6) = 36x$	*Middle term $(25x) \neq 2ab$.*

STOP
Because $25x$ does not equal $2ab$, $9x^2 - 25x + 36$ is not a perfect square trinomial.

Determine whether each trinomial is a perfect square. If so, factor it. If not, explain why.

1. $9x^2 + 30x + 100$

$a = $ _____

$b = $ _____

$2ab = $ _____

Factor or explain:

_____

2. $x^2 - 14x + 49$

$a = $ _____

$b = $ _____

$2ab = $ _____

Factor or explain:

_____

3. $25x^2 + 20x + 4$

$a = $ _____

$b = $ _____

$2ab = $ _____

Factor or explain:

_____

Holt Algebra 1

California Standards 11.0

LESSON 8-5 Review for Mastery
Factoring Special Products continued

If a binomial is a difference of squares, it can be factored using a pattern.

$$a^2 - b^2 = (a + b)(a - b)$$

Determine whether $64x^2 - 25$ is a difference of squares. If so, factor it. If not, explain why.

Step 1: Determine if the binomial is a difference.

$64x^2 - 25$ *The minus sign indicates it is a difference.*

Step 2: Find a and b.

$a = \sqrt{64x^2} = 8x$ *The first term is a perfect square.*

$b = \sqrt{25} = 5$ *The last term is a perfect square.*

Therefore, $64x^2 - 25$ is a difference of squares.

Step 3: Substitute expressions for a and b into $(a + b)(a - b)$.

$(8x + 5)(8x - 5)$

Determine whether $4x^2 + 25$ is a difference of squares. If so, factor it. If not, explain why.

Step 1: Determine if the binomial is a difference.

$4x^2 + 25$ *The plus sign indicates a sum.*

STOP. The binomial is not a difference, so it cannot be a difference of squares. It does not have a GCF either, so $4x^2 + 25$ cannot be factored.

Determine whether each binomial is a difference of squares. If so, factor it. If not, explain why.

4. $25x^2 - 81$ **5.** $30x^2 - 49$ **6.** $4x^2 - 121$

Difference? _____   Difference? _____   Difference?

_____

$a =$ _____ $a =$ _____ $a =$ _____

$b =$ _____ $b =$ _____ $b =$ _____

Factor or explain: Factor or explain: Factor or explain:

_____   _____   _____

Factor.

7. $x^2 - 100$ **8.** $x^2 - y^2$ **9.** $9x^4 - 64$

_____   _____   _____

Holt Algebra 1

California Standards 11.0

Review for Mastery

LESSON 8-6

Choosing a Factoring Method

Use the following table to help you choose a factoring method.

First factor out a GCF if possible. Then,

If binomial,	check for difference of squares.	→ yes → Use $(a + b)(a - b)$. → no → If no GCF, it cannot be factored.
If trinomial,	check for perfect square trinomial.	→ yes → Factor using $(a + b)^2$ or $(a - b)^2$. → no → If $a = 1$, check factors of c that sum to b. If $a \neq 1$, check inner plus outer factors of a and c that sum to b.
If 4 or more terms,	————————————→	Try to factor by grouping.

Explain how to choose a factoring method for $x^2 - x - 30$. Then state the method.

- There is no GCF.

- $x^2 - x - 30$ is a trinomial.

- The terms a and b are not perfect squares, therefore this is not a perfect square trinomial.

- $a = 1$

Method: Factor by checking factors of c that sum to b.

Explain how to choose a factoring method for $2x^2 - 50$. Then state the method.

- Factor out the GCF: $2(x^2 - 25)$

- $x^2 - 25$ is a binomial.

- a and b are perfect squares. This is a difference of squares.

Method: Factor out GCF. Then use $(a + b)(a - b)$.

Explain how to choose a factoring method for each polynomial. Then state the method.

1. $x^2 + 14x + 49$ _____

_____

2. $4x^2 - 40$ _____

_____

3. $2x^2 + 8x + 6$ _____

_____

Holt Algebra 1

California Standards 11.0

Review for Mastery
LESSON 8-6
Choosing a Factoring Method continued

It is often necessary to use more than one factoring method to factor a polynomial completely.

Factor $5x^2 - 5x - 60$ completely.
Check your answer.

Step 1: Factor out the GCF.

$5x^2 - 5x - 60$

$5(x^2 - x - 12)$

Step 2: Choose a method for factoring.

• $x^2 - x - 12$ is a trinomial.

• It is not a perfect square.

Method: Find factors of c that will sum to b.

Step 3: Factor.

Factors of -12	Sum
2 and -6	-4 ✗
3 and -4	-1 ✓
$(x + 3)(x - 4)$	

Step 4: Write the complete factorization.

$5(x + 3)(x - 4)$

Check:

$5(x + 3)(x - 4) = 5(x^2 - 4x + 3x - 12)$
$= 5(x^2 - x - 12)$
$= 5x^2 - 5x - 60$ ✓

Factor $16x^2 - 36$ completely.
Check your answer.

Step 1: Factor out the GCF.

$16x^2 - 36$

$4(4x^2 - 9)$

Step 2: Choose a method for factoring.

• $4x^2 - 9$ is a binomial.

• It is a difference of squares.

Method: Use $(a + b)(a - b)$.

Step 3: Factor.

$4x^2 - 9$

$a = 2x, b = 3$

$(2x + 3)(2x - 3)$

Step 4: Write the complete factorization.

$4(2x + 3)(2x - 3)$

Check:

$4(2x + 3)(2x - 3) = 4(4x^2 - 6x + 6x - 9)$
$= 4(4x^2 - 9)$
$= 16x^2 - 36$ ✓

Factor each polynomial completely.

4. $3x^2 - 300$

5. $4x^2 - 20x - 24$

6. $8x^2 - 40x + 50$

_____   _____   _____

7. $-7x^2 - 21x + 28$

8. $8x^2 - 18$

9. $20x^2 + 50x + 30$

_____   _____   _____

Holt Algebra 1

California Standards 17.0, •—21.0

LESSON
9-1
Review for Mastery
Quadratic Equations and Functions

There are three steps to graphing a quadratic function.

Graph $y = 2x^2 - 3$.

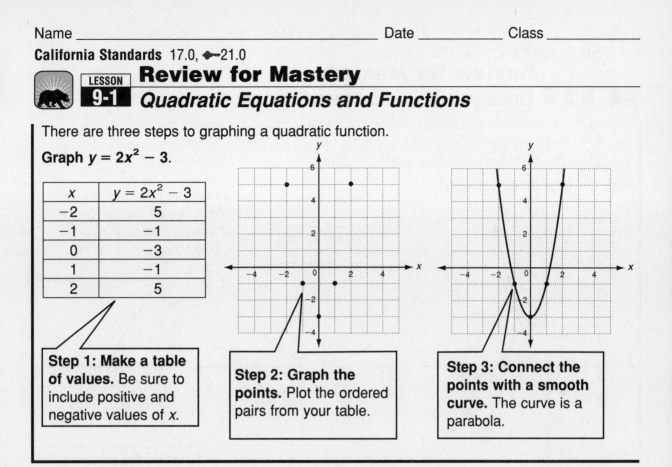

x	$y = 2x^2 - 3$
−2	5
−1	−1
0	−3
1	−1
2	5

Step 1: Make a table of values. Be sure to include positive and negative values of *x*.

Step 2: Graph the points. Plot the ordered pairs from your table.

Step 3: Connect the points with a smooth curve. The curve is a parabola.

Complete each table and then graph the quadratic function.

1. $y = -2x^2 + 1$

x	$y = -2x^2 + 1$
−2	
−1	
0	
1	
2	

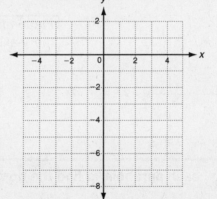

2. $y = \frac{1}{2}x^2 - 2$

x	$y = \frac{1}{2}x^2 - 2$
−4	
−2	
0	
2	
4	

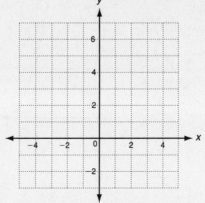

Holt Algebra 1

California Standards 17.0, ◄—21.0

LESSON 9-1

Review for Mastery

Quadratic Equations and Functions continued

To find the domain of a quadratic function, "flatten" the parabola toward the x-axis. To find the range, "flatten" the parabola toward the y-axis. Then read the domain and range from the inequality graphs.

Find the domain and range.

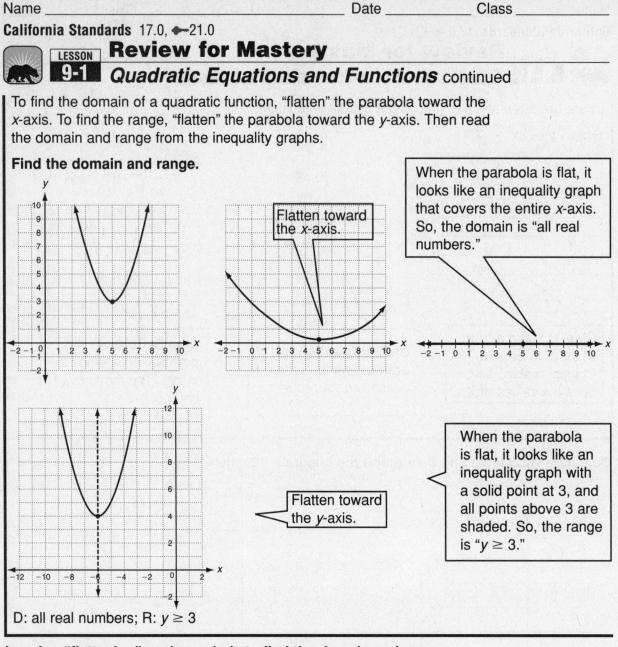

When the parabola is flat, it looks like an inequality graph that covers the entire x-axis. So, the domain is "all real numbers."

Flatten toward the x-axis.

Flatten toward the y-axis.

When the parabola is flat, it looks like an inequality graph with a solid point at 3, and all points above 3 are shaded. So, the range is "$y \geq 3$."

D: all real numbers; R: $y \geq 3$

Imagine "flattening" each parabola to find the domain and range.

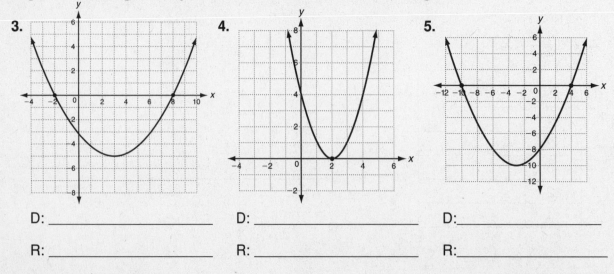

3.

D: _____

R: _____

4.

D: _____

R: _____

5.

D: _____

R: _____

Holt Algebra 1

Name _____ Date _____ Class _____

California Standards ←21.0, ←23.0

Review for Mastery

LESSON 9-2

Characteristics of Quadratic Functions

You find the **axis of symmetry** of a parabola by averaging the two zeros.
If there is only one zero or no zeros, use the *x*-value of the vertex.

Find the axis of symmetry of each parabola.

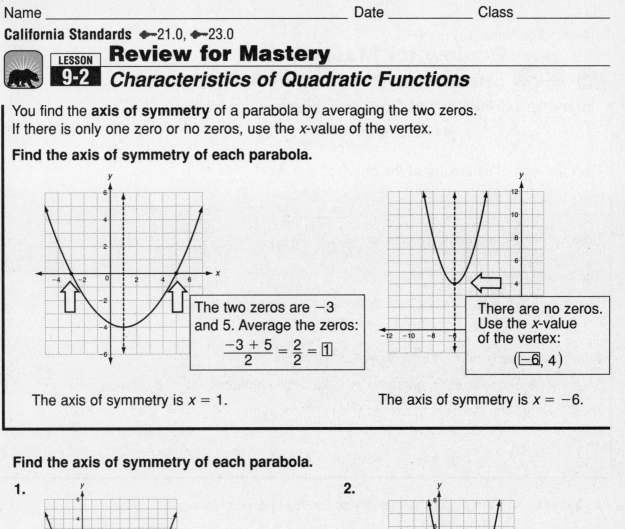

The two zeros are -3 and 5. Average the zeros:
$$\frac{-3+5}{2} = \frac{2}{2} = \boxed{1}$$

There are no zeros. Use the *x*-value of the vertex:
$(\boxed{-6}, 4)$

The axis of symmetry is $x = 1$.

The axis of symmetry is $x = -6$.

Find the axis of symmetry of each parabola.

1.

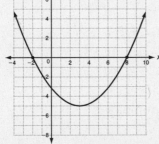

The axis of symmetry is _____.

2.

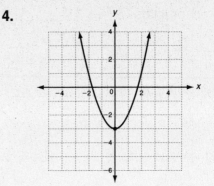

The axis of symmetry is _____.

3.

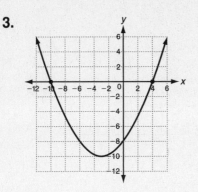

4.

Holt Algebra 1

California Standards ◆—21.0, ◆—23.0

LESSON 9-2 **Review for Mastery**

Characteristics of Quadratic Functions continued

You find the axis of symmetry of a quadratic function with this formula:

axis of symmetry $x = \dfrac{-b}{2a}$

Find the axis of symmetry of the graph of $y = -2x^2 + 8x - 5$.

Step 1: Identify the coefficients.

$$\boxed{a = -2} \quad \boxed{b = 8} \quad \boxed{c = -5}$$

Step 2: Substitute a and b into the formula. $\quad x = \dfrac{-(8)}{2(-2)} = \dfrac{-8}{-4} = 2$

The axis of symmetry is $x = 2$.

The axis of symmetry always passes through the vertex. Once you know the axis of symmetry, you can find the vertex.

Find the vertex of $y = -2x^2 + 8x - 5$.

Step 1: The x-coordinate is the same as the axis of symmetry. $\quad x = 2$ (see above)

Step 2: Substitute the x-coordinate to find the y-coordinate. $\quad y = -2(2)^2 + 8(2) - 5$
$$y = -8 + 16 - 5$$
$$y = 3$$

The vertex is $(2, 3)$.

For 5 and 6, find the axis of symmetry of the function's graph.

5. $y = x^2 - 10x + 25$

$$x = \dfrac{-b}{2a} = \dfrac{-(\boxed{})}{2(\boxed{})} = \dfrac{\boxed{}}{\boxed{}} = \boxed{}$$

The axis of symmetry is _____.

6. $y = -3x^2 + 6x + 5$

The axis of symmetry is _____.

For 7 and 8, find the vertex. (*Hint*: Refer back to problems 5 and 6.)

7. $y = x^2 - 10x + 25$

The x-coordinate is _____.

$$y = (\boxed{})^2 - 10(\boxed{}) + 25 = \boxed{}$$

The y-coordinate is _____.

The vertex is _____.

8. $y = -3x^2 + 6x + 5$

The vertex is _____.

9. Find the vertex of $y = 2x^2 + 12x - 9$.

_____

Holt Algebra 1

California Standards ←21.0, ←23.0

LESSON 9-3 Review for Mastery
Graphing Quadratic Functions

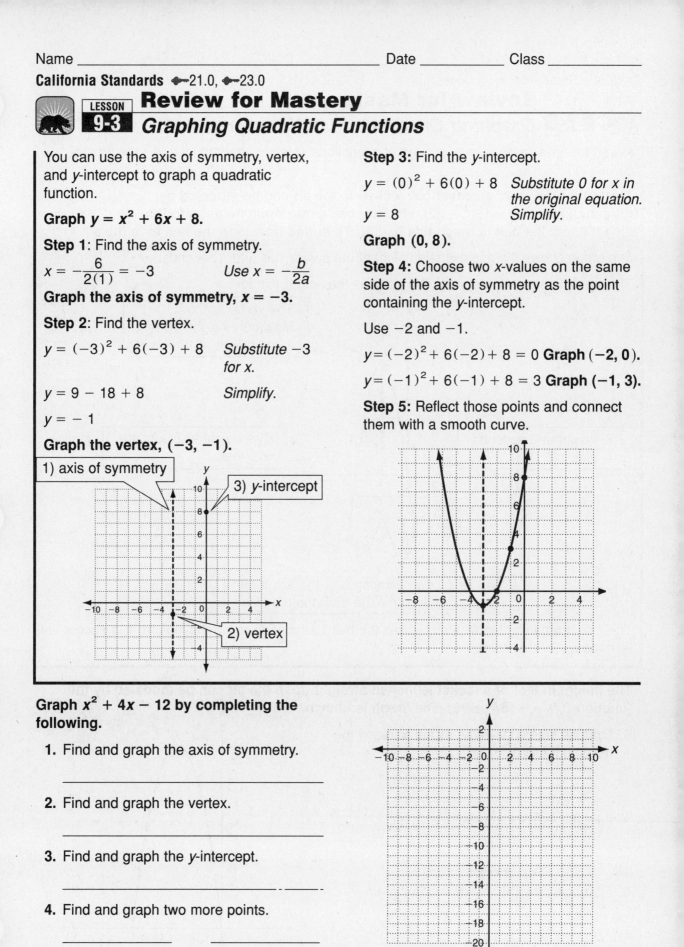

You can use the axis of symmetry, vertex, and y-intercept to graph a quadratic function.

Graph $y = x^2 + 6x + 8$.

Step 1: Find the axis of symmetry.

$x = -\dfrac{6}{2(1)} = -3$ *Use $x = -\dfrac{b}{2a}$*

Graph the axis of symmetry, $x = -3$.

Step 2: Find the vertex.

$y = (-3)^2 + 6(-3) + 8$ *Substitute −3 for x.*

$y = 9 - 18 + 8$ *Simplify.*

$y = -1$

Graph the vertex, $(-3, -1)$.

1) axis of symmetry

3) y-intercept

2) vertex

Step 3: Find the y-intercept.

$y = (0)^2 + 6(0) + 8$ *Substitute 0 for x in the original equation.*

$y = 8$ *Simplify.*

Graph (0, 8).

Step 4: Choose two x-values on the same side of the axis of symmetry as the point containing the y-intercept.

Use −2 and −1.

$y = (-2)^2 + 6(-2) + 8 = 0$ **Graph $(-2, 0)$.**

$y = (-1)^2 + 6(-1) + 8 = 3$ **Graph $(-1, 3)$.**

Step 5: Reflect those points and connect them with a smooth curve.

Graph $x^2 + 4x - 12$ by completing the following.

1. Find and graph the axis of symmetry.

   _____

2. Find and graph the vertex.

   _____

3. Find and graph the y-intercept.

   _____

4. Find and graph two more points.

   _____   _____

5. Reflect the points and draw the graph.

       Holt Algebra 1

California Standards ←—21.0, ←—23.0

LESSON 9-3 **Review for Mastery**

Graphing Quadratic Functions continued

Many real life situations involve quadratic functions. It is important to interpret the graphs correctly.

The height in feet of a soccer ball kicked in the air can be modeled by the function $f(t) = -16t^2 + 32t$. Find the ball's maximum height and the time it takes the ball to reach this height. Then find how long the ball is in the air.

The graph shows the approximate height of the soccer ball after *t* seconds.

The *x*-axis is time *t* in seconds. The *y*-axis is the height *h* in feet.

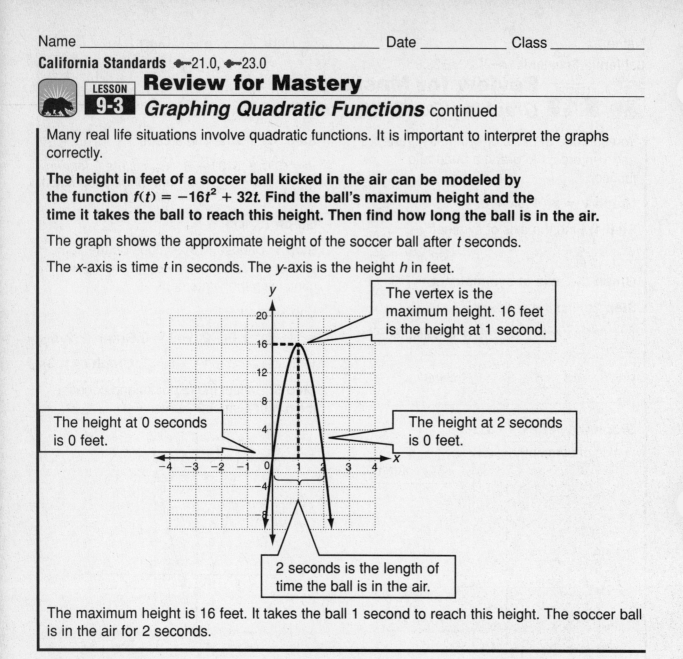

The vertex is the maximum height. 16 feet is the height at 1 second.

The height at 0 seconds is 0 feet.

The height at 2 seconds is 0 feet.

2 seconds is the length of time the ball is in the air.

The maximum height is 16 feet. It takes the ball 1 second to reach this height. The soccer ball is in the air for 2 seconds.

The height in feet of a rocket launched straight up in the air can be modeled by the function $f(t) = -16t^2 + 96t$. The graph is shown.

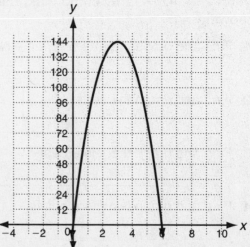

6. Find the time it takes the rocket to reach the maximum height.

_____

7. Find the rocket's maximum height.

_____

8. Find how long the rocket was in the air.

_____

Holt Algebra 1

California Standards ⬦—21.0, ⬦—23.0

LESSON 9-4

Review for Mastery
Solving Quadratic Equations by Graphing

You can find solutions to a quadratic equation by looking at the graph of the related function.

Find the solutions of $x^2 + x - 6 = 0$ from the graph of the related function.

Solutions occur where the graph crosses the *x*-axis.

Check:

$x = -3$

$x^2 + x - 6 = 0$	
$(-3)^2 + (-3) - 6$	0
$9 + (-3) - 6$	0
0	0 ✓

$x = 2$

$x^2 + x - 6 = 0$	
$(2)^2 + (2) - 6$	0
$4 + (2) - 6$	0
0	0 ✓

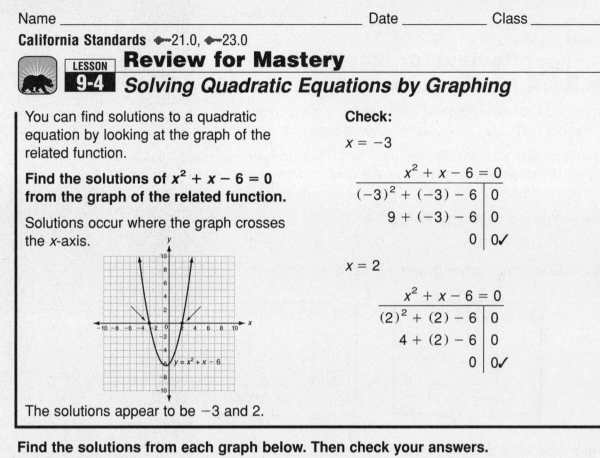

The solutions appear to be -3 and 2.

Find the solutions from each graph below. Then check your answers.

1. $3x^2 + 9x = 0$

2. $x^2 - 4x + 4 = 0$

3. $-2x^2 + 6x = 0$

_____

Check:

$$3x^2 + 9x = 0$$

$$3x^2 + 9x = 0$$

Check:

$$x^2 - 4x + 4 = 0$$

Check:

$$-2x^2 + 6x = 0$$

$$-2x^2 + 6x = 0$$

Holt Algebra 1

California Standards ⬦—21.0, ⬦—23.0

Review for Mastery

LESSON 9-4

Solving Quadratic Equations by Graphing continued

It is possible to use a graphing calculator to find the solutions of a quadratic equation. Remember that using the trace key gives an estimate of the solutions.

A dancer leaps straight into the air. The quadratic function $y = -16x^2 + 8x$ models the dancer's height above the ground after x seconds. About how long is the dancer in the air?

Step 1: Write the related function.

$y = -16x^2 + 8x$

Step 2: Graph the function by using a graphing calculator.

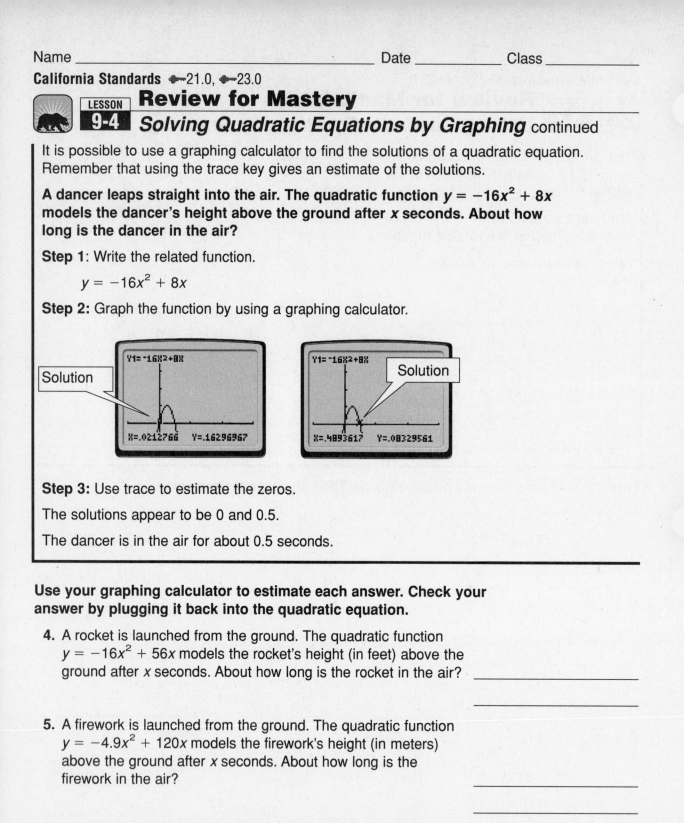

Step 3: Use trace to estimate the zeros.

The solutions appear to be 0 and 0.5.

The dancer is in the air for about 0.5 seconds.

Use your graphing calculator to estimate each answer. Check your answer by plugging it back into the quadratic equation.

4. A rocket is launched from the ground. The quadratic function $y = -16x^2 + 56x$ models the rocket's height (in feet) above the ground after x seconds. About how long is the rocket in the air? _____

   _____

5. A firework is launched from the ground. The quadratic function $y = -4.9x^2 + 120x$ models the firework's height (in meters) above the ground after x seconds. About how long is the firework in the air? _____

   _____

6. A football is kicked from the ground. The quadratic function $y = -16x^2 + 90x$ models the football's height above the ground after x seconds. About how long is the football in the air? _____

   _____

Holt Algebra 1

California Standards ◆—14.0, ◆—23.0

Review for Mastery

LESSON 9-5

Solving Quadratic Equations by Factoring

Quadratic Equations can be solved by factoring and using the Zero Product Property.

If the product of two quantities equals zero, at least one of the quantities must equal zero.

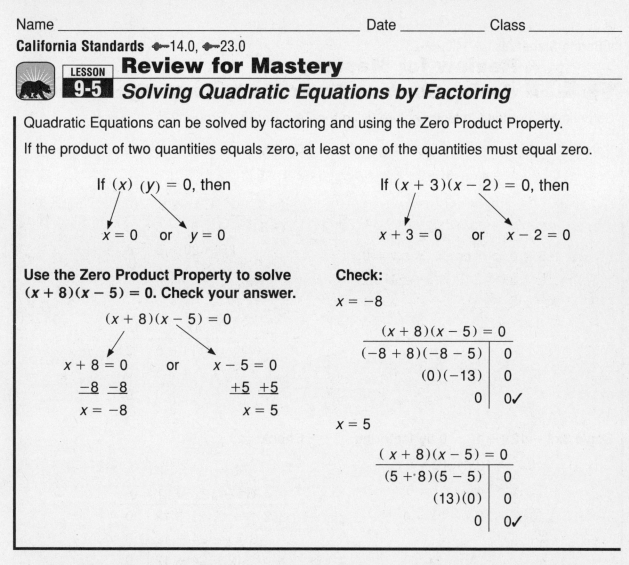

If $(x)(y) = 0$, then

$x = 0$ or $y = 0$

If $(x + 3)(x - 2) = 0$, then

$x + 3 = 0$ or $x - 2 = 0$

Use the Zero Product Property to solve $(x + 8)(x - 5) = 0$. Check your answer.

$$(x + 8)(x - 5) = 0$$

$x + 8 = 0$ or $x - 5 = 0$

$\underline{-8 \ -8}$ $\underline{+5 \ +5}$

$x = -8$ $x = 5$

Check:

$x = -8$

$(x + 8)(x - 5) = 0$	
$(-8 + 8)(-8 - 5)$	0
$(0)(-13)$	0
	0 0✓

$x = 5$

$(x + 8)(x - 5) = 0$	
$(5 + 8)(5 - 5)$	0
$(13)(0)$	0
	0 0✓

Use the Zero Product Property to solve each equation by filling in the boxes below. Then find the solutions. Check your answer.

1. $(x - 6)(x - 3) = 0$

[＿＿＿] = 0 or [＿＿＿] = 0

2. $(x + 8)(x - 5) = 0$

[＿＿＿] = 0 or [＿＿＿] = 0

3. $3x(x - 7) = 0$

[＿＿＿] = 0 or [＿＿＿] = 0

4. $(2x - 3)(x + 9) = 0$

[＿＿＿] = 0 or [＿＿＿] = 0

5. $(5x - 1)(x + 2) = 0$

6. $(x + 4)(2 - x) = 0$

Holt Algebra 1

California Standards ●—14.0, ●—23.0

LESSON 9-5 Review for Mastery
Solving Quadratic Equations by Factoring continued

Sometimes you need to factor before using the Zero Product Property.

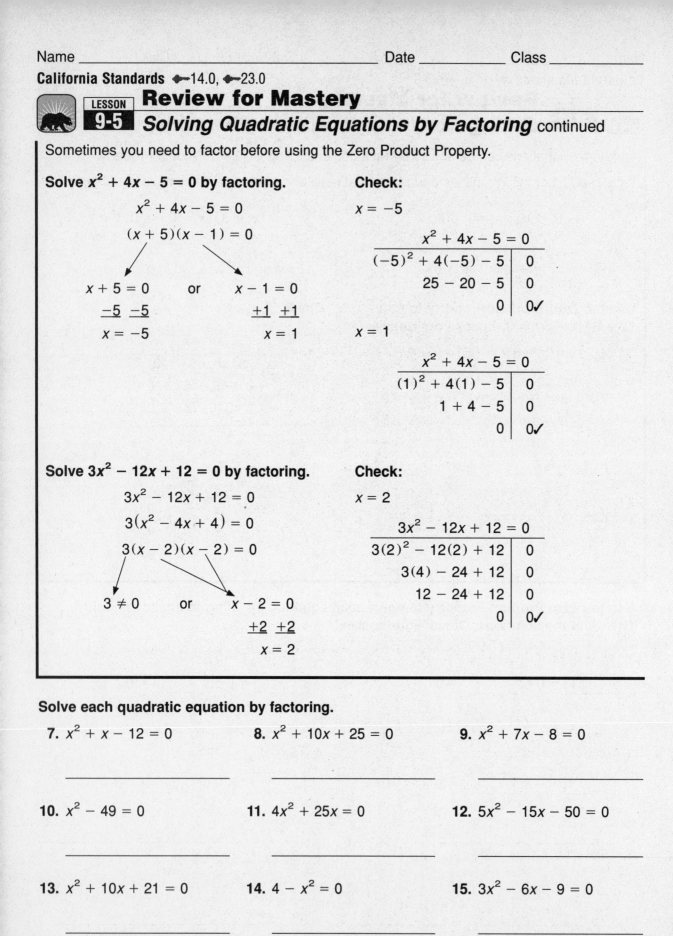

Solve $x^2 + 4x - 5 = 0$ by factoring.

$$x^2 + 4x - 5 = 0$$
$$(x + 5)(x - 1) = 0$$

$x + 5 = 0$ or $x - 1 = 0$
$\underline{-5\ -5}$ $\underline{+1\ +1}$
$x = -5$ $x = 1$

Check:

$x = -5$

$x^2 + 4x - 5 = 0$	
$(-5)^2 + 4(-5) - 5$	0
$25 - 20 - 5$	0
	0 ✓

$x = 1$

$x^2 + 4x - 5 = 0$	
$(1)^2 + 4(1) - 5$	0
$1 + 4 - 5$	0
	0 ✓

Solve $3x^2 - 12x + 12 = 0$ by factoring.

$$3x^2 - 12x + 12 = 0$$
$$3(x^2 - 4x + 4) = 0$$
$$3(x - 2)(x - 2) = 0$$

$3 \neq 0$ or $x - 2 = 0$
$\underline{+2\ +2}$
$x = 2$

Check:

$x = 2$

$3x^2 - 12x + 12 = 0$	
$3(2)^2 - 12(2) + 12$	0
$3(4) - 24 + 12$	0
$12 - 24 + 12$	0
	0 ✓

Solve each quadratic equation by factoring.

7. $x^2 + x - 12 = 0$

8. $x^2 + 10x + 25 = 0$

9. $x^2 + 7x - 8 = 0$

_____

_____

_____

10. $x^2 - 49 = 0$

11. $4x^2 + 25x = 0$

12. $5x^2 - 15x - 50 = 0$

_____

_____

_____

13. $x^2 + 10x + 21 = 0$

14. $4 - x^2 = 0$

15. $3x^2 - 6x - 9 = 0$

_____

_____

_____

Holt Algebra 1

Name _____ Date _____ Class _____

California Standards ⬅2.0, ⬅23.0

Review for Mastery

LESSON 9-6

Solving Quadratic Equations by Using Square Roots

If a quadratic equation is in the form $x^2 = a$, you must take the square root of both sides to find the solutions. Remember to find both the positive and negative square roots.

Solve $x^2 = 36$ using square roots.

$x^2 = 36$

$\sqrt{x^2} = \pm\sqrt{36}$ *Take the square root of both sides.*

$x = \pm 6$

The solutions are 6 and −6.

Check:

$x = 6$	$x = -6$
$x^2 = 36$	$x^2 = 36$
$(6)^2 \overset{?}{=} 36$	$(-6)^2 \overset{?}{=} 36$
$36 \overset{?}{=} 36$ ✓	$36 \overset{?}{=} 36$ ✓

Solve $2x^2 + 7 = 207$ using square roots.

$2x^2 + 7 = 207$

$\underline{\quad -7 \quad -7}$ *Add −7 to both sides.*

$2x^2 = 200$

$\dfrac{2x^2}{2} = \dfrac{200}{2}$ *Divide both sides by 2.*

$\sqrt{x^2} = \pm\sqrt{100}$ *Take the square root of both sides.*

$x = \pm 10$

The solutions are 10 and −10.

Check:

$x = 10$	$x = -10$
$2x^2 + 7 \overset{?}{=} 207$	$2x^2 + 7 \overset{?}{=} 207$
$2(10)^2 + 7 \overset{?}{=} 207$	$2(-10)^2 + 7 \overset{?}{=} 207$
$2(100) + 7 \overset{?}{=} 207$	$2(100) + 7 \overset{?}{=} 207$
$200 + 7 \overset{?}{=} 207$	$200 + 7 \overset{?}{=} 207$
$207 \overset{?}{=} 207$ ✓	$207 \overset{?}{=} 207$ ✓

Solve using square roots.

1. $x^2 = 81$

2. $x^2 = 9$

3. $x^2 = -64$

_____

_____

_____

4. $x^2 + 44 = 188$

5. $x^2 - 12 = 37$

6. $x^2 + 10 = 131$

_____

_____

_____

7. $3x^2 + 25 = 73$

8. $5x^2 - 9 = 116$

9. $-4x^2 + 42 = -102$

_____

_____

_____

10. $4x^2 - 11 = 25$

11. $x^2 - 13 = 87$

12. $-3x^2 + 200 = 8$

_____

_____

_____

Holt Algebra 1

California Standards ⬤—2.0, ⬤—23.0

![Bear logo] **LESSON 9-6** **Review for Mastery**

Solving Quadratic Equations by Using Square Roots continued

Remember, the square root of a number is not always a perfect square. You can use a calculator to approximate the answer.

Solve $x^2 + 6 = 24$. Round to the nearest hundredth.

$x^2 + 6 = 24$

$\underline{-6 \quad -6}$ *Add −6 to both sides.*

$ x^2 = 18$

$\sqrt{x^2} = \pm\sqrt{18}$ *Take the square root of both sides.*

$x^2 = \pm\sqrt{18}$

$ x = \pm 4.24$ *Evaluate $\sqrt{18}$ on a calculator.*

The approximate solutions are 4.24 and −4.24.

When solving application problems by using square roots, one of the solutions may not make sense.

The length of a rectangle is 5 times the width. The area of the rectangle is 210 square feet. Find the width. Round to the nearest tenth of a foot.

$(5w)(w) = 210$ $lw = A$

$5w^2 = 210$

$\dfrac{5w^2}{5} = \dfrac{210}{5}$

$w^2 = 42$

$w^2 = \pm\sqrt{42}$

$w = \pm 6.5$

```
          5w
 ┌─────────────────┐
 │                 │ w
 └─────────────────┘
```

It does not make sense for the width to be a negative number.
Therefore, the only solution is 6.5 feet.

Solve. Round to the nearest hundredth.

13. $x^2 = 50$ **14.** $x^2 + 8 = 20$ **15.** $2x^2 + 21 = 81$

_____   _____   _____

16. A triangle has a base that is 3 times the height. The area of the triangle is 63 cm^2. Find the height of the triangle. Round your answer to the nearest tenth of a centimeter. $\left(A = \dfrac{1}{2}bh\right)$. _____

17. The length of a rectangle is 4 times the width. The area of the rectangle is 850 square inches. Find the width. Round to the nearest tenth of an inch. _____

     Holt Algebra 1

California Standards ●–2.0, ●–14.0, ●–23.0

LESSON 9-7

Review for Mastery

Completing the Square

You have already learned to solve quadratic equations by using square roots. This only works if the quadratic expression is a perfect square. Remember that perfect square trinomials can be written as perfect squares.

$$x^2 + 8x + 16 = (x + 4)^2 \qquad x^2 - 10x + 25 = (x - 5)^2$$

If you have an equation of the form $x^2 + bx$, you can add the term $\left(\dfrac{b}{2}\right)^2$ to make a perfect square trinomial. This makes it possible to solve by using square roots.

Complete the square of $x^2 + 12x$ to form a perfect square trinomial. Then factor.

$x^2 + 12x$	*Identify b.*
$\left(\dfrac{12}{2}\right)^2 = 6^2 = 36$	*Find $\left(\dfrac{b}{2}\right)^2$.*
$x^2 + 12x + 36$	*Add $\left(\dfrac{b}{2}\right)^2$.*
$(x + 6)^2$	*Factor.*

Complete the square of $x^2 + 7x$ to form a perfect square trinomial. Then factor.

$x^2 + 7x$	*Identify b.*
$\left(\dfrac{7}{2}\right)^2 = \dfrac{49}{4}$	*Find $\left(\dfrac{b}{2}\right)^2$.*
$x^2 + 7x + \dfrac{49}{4}$	*Add $\left(\dfrac{b}{2}\right)^2$.*
$\left(x + \dfrac{7}{2}\right)^2$	*Factor.*

Complete the square to form a perfect square trinomial by filling in the blanks. Then factor.

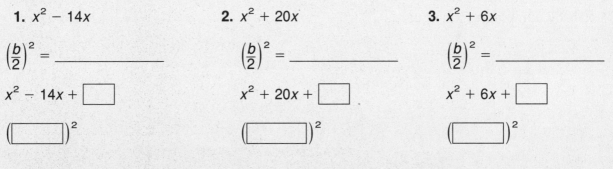

1. $x^2 - 14x$

$$\left(\dfrac{b}{2}\right)^2 = \underline{\hspace{2cm}}$$

$$x^2 - 14x + \boxed{}$$

$$\left(\boxed{}\right)^2$$

2. $x^2 + 20x$

$$\left(\dfrac{b}{2}\right)^2 = \underline{\hspace{2cm}}$$

$$x^2 + 20x + \boxed{}$$

$$\left(\boxed{}\right)^2$$

3. $x^2 + 6x$

$$\left(\dfrac{b}{2}\right)^2 = \underline{\hspace{2cm}}$$

$$x^2 + 6x + \boxed{}$$

$$\left(\boxed{}\right)^2$$

Complete the square to form a perfect square trinomial. Then factor.

4. $x^2 + 18x$

5. $x^2 - 16x$

6. $x^2 + 5x$

Holt Algebra 1

California Standards ✦2.0, ✦14.0, ✦23.0

LESSON 9-7
Review for Mastery
Completing the Square continued

To solve a quadratic equation in the form $x^2 + bx = c$, first complete the square of $x^2 + bx$. Then solve using square roots.

Solve $x^2 + 10x = -24$ by completing the square.

Step 1: Write equation in form $x^2 + bx = c$. Identify b.

$x^2 + 10x = -24$

Step 2: Find $\left(\dfrac{b}{2}\right)^2$.

$\left(\dfrac{10}{2}\right)^2 = 5^2 = 25$

Step 3: Add $\left(\dfrac{b}{2}\right)^2$ to both sides.

$x^2 + 10x = -24$

$\underline{ +25 \quad +25}$

$x^2 + 10x + 25 = 1$

Step 4: Factor the perfect square trinomial on the left.

$x^2 + 10x + 25 = 1$

$(x + 5)^2 = 1$

Step 5: Take the square root of both sides.

$\sqrt{(x + 5)^2} = \pm\sqrt{1}$

$x + 5 = \pm 1$

Step 6: Write and solve two equations.

$\begin{array}{lll} x + 5 = 1 & \text{OR} & x + 5 = -1 \\ \underline{-5 \ -5} & & \underline{-5 \ -5} \\ x = -4 & \text{OR} & x = -6 \end{array}$

The solutions are -4 and -6.

Solve by completing the square.

7. $x^2 - 6x = 7$

8. $x^2 + 8x = -12$

9. $x^2 - 2x - 63 = 0$

10. $x^2 + 4x - 32 = 0$

Holt Algebra 1

Name _____ Date _____ Class _____

California Standards ◆─19.0, ◆─20.0

LESSON 9-8 ## Review for Mastery
The Quadratic Formula

The Quadratic Formula is the only method that can be used to solve any quadratic equation.

$$x = \frac{-b \pm \sqrt{b^2 - 4ac}}{2a}$$

Solve $2x^2 - 5x - 12 = 0$ using the quadratic formula.

$$2x^2 - 5x - 12 = 0$$

Step 1: Identify a, b, and c.

$a = 2$

$b = -5$

$c = -12$

Step 2: Substitute into the quadratic formula.

$$x = \frac{-(-5) \pm \sqrt{(-5)^2 - 4(2)(-12)}}{2(2)}$$

Step 3: Simplify.

$$x = \frac{-(-5) \pm \sqrt{(-5)^2 - 4(2)(-12)}}{2(2)}$$

$$x = \frac{5 \pm \sqrt{25 - (-96)}}{4}$$

$$x = \frac{5 \pm \sqrt{121}}{4}$$

$$x = \frac{5 \pm 11}{4}$$

Step 4: Write two equations and solve.

$$x = \frac{5 + 11}{4} \quad \text{or} \quad x = \frac{5 - 11}{4}$$

$$x = 4 \qquad \text{or} \qquad x = -\frac{3}{2}$$

Solve using the quadratic equation by filling in the blanks below.

1. $x^2 + 2x - 35 = 0$

$a =$ ____; $b =$ ____; $c =$ ____

$$x = \frac{-(\boxed{}) \pm \sqrt{(\boxed{})^2 - 4(\boxed{})(\boxed{})}}{2\boxed{}}$$

Simplify:

_____

2. $3x^2 + 7x + 2 = 0$

$a =$ ____; $b =$ ____; $c =$ ____

$$x = \frac{-(\boxed{}) \pm \sqrt{(\boxed{})^2 - 4(\boxed{})(\boxed{})}}{2\boxed{}}$$

Simplify:

_____

3. $x^2 + x - 20 = 0$

$a =$ ____; $b =$ ____; $c =$ ____

$$x = \frac{-(\boxed{}) \pm \sqrt{(\boxed{})^2 - 4(\boxed{})(\boxed{})}}{2\boxed{}}$$

Simplify:

_____

4. $2x^2 - 9x - 5 = 0$

$a =$ ____; $b =$ ____; $c =$ ____

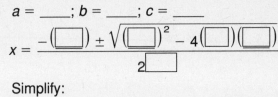

$$x = \frac{-(\boxed{}) \pm \sqrt{(\boxed{})^2 - 4(\boxed{})(\boxed{})}}{2\boxed{}}$$

Simplify:

_____

Holt Algebra 1

California Standards ←19.0, ←20.0

LESSON 9-8 Review for Mastery

The Quadratic Formula continued

Many quadratic equations can be solved by more than one method.

Solve $x^2 - 3x - 4 = 0$.

Method 1: Graphing

Graph $y = x^2 - 3x - 4$.
The solutions are the x-intercepts, -1 and 4.

Method 2: Factoring

$x^2 - 3x - 4 = 0$
$(x - 4)(x + 1) = 0$
$x - 4 = 0$ or $x + 1 = 0$
$x = 4$ or $x = -1$

Method 3: Completing the Square

$x^2 - 3x - 4 = 0$

$x^2 - 3x = 4$

$x^2 - 3x + \dfrac{9}{4} = 4 + \dfrac{9}{4}$ Add $\left(\dfrac{b}{2}\right)^2$ to both sides.

$\left(x - \dfrac{3}{2}\right)^2 = \dfrac{25}{4}$ Factor and simplify.

$x - \dfrac{3}{2} = \pm\dfrac{5}{2}$ Take square roots.

$x - \dfrac{3}{2} = \dfrac{5}{2}$ or $x - \dfrac{3}{2} = -\dfrac{5}{2}$

$x = 4$ or $x = -1$

Method 4: Using the Quadratic Formula

$x^2 - 3x - 4 = 0$

$a = 1, b = -3, c = -4$

$x = \dfrac{-b \pm \sqrt{b^2 - 4ac}}{2a}$

$x = \dfrac{-(-3) \pm \sqrt{(-3)^2 - 4(1)(-4)}}{2(1)}$ Substitute.

$x = \dfrac{3 \pm \sqrt{9 + 16}}{2} = \dfrac{3 \pm \sqrt{25}}{2} = \dfrac{3 \pm 5}{2}$ Simplify.

$x = 4$ or $x = -1$

Solve each equation using any method. Tell which method you used.

5. $x^2 - 7x - 8 = 0$

6. $-x^2 + 16 = 0$

_____

_____

7. $x^2 - 6x = 72$

8. $6x^2 + x - 1 = 0$

_____

_____

Holt Algebra 1

Name _____ Date _____ Class _____

California Standards 22.0, ◆23.0

Review for Mastery

LESSON 9-9

The Discriminant

The discriminant of a quadratic equation is $b^2 - 4ac$. The discriminant will indicate the number of solutions in a quadratic equation.

If $b^2 - 4ac > 0$	the equation has 2 real solutions.
If $b^2 - 4ac = 0$	the equation has 1 real solution.
If $b^2 - 4ac < 0$	the equation has 0 real solutions.

Find the number of solutions of $4x^2 - 8x + 5 = 0$ using the discriminant.

$4x^2 - 8x + 5 = 0$

Step 1: Identify a, b, and c.

$a = 4$, $b = -8$, $c = 5$

Step 2: Substitute into $b^2 - 4ac$.

$(-8)^2 - 4(4)(5)$

Step 3: Simplify.

$64 - 80 = -16$

$b^2 - 4ac$ is negative.
There are no real solutions.

Find the number of solutions of $9x^2 - 49 = 0$ using the discriminant.

$9x^2 - 49 = 0$

Step 1: Identify a, b, and c.

$a = 4$, $b = 0$, $c = -49$

Step 2: Substitute into $b^2 - 4ac$.

$(0)^2 - 4(9)(-49)$

Step 3: Simplify.

$0 + 1764 = 1764$

$b^2 - 4ac$ is positive.
There are two real solutions.

Find the number of solutions of each equation using the discriminant by filling in the boxes below.

1. $4x^2 + 20x + 25 = 0$

$a = \boxed{}$; $b = \boxed{}$; $c = \boxed{}$

$(\boxed{})^2 - 4(\boxed{})(\boxed{})$

2. $15x^2 + 8x + -1 = 0$

$a = \boxed{}$; $b = \boxed{}$; $c = \boxed{}$

$(\boxed{})^2 - 4(\boxed{})(\boxed{})$

_____   _____

Find the number of solutions of each equation using the discriminant.

3. $x^2 + 9x - 36 = 0$

4. $25x^2 + 4 = 0$

_____   _____

Holt Algebra 1

California Standards 22.0, ◆—23.0

LESSON 9-9 **Review for Mastery**

The Discriminant continued

You can use the discriminant to determine the number of *x*-intercepts of a quadratic function.

Find the number of *x*-intercepts of $y = 2x^2 - 2x + 3$ by using the discriminant.

$a = 2, b = -2, c = 3$

$$b^2 - 4ac = (-2)^2 - 4(2)(3)$$
$$= 4 - 24$$
$$= -20$$

The discriminant is negative, so there are no real solutions.

Therefore, the graph does not intersect the *x*-axis and there are no *x*-intercepts.

Check by graphing:

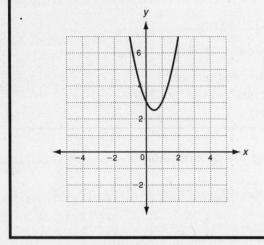

Find the number of *x*-intercepts of $y = -x^2 + 3x + 2$ by using the discriminant.

$a = -1, b = 3, c = 2$

$$b^2 - 4ac = (3)^2 - 4(-1)(2)$$
$$= 9 - (-8)$$
$$= 17$$

The discriminant is positive, so there are two real solutions.

Therefore, the graph intersects the *x*-axis in two places. There are two *x*-intercepts.

Check by graphing:

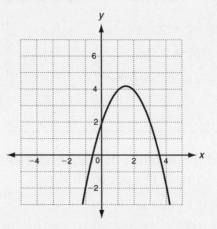

Find the number of *x*-intercepts of each function by using the discriminant.

5. $y = x^2 + x - 2$

6. $y = 4x^2 - 4x + 1$

_____

7. $y = 3x^2 - 2x + 7$

8. $y = 6x^2 + 7x - 3$

_____

Holt Algebra 1

LESSON 10-1
Review for Mastery
Inverse Variation

In an **inverse variation**, one quantity increases while the other quantity decreases. There are two ways to tell if a relationship is an inverse variation.

If the product of each ordered pair is constant, then the relationship is an inverse variation.

Tell whether the relationship in the table is an inverse variation.

Find xy for each ordered pair.

x	y
1	18	$1 \times 18 = \mathbf{18}$
2	9	$2 \times 9 = \mathbf{18}$
3	6	$3 \times 6 = \mathbf{18}$

Because the product is a constant, the relationship is an inverse variation.

If you can write the function rule in $y = \frac{k}{x}$ form, the relationship is an inverse variation.

Tell whether $xy = 4$ is an inverse variation.

$xy = 4$

$\frac{xy}{x} = \frac{4}{x}$ *Divide both sides by x.*

$y = \frac{4}{x}$

This function is an inverse relation.

If (x_1, y_1) and (x_2, y_2) are solutions of an inverse variation, then $x_1y_1 = x_2y_2$.

Let $x_1 = 4$, $y_1 = 3$, and $y_2 = 6$. Let y vary inversely as x. Find x_2.

$x_1y_1 = x_2y_2$ *Write the product rule for inverse variation.*

$(4)(3) = (x_2)(6)$ *Substitute $x_1 = 4$, $y_1 = 3$, and $y_2 = 6$.*

$12 = 6x_2$ *Multiply.*

$2 = x_2$ *Divide both sides by 6.*

Tell whether each relationship is an inverse variation.

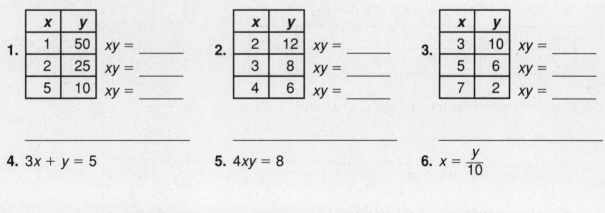

1.
x	y
1	50	$xy =$ _____
2	25	$xy =$ _____
5	10	$xy =$ _____

2.
x	y
2	12	$xy =$ _____
3	8	$xy =$ _____
4	6	$xy =$ _____

3.
x	y
3	10	$xy =$ _____
5	6	$xy =$ _____
7	2	$xy =$ _____

_____

4. $3x + y = 5$

5. $4xy = 8$

6. $x = \frac{y}{10}$

_____

7. Let $x_1 = 5$, $y_1 = 12$, and $y_2 = 6$. Let y vary inversely as x. Find x_2. _____

8. Let $x_1 = 2$, $y_1 = 15$, and $x_2 = 10$. Let y vary inversely as x. Find y_2. _____

Holt Algebra 1

California Standards Prep for ◆―13.0; 17.0

LESSON 10-1 Review for Mastery
Inverse Variation continued

You can also identify an inverse relation by its graph.

The graph of an inverse relation:
- has two parts that are not connected.
- does not contain (0, 0).

Write and graph the inverse variation in which $y = 5$ when $x = 2$.

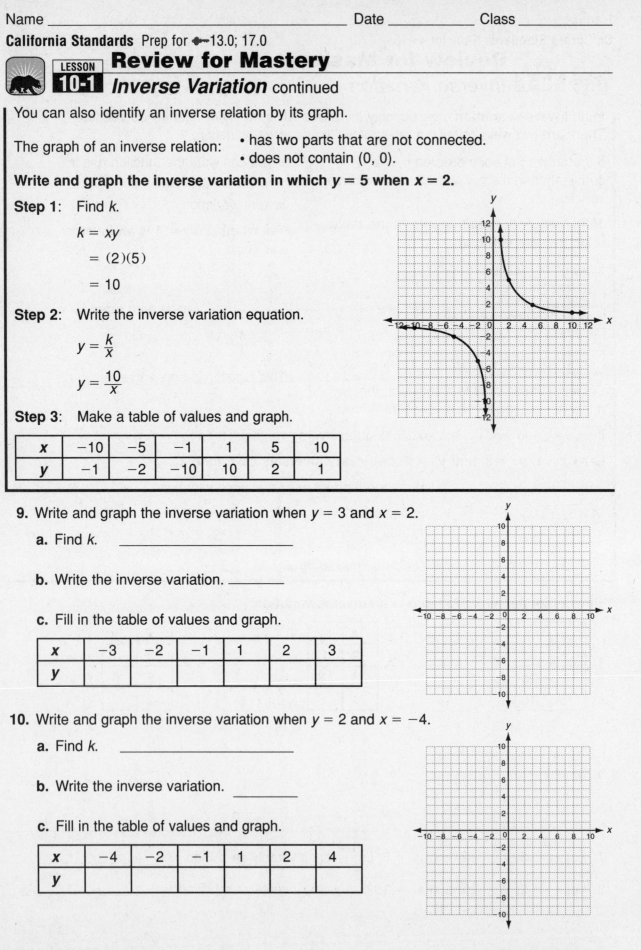

Step 1: Find k.

$$k = xy$$
$$= (2)(5)$$
$$= 10$$

Step 2: Write the inverse variation equation.

$$y = \frac{k}{x}$$
$$y = \frac{10}{x}$$

Step 3: Make a table of values and graph.

x	−10	−5	−1	1	5	10
y	−1	−2	−10	10	2	1

9. Write and graph the inverse variation when $y = 3$ and $x = 2$.

   a. Find k. _____

   b. Write the inverse variation. _____

   c. Fill in the table of values and graph.

x	−3	−2	−1	1	2	3
y						

10. Write and graph the inverse variation when $y = 2$ and $x = -4$.

   a. Find k. _____

   b. Write the inverse variation. _____

   c. Fill in the table of values and graph.

x	−4	−2	−1	1	2	4
y						

Holt Algebra 1

California Standards ✏️—13.0, 17.0

LESSON 10-2 **Review for Mastery**
Rational Functions

Remember that division by zero is undefined. Because rational functions have x in the denominator, we must exclude any values that make the denominator equal to zero.

Identify the excluded value for $y = \dfrac{3}{x - 2}$.

The function will be undefined when $x - 2 = 0$.

$$x - 2 = 0$$
$$\underline{+2 \quad +2}$$
$$x = 2 \qquad \text{The excluded value is 2.}$$

For rational functions, a vertical asymptote will occur at excluded values. An asymptote is a line that a graph gets close to, but never touches. Most rational functions have a vertical and a horizontal asymptote.

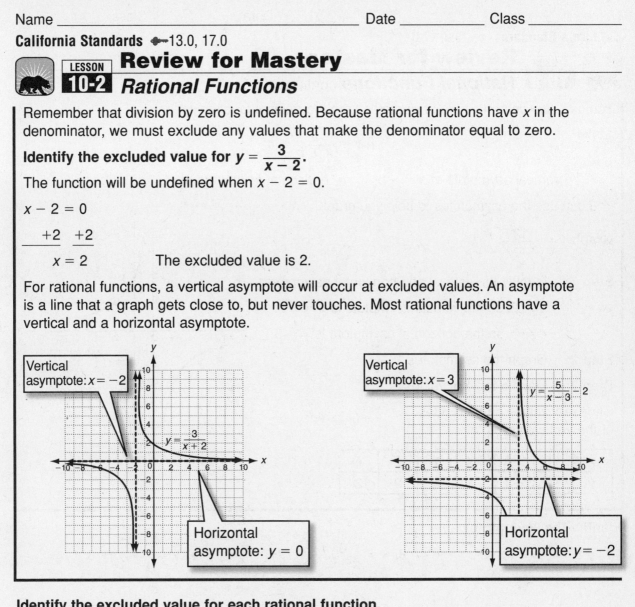

Vertical asymptote: $x = -2$

$y = \dfrac{3}{x + 2}$

Horizontal asymptote: $y = 0$

Vertical asymptote: $x = 3$

$y = \dfrac{5}{x - 3} - 2$

Horizontal asymptote: $y = -2$

Identify the excluded value for each rational function.

1. $y = \dfrac{5}{x}$

2. $y = -\dfrac{6}{x - 5}$

3. $y = \dfrac{4}{x + 7}$

_____ _____ _____

State the asymptotes for each graph below.

4.

5.

6.

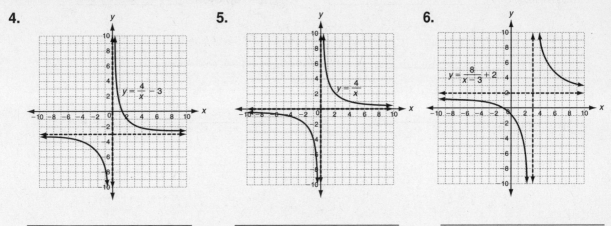

$y = \dfrac{4}{x} - 3$

$y = \dfrac{4}{x}$

$y = \dfrac{8}{x - 3} + 2$

_____ _____ _____

Holt Algebra 1

California Standards ✏️ 13.0, 17.0

LESSON 10-2 Review for Mastery
Rational Functions continued

You can also determine the asymptotes from the rational function itself.

$$y = \frac{a}{x + b} + c$$

- vertical asymptote at $x = -b$ • horizontal asymptote at $y = c$

You can use the asymptotes to help you graph.

Graph $y = \frac{12}{x + 2}$.

Step 1: Identify the vertical and horizontal asymptotes.

$b = 2$, so the vertical asymptote is $x = -2$.

$c = 0$, so the horizontal asymptote is $y = 0$.

Step 2: Graph the asymptotes.

Step 3: Make a table of values.

Choose x values on both sides
of the vertical asymptote.

x	-8	-6	-4	1	2	4
y	-2	-3	-6	4	3	2

Identify the asymptotes.

7. $y = \frac{4}{x + 5}$

8. $y = \frac{3}{x + 2} - 6$

9. $y = \frac{1}{x - 3} + 8$

_____   _____   _____

Graph each function.

10. $y = \frac{4}{x - 1}$

11. $y = \frac{8}{x + 2} + 3$

asymptotes: _____

asymptotes: _____

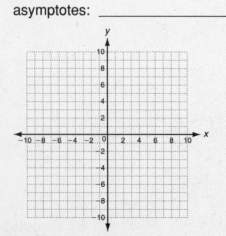

Holt Algebra 1

California Standards ☚ 12.0

LESSON 10-3 **Review for Mastery**

Simplifying Rational Expressions

A **rational expression** is an algebraic expression whose numerator and denominator are polynomials.

Exclude any values from a rational expression that make the denominator equal zero.

Find any excluded value of $\dfrac{6x}{x^2 - 5x}$.

$$\dfrac{6x}{x^2 - 5x}$$

$x^2 - 5x = 0$ *Set denominator = 0.*

$x(x - 5) = 0$ *Factor.*

$x = 0$ or $x - 5 = 0$ *Zero Product*

     $\underline{+5 \quad +5}$ *Property*

        $x = 5$

The excluded values are 0 and 5.

Simplify $\dfrac{x + 4}{2x^2 + 8x}$, **if possible. Identify any excluded values.**

$$\dfrac{x + 4}{2x^2 + 8x}$$

$$\dfrac{x + 4}{2x(x + 4)}$$ Factor the denominator.

Find excluded values here.

$$\dfrac{\cancel{x + 4}^{\,1}}{2x\,\cancel{(x + 4)}^{\,1}}$$ Divide out common factors.

$$\dfrac{1}{2x}$$ Simplify.

Remember to find the excluded value from the original equation (not the simplified one). **The excluded values are 0 and −4.**

Identify any excluded values.

1. $\dfrac{3}{4x}$

2. $\dfrac{5x}{3x^2 + 15x}$

3. $\dfrac{6}{x^2 - 5x - 14}$

_____   _____   _____

Simplify each rational expression, if possible. Identify any excluded values.

4. $\dfrac{4x}{20x^3}$

5. $\dfrac{x + 3}{x - 4}$

6. $\dfrac{27x}{3x^2}$

_____   _____   _____

7. $\dfrac{6}{3x + 9}$

8. $\dfrac{x + 4}{2x^2 + 8x}$

9. $\dfrac{5x^2 - 20x}{x - 4}$

_____   _____   _____

Holt Algebra 1

California Standards ✦―12.0

LESSON 10-3 Review for Mastery
Simplifying Rational Expressions continued

Rational expressions with binomials, trinomials and opposite binomials can also be simplified.

Simplify $\dfrac{x^2 - 4}{x^2 + 9x + 14}$, if possible.

$\dfrac{x^2 - 4}{x^2 + 9x + 14}$

$\dfrac{(x + 2)(x - 2)}{(x + 2)(x + 7)}$ *Factor.*

$\dfrac{(\cancel{x + 2})^1(x - 2)}{(\cancel{x + 2})^1(x + 7)}$ *Divide out the common factors.*

$\dfrac{x - 2}{x + 7}$ *Simplify.*

Simplify $\dfrac{3 - x}{x^2 - 7x + 12}$, if possible.

$\dfrac{3 - x}{x^2 - 7x + 12}$

$\dfrac{3 - x}{(x - 3)(x - 4)}$ *Factor.*

$\dfrac{-1(x - 3)}{(x - 3)(x - 4)}$ *Factor −1 out of the numerator.*

$\dfrac{-1(\cancel{x - 3})^1}{(\cancel{x - 3})^1(x - 4)}$ *Divide out the common factors.*

$-\dfrac{1}{x - 4}$ *Simplify.*

Simplify each rational expression, if possible.

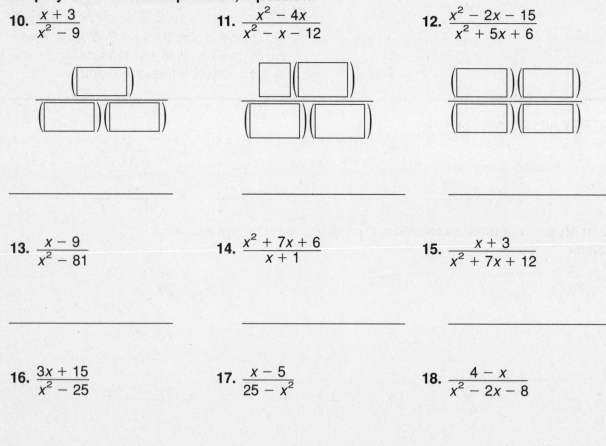

10. $\dfrac{x + 3}{x^2 - 9}$

11. $\dfrac{x^2 - 4x}{x^2 - x - 12}$

12. $\dfrac{x^2 - 2x - 15}{x^2 + 5x + 6}$

13. $\dfrac{x - 9}{x^2 - 81}$

14. $\dfrac{x^2 + 7x + 6}{x + 1}$

15. $\dfrac{x + 3}{x^2 + 7x + 12}$

16. $\dfrac{3x + 15}{x^2 - 25}$

17. $\dfrac{x - 5}{25 - x^2}$

18. $\dfrac{4 - x}{x^2 - 2x - 8}$

Holt Algebra 1

California Standards ◆—13.0

LESSON 10-4 ## Review for Mastery
Multiplying and Dividing Rational Expressions

If a, b, c, and d are nonzero polynomials, then $\dfrac{a}{b} \cdot \dfrac{c}{d} = \dfrac{ac}{bd}$.

You can make any expression rational by writing it with a denominator of 1.

Multiply $\dfrac{x+1}{7} \cdot \dfrac{5}{6x+6}$.
Simplify your answer.

$\dfrac{x+1}{7} \cdot \dfrac{5}{6x+6}$

$\dfrac{5(x+1)}{7(6x+6)}$ *Multiply the numerators and the denominators.*

$\dfrac{5(x+1)}{7 \cdot 6(x+1)}$ *Factor.*

$\dfrac{5(\cancel{x+1})^1}{7 \cdot 6(\cancel{x+1})^1}$ *Simplify.*

$\dfrac{5}{42}$

Multiply $(3x+12) \cdot \dfrac{2}{x^2-x-20}$.
Simplify your answer.

$(3x+12) \cdot \dfrac{2}{x^2-x-20}$

$\dfrac{3x+12}{1} \cdot \dfrac{2}{x^2-x-20}$ *Write as a rational expression.*

$\dfrac{3(x+4)}{1} \cdot \dfrac{2}{(x+4)(x-5)}$ *Factor.*

$\dfrac{3(\cancel{x+4})^1}{1} \cdot \dfrac{2}{(\cancel{x+4})^1(x-5)}$ *Simplify.*

$\dfrac{6}{x-5}$

Multiply. Simplify your answer.

1. $\dfrac{x+3}{5x} \cdot \dfrac{2}{4x+12}$

2. $\dfrac{3x}{x+3} \cdot \dfrac{x^2+5x+6}{x}$

3. $\dfrac{4x-12}{6x} \cdot \dfrac{x+3}{x^2-9}$

$$\dfrac{(\boxed{})}{(\boxed{})} \cdot \dfrac{(\boxed{})}{(\boxed{})(\boxed{})}$$

_____   _____   _____

4. $(4x+24)\dfrac{5}{x^2-36}$

5. $(x+7)\dfrac{3x}{x^2+13x+42}$

6. $(x^2-16)\dfrac{6}{x^2-x-12}$

_____   _____   _____

Holt Algebra 1

Name _____ Date _____ Class _____

California Standards ✦—13.0

LESSON | **Review for Mastery**
10-4 | *Multiplying and Dividing Rational Expressions* continued

If a, b, c, and d are nonzero polynomials, then $\dfrac{a}{b} \div \dfrac{c}{d} = \dfrac{a}{b} \cdot \dfrac{d}{c} = \dfrac{ad}{bc}$.

Divide $\dfrac{3}{x+2} \div \dfrac{5}{x+2}$.
Simplify your answer.

$\dfrac{3}{x+2} \div \dfrac{5}{x+2}$

$\dfrac{3}{x+2} \cdot \dfrac{x+2}{5}$ *Write as multiplication by the reciprocal.*

$\dfrac{3}{\cancel{x+2}^{1}} \cdot \dfrac{\cancel{x+2}^{1}}{5}$ *Divide out common factors.*

$\dfrac{3}{5}$ *Simplify.*

Divide $\dfrac{2x-4}{x^2} \div (x-2)$.
Simplify your answer.

$\dfrac{2x-4}{x^2} \div (x-2)$

$\dfrac{2x-4}{x^2} \div \dfrac{x-2}{1}$ *Write as a rational expression.*

$\dfrac{2x-4}{x^2} \cdot \dfrac{1}{x-2}$ *Write reciprocal.*

$\dfrac{2(x-2)}{x^2} \cdot \dfrac{1}{x-2}$ *Factor.*

$\dfrac{2(\cancel{x-2})^{1}}{x^2} \cdot \dfrac{1}{\cancel{x-2}^{1}}$ *Simplify.*

$\dfrac{2}{x^2}$

Divide. Simplify your answer.

7. $\dfrac{4x}{x^2} \div \dfrac{x^2}{7}$

$\boxed{} \cdot \dfrac{\boxed{}}{\boxed{}}$

8. $\dfrac{8x^2y^3}{2xy} \div \dfrac{xy}{3}$

9. $\dfrac{x^2}{x-3} \div \dfrac{x+5}{x^2+2x-15}$

_____ _____ _____

10. $\dfrac{x+4}{x-5} \div (x^2 - x - 20)$ **11.** $\dfrac{x^2-4x-5}{8} \div (x^2+2x+1)$ **12.** $\dfrac{x+10}{x^2} \div (x^2 - 100)$

_____ _____ _____

Holt Algebra 1

Name _____ Date _____ Class _____

California Standards ◆─13.0, ◆─15.0

LESSON 10-5 Review for Mastery
Adding and Subtracting Rational Expressions

The rules for adding and subtracting rational expressions are the same as the rules for adding and subtracting fractions.

$$\frac{2}{7} + \frac{4}{7} = \frac{2+4}{7} = \frac{6}{7} \qquad \frac{4}{5} - \frac{1}{5} = \frac{4-1}{5} = \frac{3}{5}$$

Add $\dfrac{5x+10}{x^2-16} + \dfrac{10}{x^2-16}$.

Simplify your answer.

$\dfrac{5x+10}{x^2-16} + \dfrac{10}{x^2-16}$

$\dfrac{(5x+10)+10}{x^2-16}$ *Add numerators.*

$\dfrac{5x+20}{x^2-16}$ *Add like terms.*

$\dfrac{5(x+4)}{(x+4)(x-4)}$ *Factor.*

$\dfrac{5(x+4)^1}{(x+4)^1(x-4)}$ *Simplify.*

$\dfrac{5}{x-4}$

Subtract $\dfrac{2x}{2x+6} - \dfrac{x-3}{2x+6}$.

Simplify your answer.

$\dfrac{2x}{2x+6} - \dfrac{x-3}{2x+6}$

$\dfrac{2x-(x-3)}{2x+6}$ *Subtract numerators.*

$\dfrac{2x-x+3}{2x+6}$ *Distribute −1.*

$\dfrac{x+3}{2x+6}$ *Combine like terms.*

$\dfrac{x+3}{2(x+3)}$ *Factor.*

$\dfrac{x+3^1}{2(x+3)^1}$ *Simplify.*

$\dfrac{1}{2}$

Add or subtract. Simplify your answer.

1. $\dfrac{x+2}{x^2-100} + \dfrac{8}{x^2-100}$

2. $\dfrac{x^2-18}{x+6} + \dfrac{3x}{x+6}$

3. $\dfrac{x}{5x+30} + \dfrac{6}{5x+30}$

_____   _____   _____

4. $\dfrac{x}{10x^2-20x} - \dfrac{2}{10x^2-20x}$

5. $\dfrac{x^2}{x^2+10x+25} - \dfrac{25}{x^2+10x+25}$

6. $\dfrac{x^2}{x+6} - \dfrac{12-4x}{x+6}$

_____   _____   _____

Holt Algebra 1

California Standards ◆─13.0, ◆─15.0

LESSON 10-5

Review for Mastery
Adding and Subtracting Rational Expressions *continued*

Like fractions, you may need to multiply by a form of 1 to obtain common denominators.

$$\frac{1}{6} + \frac{4}{15} = \frac{1}{6}\left(\frac{5}{5}\right) + \frac{4}{15}\left(\frac{2}{2}\right) = \frac{5}{30} + \frac{8}{30} = \frac{13}{30}$$

Add $\frac{3}{10x} + \frac{2}{5x^2}$.
Simplify your answer.

$\frac{3}{10x} + \frac{2}{5x^2}$ *The LCD is $10x^2$.*

$\frac{3}{10x}\left(\frac{x}{x}\right) + \frac{2}{5x^2}\left(\frac{2}{2}\right)$ *Multiply each term by a form of 1.*

$\frac{3x}{10x^2} + \frac{4}{10x^2}$ *Multiply.*

$\frac{3x + 4}{10x^2}$ *Add numerators.*

Subtract $\frac{3}{x-4} - \frac{5}{4-x}$.
Simplify your answer.

$\frac{3}{x-4} - \frac{5}{4-x}$ *The LCD is $x - 4$.*

$\frac{3}{x-4} - \frac{5}{4-x}\left(\frac{-1}{-1}\right)$ *Multiply the second term by a form of 1.*

$\frac{3}{x-4} - \frac{-5}{x-4}$ *Multiply.*

$\frac{8}{x-4}$ *Add numerators.*

---

7. Identify the LCD of $\frac{5}{8x^2}$ and $\frac{13}{20x}$. _____

8. Identify the LCD of $\frac{3}{5x}$ and $\frac{x}{x+7}$. _____

Add or subtract. Simplify your answer.

9. $\frac{2x}{8x^3} + \frac{5}{12x}$

$\frac{2x}{8x^3}\left(\dfrac{\boxed{}}{\boxed{}}\right) + \frac{5}{12x}\left(\dfrac{\boxed{}}{\boxed{}}\right)$

10. $\frac{5x + 11}{x^2 + 5x + 6} - \frac{4}{x + 3}$

$\frac{5x + 11}{(\boxed{})(\boxed{})} - \frac{4}{x + 3}\left(\dfrac{\boxed{}}{\boxed{}}\right)$

_____

11. $\frac{4x}{6x} + \frac{2}{x + 4}$

12. $\frac{3x - 6}{x^2 - 36} - \frac{2}{x + 6}$

13. $\frac{2x}{x^2 + 4x + 3} + \frac{1}{x + 1}$

_____ _____ _____

Holt Algebra 1

California Standards ●━10.0, ●━12.0

LESSON 10-6 **Review for Mastery**
Dividing Polynomials

To divide a polynomial by a monomial, first write the division as a rational expression.

Divide $(12x^2 + 9x) \div 3x$.

$\dfrac{12x^2 + 9x}{3x}$ *Rewrite as a rational expression.*

$\dfrac{12x^2}{3x} + \dfrac{9x}{3x}$ *Divide each term by 3x.*

$\dfrac{\cancel{12}^4 \, x\cancel{^2}^1}{\cancel{3}_1 \, \cancel{x}_1} + \dfrac{\cancel{9}^3 \, \cancel{x}^1}{\cancel{3}_1 \, \cancel{x}_1}$ *Divide out common factors.*

$4x + 3$ *Simplify.*

To divide a polynomial by a binomial, try to factor and divide out common factors.

Divide $\dfrac{x^2 + 6x + 5}{x + 1}$.

$\dfrac{x^2 + 6x + 5}{x + 1}$

$\dfrac{(x + 1)(x + 5)}{x + 1}$ *Factor the numerator.*

$\dfrac{\cancel{(x + 1)}^1 (x + 5)}{\cancel{x + 1}^1}$ *Divide out common factors.*

$x + 5$ *Simplify.*

You may find that a rational expression does not divide evenly.

Divide $(5x^2 + 10x + 3) \div 5x$.

$\dfrac{5x^2 + 10x + 3}{5x}$ *Rewrite as a rational expression.*

$\dfrac{5x^2}{5x} + \dfrac{10x}{5x} + \dfrac{3}{5x}$ *Divide each term by 5x.*

$x + 2 + \dfrac{3}{5x}$

Divide.

1. $(14x^3 + 6x) \div 2x$

2. $(6x^4 + 12x^2 + 18x) \div 6x^2$

3. $(10x^3 + 12x^2 + 2x) \div 2x$

_____   _____   _____

4. $(x^2 - 49) \div (x + 7)$

5. $(3x^2 - 15x) \div (x - 5)$

6. $(x^2 - 5x - 24) \div (x - 8)$

_____   _____   _____

Holt Algebra 1

California Standards ⬦─10.0, ⬦─12.0

LESSON 10-6 Review for Mastery
Dividing Polynomials continued

You can use long division to divide a polynomial by a binomial.

Divide $(2x^2 + 2x + 7) \div (x + 3)$.

$x + 3\overline{\smash{\big)}2x^2 + 2x + 7}$ *Write in long division form.*

$$\begin{array}{r} 2x - 4 \\ x + 3\overline{\smash{\big)}2x^2 + 2x + 7} \\ \underline{-(2x^2 + 6x)} \\ -4x + 7 \\ \underline{-(-4x - 12)} \\ 19 \end{array}$$

Think: $x \cdot ? = 2x^2$.
Use 2x.

Think: $x \cdot ? = -4x$.
Use −4.

$(2x^2 + 2x + 7) \div (x + 3) = 2x - 4 + \dfrac{19}{x + 3}$

Use a zero coefficient if the polynomial is missing a term.

Divide $(x^2 - 4) \div (x + 2)$.

$x + 2\overline{\smash{\big)}x^2 + 0x - 4}$ *Write in long division form.*

$$\begin{array}{r} x - 2 \\ x + 2\overline{\smash{\big)}x^2 + 0x - 4} \\ \underline{-(x^2 + 2x)} \\ -2x - 4 \\ \underline{-(-2x - 4)} \\ 0 \end{array}$$

Think: $x \cdot ? = x^2$.
Use x.

Think: $x \cdot ? = -2x$.
Use −2.

$(x^2 - 4) \div (x + 2) = (x - 2)$

Divide using long division.

7. $(x^2 - 4x - 12) \div (x + 2)$

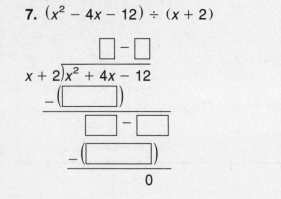

8. $(x^2 + 6x + 3) \div (x + 4)$

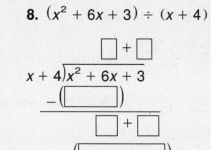

_____   _____

9. $(x^2 - 25) \div (x + 5)$

10. $(x^2 + 5x + 4) \div (x + 2)$

_____   _____

Holt Algebra 1

California Standards Prep for ✦—15.0

LESSON 10-7

Review for Mastery
Solving Rational Equations

A **rational equation** is an equation that contains one or more rational expressions. Some rational equations are proportions and can be solved using cross products. Solutions to all rational equations must be checked.

Solve $\dfrac{4}{x-3} = \dfrac{2}{x}$.

$$\dfrac{4}{x-3} \bowtie \dfrac{2}{x}$$

$4(x) = 2(x-3)$	*Multiply.*
$4x = 2x - 6$	*Distribute.*
$\underline{-2x \quad -2x}$	*Add $-2x$ to both sides.*
$2x = -6$	
$\dfrac{2x}{2} = \dfrac{-6}{2}$	*Divide.*
$x = -3$	*Simplify.*

Check:

$$\dfrac{4}{x} - 3 = \dfrac{2}{x}$$

$\dfrac{4}{(-3)-3}$	$\dfrac{2}{(-3)}$
$\dfrac{4}{-6}$	$\dfrac{2}{-3}$
$-\dfrac{2}{3}$	$-\dfrac{2}{3}$ ✓

The solution is -3.

Solve $\dfrac{x-4}{x^2-4} = \dfrac{-2}{x-2}$.

$$\dfrac{x-4}{x^2-4} \bowtie \dfrac{-2}{x-2}$$

$(x-4)(x-2) = -2(x^2-4)$

$x^2 - 6x + 8 = -2x^2 + 8$

$\underline{+2x^2 \qquad\qquad +2x^2}$

$3x^2 - 6x + 8 = 8$

$\underline{\qquad\quad -8 \quad -8}$

$3x^2 - 6x = 0$

| $3x(x-2) = 0$ | *Zero Product* |
| $x = 0$ or $x = 2$ | *Property* |

Check:

$\dfrac{x-4}{x^2-4} = \dfrac{-2}{x-2}$		$\dfrac{x-4}{x^2-4} = \dfrac{-2}{x-2}$	
$\dfrac{(0)-4}{(0)^2-4}$	$\dfrac{-2}{(0)-2}$	$\dfrac{(2)-4}{(2)^2-4}$	$\dfrac{-2}{(2)-2}$
$\dfrac{-4}{-4}$	$\dfrac{-2}{-2}$	$\dfrac{-2}{0}$	$\dfrac{-2}{0}$ ✗
1	1 ✓	undefined	

The only solution is 0.

Solve. Check your answer.

1. $\dfrac{3}{x+2} = \dfrac{4}{x+1}$

2. $\dfrac{x}{6} = \dfrac{x}{x+4}$

3. $\dfrac{5}{x+3} = \dfrac{6}{x+1}$

_____ _____ _____

4. $\dfrac{2x}{6} = \dfrac{x}{x+1}$

5. $\dfrac{8}{x^2-64} = \dfrac{1}{x-8}$

6. $\dfrac{x+2}{x-2} = \dfrac{4}{x-4}$

_____ _____ _____

Holt Algebra 1

California Standards Prep for ✦─15.0

LESSON 10-7

Review for Mastery

Solving Rational Equations continued

If a rational equation contains sums or differences of rational expressions, multiply every term by the LCD to eliminate the fractions.

Solve $\dfrac{1}{x} + \dfrac{2}{x+3} = \dfrac{3}{2x}$.

$\dfrac{1}{x} + \dfrac{2}{x+3} = \dfrac{3}{2x}$ ⟶ The LCD is $2x(x+3)$.

$2x(x+3)\left(\dfrac{1}{x}\right) + 2x(x+3)\left(\dfrac{2}{x+3}\right) = 2x(x+3)\left(\dfrac{3}{2x}\right)$ ⟶ Multiply every term by the LCD.

$2x^1(x+3)\left(\dfrac{1}{x^1}\right) + 2x(x+3)^1\left(\dfrac{2}{x+3^1}\right) = 2x^1(x+3)\left(\dfrac{3}{2x^1}\right)$ ⟶ Divide out common factors.

$2(x+3) + 2x(2) = (x+3)(3)$ ⟵ All fractions have been eliminated.

$2x + 6 + 4x = 3x + 9$

$6x + 6 = 3x + 9$

$\underline{-3x-3x}$

$3x + 6 = 9$

$\underline{-6-6}$

$\dfrac{3x}{3} = \dfrac{3}{3}$

$x = 1$

Check:

$\dfrac{1}{x} + \dfrac{2}{x+3} = \dfrac{3}{2x}$

$\dfrac{1}{1} + \dfrac{2}{1+3} = \dfrac{3}{2(1)}$

$1 + \dfrac{1}{2} = \dfrac{3}{2}$

$\dfrac{3}{2} = \dfrac{3}{2}$ ✓

Solve. Check your answer.

7. $\dfrac{3}{x} + \dfrac{2}{x+2} = \dfrac{4}{x}$

LCD: _____

_____

8. $\dfrac{10}{x} - \dfrac{8}{x} = \dfrac{6}{x+1}$

LCD: _____

_____

9. $\dfrac{1}{4} + \dfrac{1}{4x} = \dfrac{5}{x^2}$

LCD: _____

_____

10. $\dfrac{22}{(x+1)(x-1)} + \dfrac{2}{x+1} = \dfrac{8}{x-1}$

LCD: _____

_____

Holt Algebra 1

California Standards ←15.0

LESSON 10-8 Review for Mastery
Applying Rational Equations

You can use these steps to solve work problems.

Kyle can paint the living room in his apartment in 3 hours. Jemma can paint the same room in 4 hours. How long will it take them to paint the room if they work together?

Let *h* be the number of hours it takes Kyle and Jemma to paint the room.

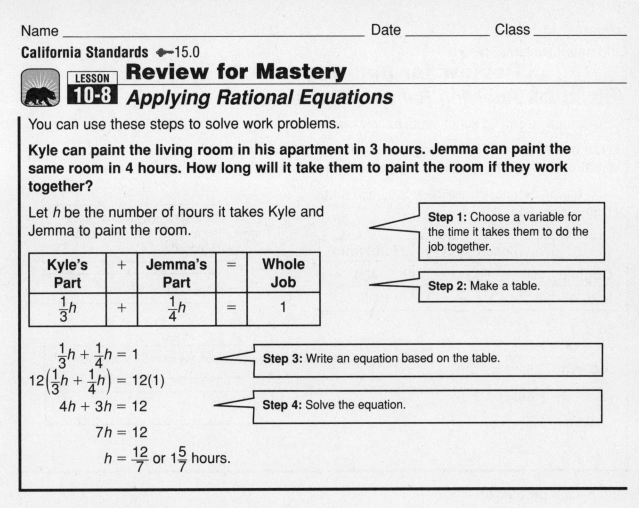

Kyle's Part	+	Jemma's Part	=	Whole Job
$\frac{1}{3}h$	+	$\frac{1}{4}h$	=	1

Step 1: Choose a variable for the time it takes them to do the job together.

Step 2: Make a table.

$$\frac{1}{3}h + \frac{1}{4}h = 1$$
$$12\left(\frac{1}{3}h + \frac{1}{4}h\right) = 12(1)$$
$$4h + 3h = 12$$
$$7h = 12$$
$$h = \frac{12}{7} \text{ or } 1\frac{5}{7} \text{ hours.}$$

Step 3: Write an equation based on the table.

Step 4: Solve the equation.

Solve each problem.

1. Zack can wash all the windows in his house in 3 hours. His brother Cory can do the same job in 5 hours. How long will it take them to wash all the windows if they work together?

2. Brenda and Leonard work in a sandwich shop. Brenda can prepare sandwiches for an office party in 40 minutes. Leonard can prepare sandwiches for the same party in 50 minutes. How long will it take them to prepare the sandwiches if they work together?

3. At an aquarium, two different pipes can be used to fill one of the large tanks. Pipe A can fill the tank in 7 hours. Pipe B can fill the tank in 9 hours. The aquarium's manager would like to fill the tank in less than 4 hours. Is it possible to do this by using both pipes at the same time? Explain your answer.

Holt Algebra 1

California Standards ⟵15.0

LESSON 10-8

Review for Mastery
Applying Rational Equations continued

You can use a similar set of steps to solve percent mixture problems.

Ryan has 400 mL of a cleaning solution that is 20% bleach. He wants to make a solution that is 50% bleach. How much bleach should he add to the solution?

Let *a* be the number of milliliters of bleach that Ryan should add.

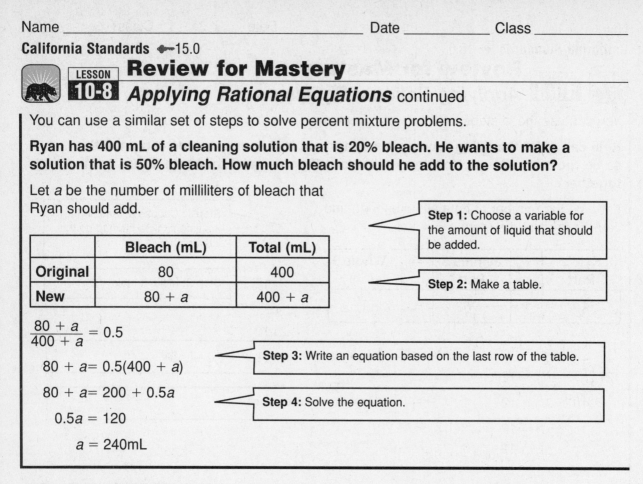

	Bleach (mL)	Total (mL)
Original	80	400
New	80 + a	400 + a

Step 1: Choose a variable for the amount of liquid that should be added.

Step 2: Make a table.

$\dfrac{80 + a}{400 + a} = 0.5$

$80 + a = 0.5(400 + a)$

Step 3: Write an equation based on the last row of the table.

$80 + a = 200 + 0.5a$

Step 4: Solve the equation.

$0.5a = 120$

$a = 240\text{mL}$

Solve each problem.

4. A chemist has 600 mL of a solution that is 25% acid. She wants to make a solution that is 40% acid. How much acid should she add to the original solution?

_____

5. A cook at a restaurant has 20 quarts of soup. The soup is 10% chicken stock. The cook wants to make a soup that is 20% chicken stock. How much chicken stock should he add to the original soup?

_____

6. LaTonya has 20 ounces of trail mix that contains 20% raisins. She wants to make a mix that contains 40% raisins. How many ounces of raisins should she add to the original trail mix?

_____

7. Jay has 1 liter of a solution that is 30% alcohol. He needs a solution that is 50% alcohol. How many milliliters of alcohol should he add to the original solution? (*Hint:* 1L = 1000 mL)

_____

Holt Algebra 1

California Standards Ext. of ⊶2.0; 17.0

Review for Mastery
LESSON 11-1 *Square-Root Functions*

A square-root function is a function in which the independent variable is under the square-root sign.

Square-root functions	Not square-root functions
$y = \sqrt{2x + 3}$	$y = 2x + \sqrt{3}$
$y = 4 + \sqrt{x}$	$y = \sqrt{4x}$

Determine whether $y = 5 + \dfrac{\sqrt{x}}{2}$ is a square root function. Explain.

Because x is under the square-root sign, this is a square root function.

The square root of a negative number is not a real number. Therefore, the x-values must be restricted to numbers that make the value under the radical sign greater than or equal to 0.

Find the domain of $y = \sqrt{x + 5}$.

$x + 5$ is under the radical sign.
$x + 5$ must be greater than or equal to zero.
$x + 5 \geq 0$

$\dfrac{-5 \quad -5}{x \geq -5}$ *Add −5 to both sides.*

The domain is the set of all real numbers greater than or equal to −5.

Find the domain of $y = 3 - \sqrt{4x - 12}$.

$4x - 12$ is under the radical sign.
$4x - 12$ must be greater than or equal to zero.
$4x - 12 \geq 0$

$\dfrac{+12 \quad +12}{4x \geq 12}$ *Add 12 to both sides.*

$\dfrac{4x}{4} \geq \dfrac{12}{4}$ *Divide each side by 4.*

$x \geq 3$

The domain is the set of all real numbers greater than or equal to 3.

Determine whether the following are square-root functions. Explain.

1. $y = \sqrt{8} + x$ _____

2. $y = \sqrt{8 + x}$ _____

Find the domain of each square-root function.

3. $y = \sqrt{5x - 8}$ **4.** $y = 6 + \sqrt{x}$ **5.** $y = \sqrt{3x} - 5$

_____   _____   _____

6. $y = \sqrt{2(x - 5)}$ **7.** $y = \sqrt{\dfrac{x}{5}} - 8$ **8.** $y = \sqrt{\dfrac{x}{3} + 2}$

_____   _____   _____

Holt Algebra 1

Name _____ Date _____ Class _____

California Standards Ext. of ☞2.0; 17.0

LESSON **Review for Mastery**
11-1 *Square-Root Functions* continued

You can use the domain of the square-root function to help you graph.

Graph $f(x) = \sqrt{3x - 6}$.

Step 1: Find the domain of the function.

$$3x - 6 \geq 0$$

3x – 6 must be greater than or equal to zero.

$$\underline{ +6 \quad +6}$$
$$3x \geq 6$$

$$\frac{3x}{3} \geq \frac{6}{3}$$

$$x \geq 2$$

x	$f(x) = \sqrt{3x - 6}$
2	0
5	3
14	6
29	9

The domain is the set of all real numbers greater than or equal to 2.

Step 2: Choose *x*-values greater than or equal to 2 to generate ordered pairs.

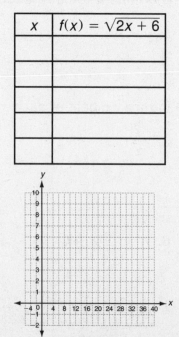

Graph each square-root function.

9. $y = \sqrt{2x}$

Domain: _____

x	$f(x) = \sqrt{2x}$

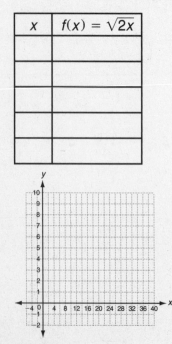

10. $y = \sqrt{x + 3}$

Domain: _____

x	$f(x) = \sqrt{x + 3}$

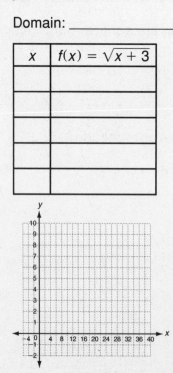

11. $y = \sqrt{2x + 6}$

Domain: _____

x	$f(x) = \sqrt{2x + 6}$

Holt Algebra 1

California Standards Ext. of ◆–2.0

LESSON **11-2**

Review for Mastery
Radical Expressions

A **radical expression** is an expression that contains a radical sign.

$$\sqrt{14x}$$

> The expression under the radical sign is the **radicand**.

A radical expression is in simplest form if:

- the radicand has no perfect square factors other than 1
- the radicand has no fractions
- there are no square roots in the denominator

Product Property of Square Roots	Quotient Property of Square Roots

$\sqrt{ab} = \sqrt{a} \cdot \sqrt{b}$; where $a \geq 0$ and $b \geq 0$

$\sqrt{\dfrac{a}{b}} = \dfrac{\sqrt{a}}{\sqrt{b}}$; where $a \geq 0$ and $b > 0$

Simplify $\sqrt{50}$.

$\sqrt{50} = \sqrt{25 \cdot 2}$ *Write the radicand as a product.*

$\quad = \sqrt{25} \cdot \sqrt{2}$ *Use Product Property of Square Roots*

$\quad = 5\sqrt{2}$ *Simplify.*

Simplify $\sqrt{x^2 y}$.

$\sqrt{x^2 y} = \sqrt{x^2}\,\sqrt{y}$

$\quad = x\sqrt{y}$

Simplify $\sqrt{\dfrac{3}{49}}$.

$\sqrt{\dfrac{3}{49}} = \dfrac{\sqrt{3}}{\sqrt{49}}$ *Use Quotient Property of Square Roots.*

$\quad = \dfrac{\sqrt{3}}{7}$ *Simplify.*

Simplify $\sqrt{\dfrac{x^6}{16}}$.

$\sqrt{\dfrac{x^6}{16}} = \dfrac{\sqrt{x^6}}{\sqrt{16}}$

$\quad = \dfrac{x^3}{4}$

Simplify. All variables represent nonnegative numbers.

1. $\sqrt{20}$ **2.** $\sqrt{300}$ **3.** $\sqrt{54x^4}$

_____   _____   _____

4. $\sqrt{\dfrac{7}{81}}$ **5.** $\sqrt{\dfrac{10}{9}}$ **6.** $\sqrt{\dfrac{9x^8}{25y^6}}$

_____   _____   _____

California Standards Ext. of ◆―2.0

LESSON 11-2

Review for Mastery
Radical Expressions continued

The Product and Quotient Properties can be used together to simplify radical expressions.

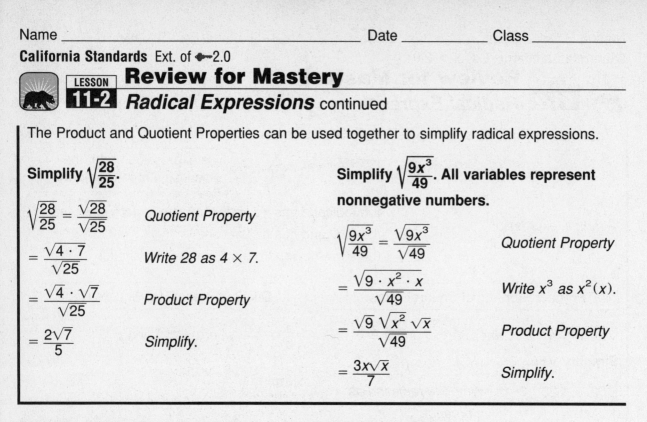

Simplify $\sqrt{\dfrac{28}{25}}$.

$\sqrt{\dfrac{28}{25}} = \dfrac{\sqrt{28}}{\sqrt{25}}$ *Quotient Property*

$= \dfrac{\sqrt{4 \cdot 7}}{\sqrt{25}}$ *Write 28 as 4 × 7.*

$= \dfrac{\sqrt{4} \cdot \sqrt{7}}{\sqrt{25}}$ *Product Property*

$= \dfrac{2\sqrt{7}}{5}$ *Simplify.*

Simplify $\sqrt{\dfrac{9x^3}{49}}$. **All variables represent nonnegative numbers.**

$\sqrt{\dfrac{9x^3}{49}} = \dfrac{\sqrt{9x^3}}{\sqrt{49}}$ *Quotient Property*

$= \dfrac{\sqrt{9 \cdot x^2 \cdot x}}{\sqrt{49}}$ *Write x^3 as $x^2(x)$.*

$= \dfrac{\sqrt{9} \, \sqrt{x^2} \, \sqrt{x}}{\sqrt{49}}$ *Product Property*

$= \dfrac{3x\sqrt{x}}{7}$ *Simplify.*

Simplify by filling in the blanks below. All variables represent nonnegative numbers.

7. $\sqrt{\dfrac{75}{4}} = \dfrac{\sqrt{\Box}}{\sqrt{\Box}}$

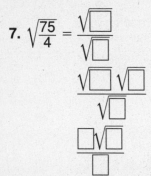

8. $\sqrt{\dfrac{288}{25}} = \dfrac{\sqrt{\Box}}{\sqrt{\Box}}$

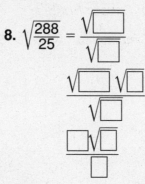

Simplify. All variables represent nonnegative numbers.

9. $\sqrt{\dfrac{8}{81}}$

10. $\sqrt{\dfrac{18}{49}}$

11. $\sqrt{\dfrac{500}{36}}$

_____   _____   _____

12. $\sqrt{\dfrac{242x^2}{9}}$

13. $\sqrt{\dfrac{m^7}{16n^2}}$

14. $\sqrt{\dfrac{200x^2}{49y^2}}$

_____   _____   _____

Holt Algebra 1

Name _____ Date _____ Class _____

California Standards Ext. of ◆━2.0

LESSON 11-3 Review for Mastery
Adding and Subtracting Radical Expressions

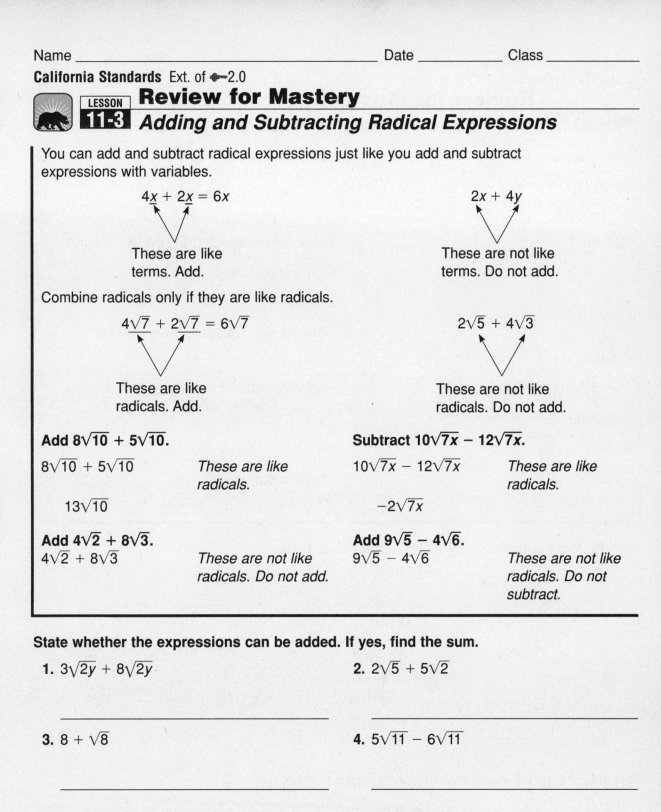

You can add and subtract radical expressions just like you add and subtract expressions with variables.

$4\underline{x} + 2\underline{x} = 6x$

These are like terms. Add.

$2x + 4y$

These are not like terms. Do not add.

Combine radicals only if they are like radicals.

$4\underline{\sqrt{7}} + 2\underline{\sqrt{7}} = 6\sqrt{7}$

These are like radicals. Add.

$2\sqrt{5} + 4\sqrt{3}$

These are not like radicals. Do not add.

Add $8\sqrt{10} + 5\sqrt{10}$.

$8\sqrt{10} + 5\sqrt{10}$ *These are like radicals.*

$13\sqrt{10}$

Subtract $10\sqrt{7x} - 12\sqrt{7x}$.

$10\sqrt{7x} - 12\sqrt{7x}$ *These are like radicals.*

$-2\sqrt{7x}$

Add $4\sqrt{2} + 8\sqrt{3}$.

$4\sqrt{2} + 8\sqrt{3}$ *These are not like radicals. Do not add.*

Add $9\sqrt{5} - 4\sqrt{6}$.

$9\sqrt{5} - 4\sqrt{6}$ *These are not like radicals. Do not subtract.*

State whether the expressions can be added. If yes, find the sum.

1. $3\sqrt{2y} + 8\sqrt{2y}$

2. $2\sqrt{5} + 5\sqrt{2}$

_____   _____

3. $8 + \sqrt{8}$

4. $5\sqrt{11} - 6\sqrt{11}$

_____   _____

Add or subtract. All variables represent nonnegative numbers.

5. $4\sqrt{13} + 2\sqrt{13}$

6. $8\sqrt{2} - 3\sqrt{2}$

7. $5\sqrt{5} + 6\sqrt{5}$

_____   _____   _____

8. $12\sqrt{3a} - 2\sqrt{3a}$

9. $7\sqrt{x} + \sqrt{x}$

10. $10\sqrt{6} - 3\sqrt{6}$

_____   _____   _____

Holt Algebra 1

California Standards Ext. of ⬦2.0

LESSON 11-3 Review for Mastery
Adding and Subtracting Radical Expressions continued

Sometimes it is necessary to simplify expressions before adding or subtracting.

Simplify $\sqrt{50} + \sqrt{18}$.

$\sqrt{50} + \sqrt{18}$

$\sqrt{25 \cdot 2} + \sqrt{9 \cdot 2}$ *Factor the radicands using perfect squares.*

$\sqrt{25} \cdot \sqrt{2} + \sqrt{9} \cdot \sqrt{2}$ *Product Property*

$5\sqrt{2} + 3\sqrt{2}$ *Simplify.*

$8\sqrt{2}$ *Combine like radicals.*

Simplify $\sqrt{45a} + \sqrt{80a} - \sqrt{20}$.

$\sqrt{9 \cdot 5a} + \sqrt{16 \cdot 5a} - \sqrt{4 \cdot 5}$ *Factor the radicands using perfect squares.*

$\sqrt{9} \cdot \sqrt{5a} + \sqrt{16} \cdot \sqrt{5a} - \sqrt{4} \cdot \sqrt{5}$ *Product Property*

$3\sqrt{5a} + 4\sqrt{5a} - 2\sqrt{5}$ *Simplify.*

$7\sqrt{5a} - 2\sqrt{5}$ *Combine like radicals.*
Notice that $\sqrt{5a}$ and $\sqrt{5}$ are not like radicals.

Simplify each expression by filling in the boxes below.

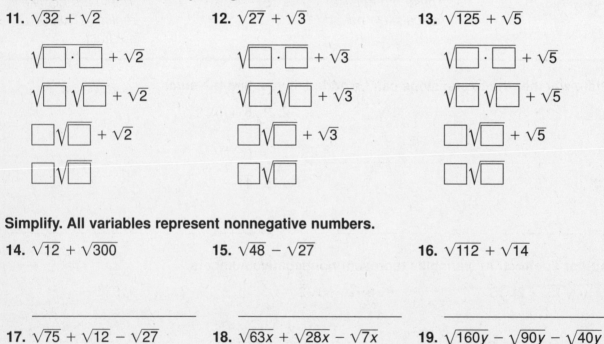

11. $\sqrt{32} + \sqrt{2}$

$\sqrt{\boxed{} \cdot \boxed{}} + \sqrt{2}$

$\sqrt{\boxed{}}\sqrt{\boxed{}} + \sqrt{2}$

$\boxed{}\sqrt{\boxed{}} + \sqrt{2}$

$\boxed{}\sqrt{\boxed{}}$

12. $\sqrt{27} + \sqrt{3}$

$\sqrt{\boxed{} \cdot \boxed{}} + \sqrt{3}$

$\sqrt{\boxed{}}\sqrt{\boxed{}} + \sqrt{3}$

$\boxed{}\sqrt{\boxed{}} + \sqrt{3}$

$\boxed{}\sqrt{\boxed{}}$

13. $\sqrt{125} + \sqrt{5}$

$\sqrt{\boxed{} \cdot \boxed{}} + \sqrt{5}$

$\sqrt{\boxed{}}\sqrt{\boxed{}} + \sqrt{5}$

$\boxed{}\sqrt{\boxed{}} + \sqrt{5}$

$\boxed{}\sqrt{\boxed{}}$

Simplify. All variables represent nonnegative numbers.

14. $\sqrt{12} + \sqrt{300}$

15. $\sqrt{48} - \sqrt{27}$

16. $\sqrt{112} + \sqrt{14}$

_____   _____   _____

17. $\sqrt{75} + \sqrt{12} - \sqrt{27}$

18. $\sqrt{63x} + \sqrt{28x} - \sqrt{7x}$

19. $\sqrt{160y} - \sqrt{90y} - \sqrt{40y}$

_____   _____   _____

Holt Algebra 1

California Standards Ext. of ⬥━2.0

Review for Mastery
11-4 Multiplying and Dividing Radical Expressions

Use the Product and Quotient Properties to multiply and divide radical expressions.

Product Property of Square Roots	Quotient Property of Square Roots
$\sqrt{ab} = \sqrt{a} \cdot \sqrt{b}$; where $a \geq 0$ and $b \geq 0$	$\sqrt{\dfrac{a}{b}} = \dfrac{\sqrt{a}}{\sqrt{b}}$; where $a \geq 0$ and $b > 0$

Multiply $\sqrt{6}\ \sqrt{10}$.

$\sqrt{6}\ \sqrt{10}$

$\sqrt{6 \cdot 10}$ *Product Property of Square Roots*

$\sqrt{60}$ *Multiply the factors in the radicand.*

$\sqrt{4 \cdot 15}$ *Factor 60 using a perfect square factor.*

$\sqrt{4} \cdot \sqrt{15}$ *Product Property of Square Roots*

$2\sqrt{15}$ *Simplify.*

A quotient with a square root in the denominator is not simplified. Rationalize the denominator by multiplying by a form of 1 to get a perfect square.

Simplify $\sqrt{\dfrac{10}{3}}$.

$\sqrt{\dfrac{10}{3}} = \dfrac{\sqrt{10}}{\sqrt{3}}$ *Quotient Property*

$\dfrac{\sqrt{10}}{\sqrt{3}}\left(\dfrac{\sqrt{3}}{\sqrt{3}}\right)$ *Multiply by form of 1.*

$\dfrac{\sqrt{30}}{\sqrt{9}}$ *Product Property*

$\dfrac{\sqrt{30}}{3}$ *Simplify.*

Multiply. Then simplify.

1. $\sqrt{3}\ \sqrt{12}$

2. $\sqrt{5}\ \sqrt{10}$

3. $\sqrt{8}\ \sqrt{11}$

_____   _____   _____

Rationalize the denominator of each quotient. Then simplify.

4. $\dfrac{\sqrt{7}}{\sqrt{2}}$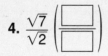

5. $\dfrac{\sqrt{8}}{\sqrt{3}}$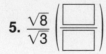

6. $\dfrac{\sqrt{12}}{\sqrt{5}}$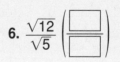

_____   _____   _____

         Holt Algebra 1

Name _____ Date _____ Class _____

California Standards Ext. of ◆2.0

Review for Mastery
11-4 *Multiplying and Dividing Radical Expressions* continued

Terms can be multiplied and divided if they are both under the radicals OR if they are both outside the radicals.

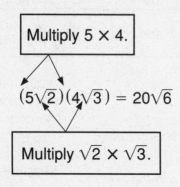

Multiply 5 × 4.

$(5\sqrt{2})(4\sqrt{3}) = 20\sqrt{6}$

Multiply $\sqrt{2} \times \sqrt{3}$.

Multiply $\sqrt{3}\,(6 + \sqrt{8})$. Write the product in simplest form.

$\sqrt{3}\,(6 + \sqrt{8})$	
$\sqrt{3}(6) + \sqrt{3}\,\sqrt{8}$	*Distribute.*
$6\sqrt{3} + \sqrt{24}$	*Multiply the factors in the radicand.*
$6\sqrt{3} + \sqrt{4 \cdot 6}$	*Factor 24 using a perfect square factor.*
$6\sqrt{3} + \sqrt{4}\,\sqrt{6}$	*Product Property of Square Roots*
$6\sqrt{3} + 2\sqrt{6}$	*Simplify.*

Use FOIL to multiply binomials with square roots.

Multiply $(3 + \sqrt{2})\,(4 + \sqrt{2})$.

$(3 + \sqrt{2})(4 + \sqrt{2})$	
$3(4) + 3\sqrt{2} + 4\sqrt{2} + \sqrt{2}\,\sqrt{2}$	*FOIL.*
$12 + 3\sqrt{2} + 4\sqrt{2} + \sqrt{4}$	*Multiply.*
$12 + 3\sqrt{2} + 4\sqrt{2} + 2$	*Simplify.*
$14 + 7\sqrt{2}$	*Add.*

Multiply. Write each product in simplest form.

7. $\sqrt{5}\,(4 + \sqrt{8})$

$\sqrt{5}\,\boxed{} + \sqrt{5}\,\boxed{}$

8. $\sqrt{2}\,(\sqrt{2} + \sqrt{14})$

_____

9. $(6 + \sqrt{3})(5 - \sqrt{3})$

$(6)(\boxed{}) - (6)(\boxed{}) + \sqrt{3}(\boxed{}) - \sqrt{3}(\boxed{})$

_____

10. $(5 + \sqrt{10})(8 + \sqrt{10})$

_____

Holt Algebra 1

California Standards Ext. of ⬦2.0

Review for Mastery
LESSON 11-5 *Solving Radical Equations*

A **radical equation** is an equation that contains a variable within a radical.
You can square both sides of an equation, and the resulting equation is still true.

Solve $\sqrt{x} = 7$.

$\sqrt{x} = 7$

$(\sqrt{x})^2 = (7)^2$ *Square both sides.*

$x = 49$

Check:

$\sqrt{x} = 7$

$\sqrt{49} \overset{?}{=} 7$ *Substitute 49 for x in the original equation.*

$7 = 7 ✓$

Sometimes you first need to isolate the variable.

Solve $4\sqrt{x} = 20$.

$4\sqrt{x} = 20$

$\dfrac{4\sqrt{x}}{4} = \dfrac{20}{4}$ *Divide both sides by 4.*

$\sqrt{x} = 5$

$(\sqrt{x})^2 = (5)^2$ *Square both sides.*

$x = 25$

Check:

$4\sqrt{x} = 20$

$4\sqrt{25} \overset{?}{=} 20$ *Substitute 25 for x in the original equation.*

$4(5) \overset{?}{=} 20$

$20 = 20 ✓$

Sometimes a solution will not check in the original equation. This is an **extraneous solution**.

Solve $\sqrt{x} + 3 = 1$.

$\sqrt{x} + 3 = 1$

$\underline{ -3 -3 }$ *Add −3 to both sides.*

$\sqrt{x} = -2$

$(\sqrt{x})^2 = (-2)^2$ *Square both sides.*

$x = 4$

Check:

$\sqrt{x} + 3 = 1$

$\sqrt{4} + 3 \overset{?}{=} 1$ *Substitute 4 for x in the original equation.*

$2 + 3 \overset{?}{=} 1$

$5 = 1 ✗$ *The solution is extraneous.*

The equation has no solution.

Solve each equation. Check your answer. All variables represent nonnegative numbers.

1. $\sqrt{x} = 12$

2. $\sqrt{x} - 6 = -1$

3. $\sqrt{x} + 8 = 2$

_____

_____

_____

4. $8\sqrt{x} = 80$

5. $\dfrac{\sqrt{x}}{4} = 2$

6. $\sqrt{4x - 7} = 9$

_____

_____

_____

Holt Algebra 1

Name _____ Date _____ Class _____

California Standards Ext. of ←─2.0

Review for Mastery

LESSON 11-5

Solving Radical Equations continued

You can also solve equations with square roots on both sides.

Solve $\sqrt{x + 2} = \sqrt{5}$.

$$\sqrt{x + 2} = \sqrt{5}$$
$$(\sqrt{x + 2})^2 = (\sqrt{5})^2 \qquad \text{Square both}$$
$$x + 2 = 5 \qquad \text{sides.}$$
$$\underline{-2 \quad -2} \qquad \text{Add } -2 \text{ to}$$
$$x = 3 \qquad \text{both sides.}$$

Check:

$$\sqrt{x + 2} = \sqrt{5}$$
$$\sqrt{3 + 2} \overset{?}{=} \sqrt{5} \qquad \text{Substitute 3 for } x \text{ in the}$$
$$\sqrt{5} = \sqrt{5} \checkmark \qquad \text{original equation.}$$

If two square root expressions are on the same side, move one of the expressions to the other side before squaring both sides.

Solve $\sqrt{x + 5} - \sqrt{19} = 0$.

$$\sqrt{x + 5} - \sqrt{19} = 0$$
$$\underline{+\sqrt{19} \quad +\sqrt{19}} \qquad \text{Add } \sqrt{19} \text{ to}$$
$$\sqrt{x + 5} = \sqrt{19} \qquad \text{both sides.}$$
$$(\sqrt{x + 5})^2 = (\sqrt{19})^2 \qquad \text{Square both}$$
$$x + 5 = 19 \qquad \text{sides.}$$
$$\underline{-5 \quad -5} \qquad \text{Add } -5 \text{ to}$$
$$x = 14 \qquad \text{both sides.}$$

Check:

$$\sqrt{x + 5} - \sqrt{19} = 0$$
$$\sqrt{14 + 5} - \sqrt{19} \overset{?}{=} 0 \qquad \text{Substitute}$$
$$\sqrt{19} - \sqrt{19} \overset{?}{=} 0 \qquad \text{14 for } x \text{ in}$$
$$\qquad\qquad\qquad\qquad \text{the original}$$
$$0 = 0 \checkmark \qquad \text{equation.}$$

Solve each equation. Check your answer. All variables represent nonnegative numbers.

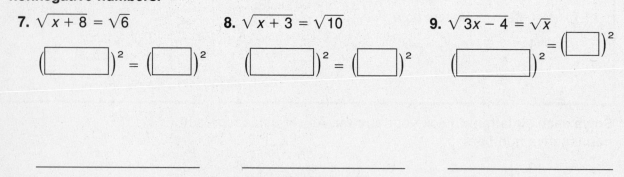

7. $\sqrt{x + 8} = \sqrt{6}$

$$\left(\boxed{}\right)^2 = \left(\boxed{}\right)^2$$

8. $\sqrt{x + 3} = \sqrt{10}$

$$\left(\boxed{}\right)^2 = \left(\boxed{}\right)^2$$

9. $\sqrt{3x - 4} = \sqrt{x}$

$$\left(\boxed{}\right)^2 = \left(\boxed{}\right)^2$$

_____   _____   _____

10. $\sqrt{5x + 3} = \sqrt{18}$

11. $\sqrt{4x - 3} = \sqrt{x + 9}$

12. $\sqrt{x + 2} = x$

_____   _____   _____

Holt Algebra 1

California Standards Prep for 2A22.0

LESSON 11-6 **Review for Mastery**

Geometric Sequences

In a **geometric sequence**, each term is *multiplied* by the same number to get to the next term. This number is called the **common ratio**.

The common ratio is 4.

Determine if the sequence 2, 6, 18, 54, ... is a geometric sequence.

Divide each term by the term before it.

$$\frac{54}{18} = 3 \qquad \frac{18}{6} = 3 \qquad \frac{6}{2} = 3$$

This is a geometric sequence; 3 is the common ratio.

Determine if the sequence 5, 10, 15, 20, ... is a geometric sequence.

Divide each term by the term before it.

$$\frac{20}{15} = \frac{4}{3} \qquad \frac{15}{10} = \frac{3}{2} \qquad \frac{10}{5} = 2$$

This is not a geometric sequence; there is no common ratio.

Find the next three terms in the geometric sequence 1, 4, 16, 64, ...

Step 1: Find the common ratio.

$$\frac{64}{16} = 4 \qquad \frac{16}{4} = 4 \qquad \frac{4}{1} = 4$$

Step 2: Continue to multiply by the common ratio.

$$64 \times 4 = 256 \qquad 256 \times 4 = 1024 \qquad 1024 \times 4 = 4096$$

The next three terms are 256, 1024, and 4096.

Determine if each sequence is a geometric sequence. Explain.

1. 2, 4, 6, 8, ... _____

2. −4, 8, −16, 32, ... _____

3. 32, 16, 8, 4,... _____

Find the common ratio in each geometric sequence below. Then find the next three terms.

4. 1, 5, 25, 125, ...

5. −6, 12, −24, 48, ...

6. 4, 6, 9, 13.5, ...

7. $\frac{1}{4}$, $\frac{1}{2}$, 1, 2, ...

Holt Algebra 1

California Standards Prep for 2A22.0

LESSON
11-6 # Review for Mastery
Geometric Sequences continued

There are two ways to find a given term of a geometric sequence.

Find the 8th term in the geometric sequence 5, 10, 20, 40, ….

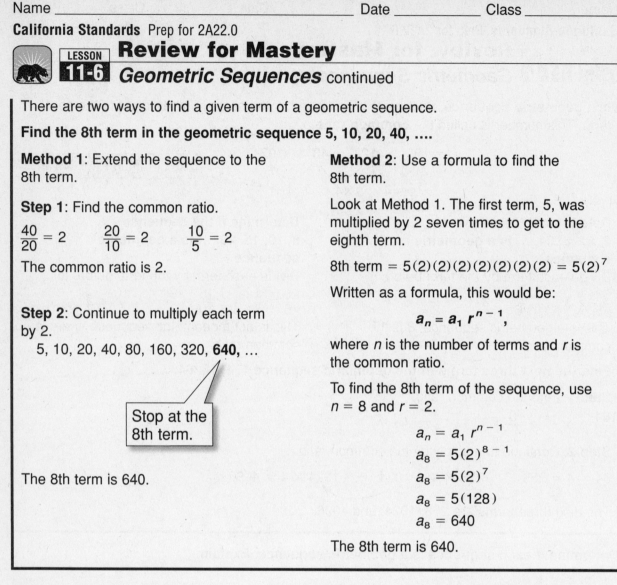

Method 1: Extend the sequence to the 8th term.

Step 1: Find the common ratio.

$\frac{40}{20} = 2$ $\frac{20}{10} = 2$ $\frac{10}{5} = 2$

The common ratio is 2.

Step 2: Continue to multiply each term by 2.

5, 10, 20, 40, 80, 160, 320, **640**, …

Stop at the 8th term.

The 8th term is 640.

Method 2: Use a formula to find the 8th term.

Look at Method 1. The first term, 5, was multiplied by 2 seven times to get to the eighth term.

8th term = $5(2)(2)(2)(2)(2)(2)(2) = 5(2)^7$

Written as a formula, this would be:

$$a_n = a_1 r^{n-1},$$

where n is the number of terms and r is the common ratio.

To find the 8th term of the sequence, use $n = 8$ and $r = 2$.

$a_n = a_1 r^{n-1}$
$a_8 = 5(2)^{8-1}$
$a_8 = 5(2)^7$
$a_8 = 5(128)$
$a_8 = 640$

The 8th term is 640.

Find the indicated term.

8. $a_1 = 7$, $r = -2$; 10th term

$a_{10} = \square (\square)^{\square - 1}$

9. $a_1 = -4$, $r = 3$; 8th term

$a_8 = \square (\square)^{\square - 1}$

_____   _____

10. The first term of a geometric sequence is 2, and the common ratio is 3. What is the 7th term?

_____

11. The first term of a geometric sequence is −3, and the common ratio is −2. What is the 9th term?

_____

12. Find the 12th term in the geometric sequence 5, −15, 45, −135, ….

_____

13. Find the 8th term in the geometric sequence 243, 81, 27, 9, ….

_____

Holt Algebra 1

Name _____ Date _____ Class _____

LESSON 11-7

Review for Mastery
Exponential Functions

An **exponential function** has the independent variable as the exponent.

$y = 3^x$ and $y = -2(0.5)^x$ are exponential functions.

A set of ordered pairs satisfies an exponential function if the y-values are multiplied by a constant amount as the x-values change by a constant amount.

Tell whether the following ordered pairs satisfy an exponential function.

x	y
3	4
5	12
7	36
9	108

Think 4 × ? = 12.
Think 12 × ? = 36.
Think 36 × ? = 108.

x	y
1	2
2	4
3	6
4	8

Think 2 × ? = 4.
Think 4 × ? = 6.
Think 6 × ? = 8.

The x-values increase by the constant amount 2.

Each y-value is multiplied by the constant amount 3.

This is an exponential function.

The x-values increase by the constant amount 1.

The y-value is multiplied by 2, then 1.5, then $1.\overline{3}$. There is no constant ratio.

This is not an exponential function.

The population of a school can be described by the function $f(x) = 1500(1.02)^x$, where x represents the number of years since the school was built. What will be the population of the school in 12 years?

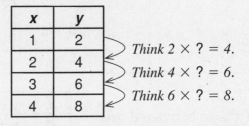

$f(x) = 1500(1.02)^x$

$f(12) = 1500(1.02)^{12}$ *Substitute 12 for x.*

≈ 1902 *Round number of people to the nearest whole number.*

Tell whether the ordered pairs satisfy an exponential function.

1.
x	y
−1	1.5
−2	3
−3	6
−4	12

2.
x	y
1	1
2	2
3	6
4	24

3.
x	y
−2	−2
−1	−10
0	−50
1	−250

_____   _____   _____

4. If a rubber ball is dropped from a height of 10 feet, the function $f(x) = 20(0.6)^x$ gives the height in feet of each bounce, where x is the bounce number. What will be the height of the 5th bounce? Round to the nearest tenth of a foot.   _____

5. A population of pigs is expected to increase at a rate of 4% each year. If the original population is 1000, the function $f(x) = 1000(1.04)^x$ gives the population in x years. What will be the population in 12 years?   _____

Holt Algebra 1

California Standards Prev. of 2A◆12.0

Review for Mastery
Exponential Functions continued

The graph of an exponential function is always a curve in two quadrants. $y = ab^x$

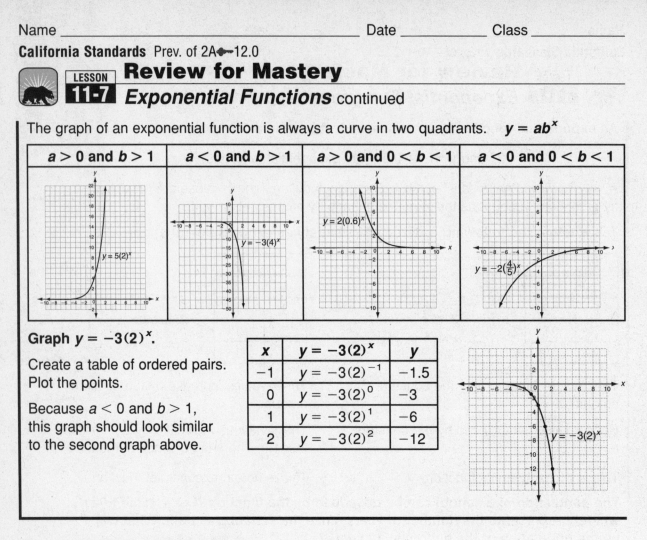

$a > 0$ and $b > 1$	$a < 0$ and $b > 1$	$a > 0$ and $0 < b < 1$	$a < 0$ and $0 < b < 1$
$y = 5(2)^x$	$y = -3(4)^x$	$y = 2(0.6)^x$	$y = -2\left(\frac{4}{5}\right)^x$

Graph $y = -3(2)^x$.

Create a table of ordered pairs. Plot the points.

Because $a < 0$ and $b > 1$, this graph should look similar to the second graph above.

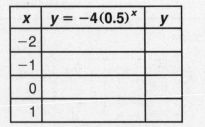

x	$y = -3(2)^x$	y
-1	$y = -3(2)^{-1}$	-1.5
0	$y = -3(2)^{0}$	-3
1	$y = -3(2)^{1}$	-6
2	$y = -3(2)^{2}$	-12

$y = -3(2)^x$

Graph each exponential function.

6. $y = -4(0.5)^x$

x	$y = -4(0.5)^x$	y
-2		
-1		
0		
1		

7. $y = 2(5)^x$

x	$y = 2(5)^x$	y
-1		
0		
1		
2		

8. $y = -1(2)^x$

x	$y = -1(2)^x$	y
-1		
0		
1		
2		

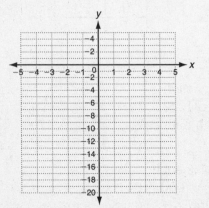

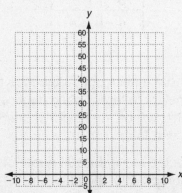

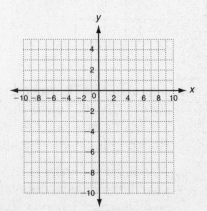

Holt Algebra 1

California Standards Prev. of 2A◆–12.0

LESSON 11-8 **Review for Mastery**
Exponential Growth and Decay

In the exponential growth and decay formulas, y = final amount, a = original amount, r = rate of growth or decay, and t = time.

Exponential growth: $y = a(1 + r)^t$

Exponential decay: $y = a(1 - r)^t$

The population of a city is increasing at a rate of 4% each year. In 2000 there were 236,000 people in the city. Write an exponential growth function to model this situation. Then find the population in 2009.	**The population of a city is decreasing at a rate of 6% each year. In 2000 there were 35,000 people in the city. Write an exponential decay function to model this situation. Then find the population in 2012.**
Step 1: Identify the variables.	**Step 1:** Identify the variables.
$a = 236{,}000 \qquad r = 0.04$	$a = 35{,}000 \quad r = 0.06$
Step 2: Substitute for a and r.	**Step 2:** Substitute for a and r.
$y = a(1 + r)^t$	$y = a(1 - r)^t$
$y = 236{,}000(1 + 0.04)^t$	$y = 35{,}000(1 - 0.06)^t$
The exponential growth function is $y = 236{,}000(1.04)^t$.	The exponential decay function is $y = 35{,}000(0.94)^t$.
Growth = greater than 1.	Decay = less than 1.
Step 3: Substitute for t.	**Step 3:** Substitute for t.
$y = 236{,}000(1.04)^9$	$y = 35{,}000(0.94)^{12}$
$\approx 335{,}902$	$\approx 16{,}657$
The population will be about 335,902.	The population will be about 16,657.

Write an exponential growth function to model each situation. Then find the value of the function after the given amount of time.

1. Annual sales at a company are $372,000 and increasing at a rate of 5% per year; 8 years

$y = \boxed{}\left(1 + \boxed{}\right)^{\boxed{}}$

_____

2. The population of a town is 4200 and increasing at a rate of 3% per year; 7 years

_____

Write an exponential decay function to model each situation. Then find the value of the function after the given amount of time.

3. Monthly car sales for a certain type of car are $350,000 and are decreasing at a rate of 3% per month; 6 months

$y = \boxed{}\left(1 - \boxed{}\right)^{\boxed{}}$;

_____

4. An internet chat room has 1200 participants and is decreasing at a rate of 2% per year; 5 years

_____

Holt Algebra 1

California Standards Prev. of 2A◆~12.0

LESSON 11-8 Review for Mastery

Exponential Growth and Decay continued

A special type of exponential growth involves finding compound interest.

$$A = P\left(1 + \frac{r}{n}\right)^{nt}$$

- where A is the total balance after t years
- P is the original amount
- r is the interest rate
- n is the number of times the interest is compounded in one year
- t is the number of years

Write a compound interest function to model \$15,000 invested at a rate of 3% compounded quarterly. Then find the balance after 8 years.

$$A = 15,000\left(1 + \frac{0.03}{4}\right)^{4t}$$

$A = 15,000(1.0075)^{4t}$ — *Compound interest function*

$A = 15,000(1.0075)^{4(8)}$ — *Substitute 8 for t.*

$A = 15,000(1.0075)^{32}$

$\approx 19,051.67$

The balance after 8 years is \$19,051.67.

A special type of exponential decay involves the half-life of substances.

$$A = P(0.5)^t$$

- where A is the final amount
- P is the original amount
- t is the number of half-lives in a given time period

Ismuth-212 has a half-life of approximately 60 seconds. Find the amount of Ismuth-212 left from a 25 gram sample after 300 seconds.

Step 1: Find t. $t = \dfrac{300}{60} = 5$

Step 2: Substitute for P and t.

$A = 25(0.5)^5$

$= 0.78125$

The amount after 300 s is 0.78125 g.

Write a compound interest function to model each situation. Then find the balance after the given number of years.

5. \$17,000 invested at 3%, compounded annually; 6 years _____

_____

6. \$23,000 invested at 2%, compounded quarterly; 8 years _____

_____

Write an exponential decay function to model each situation. Then find the value after the given amount of time.

7. A 30 gram sample of Iodine-131 has a half-life of about 8 days; 24 days _____

8. A 40 gram sample of Sodium-24 has a half-life of 15 hours; 60 hours _____

Holt Algebra 1

California Standards Ext. of ◆─7.0; Prev. of 2A◆─12.0

Review for Mastery
LESSON 11-9 *Linear, Quadratic, and Exponential Models*

Graph to decide whether a linear, quadratic or exponential function best models the data.

Graph $(-2, 0), (-1, -3), (0, -4), (1, -3), (2, 0)$. **What kind of model best describes the data?**

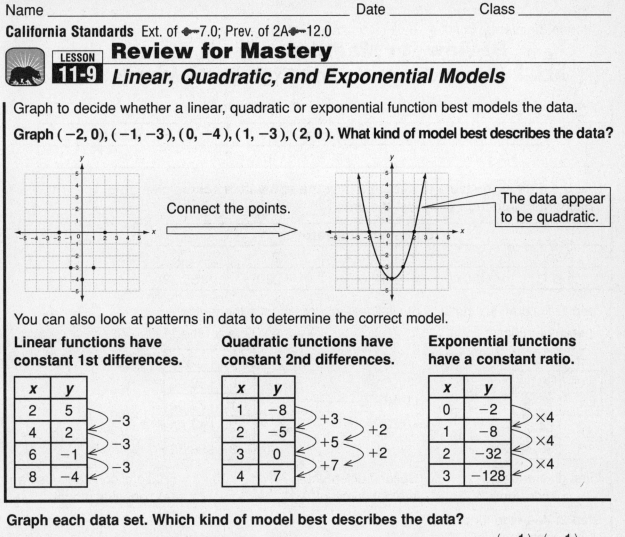

Connect the points.

The data appear to be quadratic.

You can also look at patterns in data to determine the correct model.

Linear functions have constant 1st differences.			**Quadratic functions have constant 2nd differences.**			**Exponential functions have a constant ratio.**	
x	**y**		**x**	**y**		**x**	**y**
2	5	−3	1	−8	+3 +2	0	−2	×4
4	2	−3	2	−5	+5 +2	1	−8	×4
6	−1	−3	3	0	+7 +2	2	−32	×4
8	−4		4	7		3	−128

Graph each data set. Which kind of model best describes the data?

1. $(-2, -4), (-1, -2), (0, 0), (1, 2), (2, 4)$ **2.** $(-1, 4), (0, 2), (1, 1), \left(2, \frac{1}{2}\right), \left(3, \frac{1}{4}\right)$

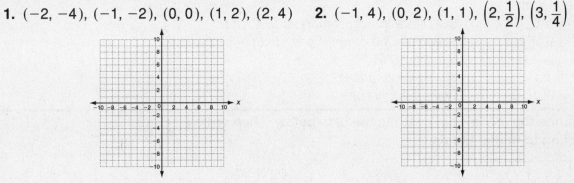

_____   _____

Look for a pattern in each data set to determine which kind of model best describes the data.

3.

x	y
0	6
1	12
2	24
3	48

4.

x	y
0	10
1	18
2	28
3	40

5.

x	y
3	4
6	−2
9	−8
12	−14

_____   _____   _____

Holt Algebra 1

California Standards Ext. of ➛7.0; Prev. of 2A➛12.0

LESSON 11-9 Review for Mastery
Linear, Quadratic, and Exponential Models continued

After deciding which model fits best, you can write a function.

Linear	Quadratic	Exponential
$y = mx + b$	$y = ax^2 + bx + c$	$y = ab^x$

Use the data in the table to describe how the software's cost is changing. Then write a function to model the data.

Computer Software				
Year	0	1	2	3
Cost ($)	80.00	72.00	64.80	58.32

Step 1: Determine whether data is linear, quadratic, or exponential.

Check differences: Check ratio:

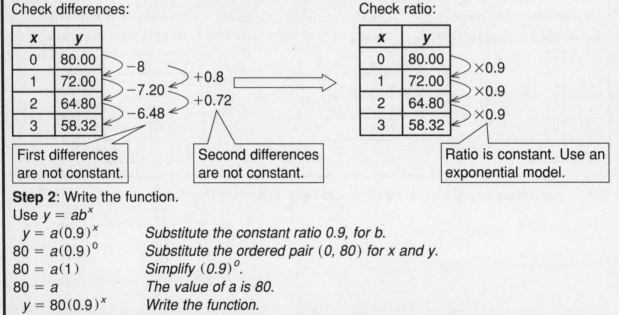

x	y
0	80.00
1	72.00
2	64.80
3	58.32

−8
−7.20   +0.8
−6.48   +0.72

x	y
0	80.00
1	72.00
2	64.80
3	58.32

×0.9
×0.9
×0.9

First differences are not constant.   Second differences are not constant.   Ratio is constant. Use an exponential model.

Step 2: Write the function.
Use $y = ab^x$

$y = a(0.9)^x$	*Substitute the constant ratio 0.9, for b.*
$80 = a(0.9)^0$	*Substitute the ordered pair (0, 80) for x and y.*
$80 = a(1)$	*Simplify $(0.9)^0$.*
$80 = a$	*The value of a is 80.*
$y = 80(0.9)^x$	*Write the function.*

Describe the model that best fits the data below. Then write a function to model the data.

6.
x	y
0	1
1	4
2	16
3	64

model: _____

function: _____

7.
x	y
0	7
1	10
2	13
3	16

model: _____

function: _____

Holt Algebra 1